KU-275-883

GEORGES BERNANOS

A Study of the Man
and the Writer

by the same author

William Poel and the Elizabethan Revival
Hilaire Belloc
William Rothenstein
Eric Gill
Teilhard de Chardin

George Eliot – *English Novelists Series*
Ronald Knox the Writer
Nature in Shakespearian Tragedy
The Christian Theatre

Vanier, Soldier, Diplomat and Governor General
The Property Basket – Autobiography

GEORGES BERNANOS

A Study of the Man and the Writer

ROBERT SPEAIGHT

COLLINS & HARVILL PRESS

London, 1973

© 1973 Robert Speaight

ISBN 0 00 261279 8

Set in Monotype Bembo
Made and printed in Great Britain by
William Collins Sons & Co Ltd Glasgow,
for Collins, St James's Place and
Harvill Press, 30A Pavilion Road,
London, SW1

TO
ANTONIA WHITE
with affection and admiration

CONTENTS

ILLUSTRATIONS

The illustrations are reproduced by kind permission
of M. Jean-Loup Bernanos

ACKNOWLEDGEMENTS

The principal sources of this book are the works and correspondence of Georges Bernanos, and the critical studies which have been devoted to him. Of the latter I am particularly indebted to Max Milner's *Georges Bernanos* which is the most complete introduction to his work which has yet appeared in French. Not only has M. Milner given me valuable help in my research, but it was at his suggestion that Mme Heurgon-Desjardins kindly invited me to attend the *colloque* devoted to Bernanos at Cérisy-la-Salle in July 1969. But for the personal contacts which I made, or renewed, there, the present work might never have been undertaken. I am equally in debt to the late Albert Béguin, Bernanos' literary executor, who gave me copies of many letters, since edited by Sister Jean Murray, OP; to Mgr Pézeril with whom I had several conversations in Paris shortly after Bernanos' death; and to M. Jean-Loup Bernanos without whose encouragement I should not have ventured upon this study. Among others who knew Bernanos well and helped me with their reminiscences I am grateful to M. and Mme Luc Estang, M. Michel Dard, Sister Jean Murray, OP, M. Guy Hattu, Sir David Scott Fox, and Senhor Pedro Octavio Carneiro da Cunha. I must also thank Senhor Antonio Olinto, Cultural Counsellor at the Brazilian Embassy in London, and Dona Thais, for facilitating my enquiries; and Mr Graham Connell for translating for me important sections of *Bernanos no Brasil*. All the other translations in the present study are my own.

I must thank the Librarian of Southampton University for so kindly lending to me several issues of *Etudes Bernanosiennes*, and my secretary, Mrs Pat Brayne, for once again typing the manuscript with her customary expedition and skill.

My grateful acknowledgements to those publishers who have given me permission to quote and translate from the works of Georges Bernanos or from publications relating to them, will be found at the end of the book.

Bernanos uses language like a flame-thrower.
Raymond Mortimer

I am between the Angel of light and the Angel of darkness, looking at them each in turn with the same enraged hunger for the absolute.
Georges Bernanos

Le démon aime les collectivités.
André Malraux

La France est une personne.
Michelet

La joie c'est aussi, 24 heures de doute moins une minute de l'espérance.
Georges Bernanos

INTRODUCTION

I MET him only once – at the French Institute, in July 1945. Writers muzzled by the Occupation, or muted – to a greater or lesser extent – by exile, had been visiting London since September 1944, and the Institute was glad to take them at whatever word they had to offer. On this occasion André Rousseaux was announced to speak to us about Charles Péguy – a man of whom the British public knew singularly little, although he had furnished the resisting and the Fighting French with the ammunition to sustain them where other ammunition was in short supply. Rousseaux was a critic of repute who had lost a leg in the 1914 war; he was also – as I discovered for myself when he dined with me – a nationalist who still harboured, even in those euphoric months after the Liberation, the suspicion that Albion was perfidious when it suited its purposes to be so. The theme of his lecture was 'Péguy – the Christian and the Revolutionary', for this was a time when revolution, of one kind or another, was very much in the air.

He was introduced by Raymond Mortimer, and these two were followed on to the platform by a man of burly physique and bronzed complexion, walking with the aid of a stick. This was Georges Bernanos. At the earnest request of General de Gaulle, he had returned from Brazil, where he had been living in voluntary exile for the past seven years, and was passing through London on his way to Paris. I very much doubt if he had ever been in London before; London was not on his map. After a tiring journey he had put up at an indifferent hotel, and he was probably not in the best of humours when he arrived at the French Embassy for luncheon. But here he fell – as only Frenchmen can fall – into the arms of his old friend, André Rousseaux, who had then brought him along to the Institute; not with the intention that he should open his mind to the audience, but that he should merely present his impressive person to many who were curious to know what he looked like and would be reassured to know that he was presently to return to

France. Raymond Mortimer introduced him briefly to the accompaniment of warm applause.

I cannot now remember how I came to be introduced to him myself. I had only recently returned from Paris, and Bernanos was anxious – anxiety is here the word – to know my impressions. They were no doubt coloured by an optimism which was then *de règle*. I spoke of Cardinal Suhard, who had redeemed the errors of his attitude under the Occupation by a quite extraordinary humility; but here Bernanos was not convinced, although conviction was to come to him afterwards. 'Ah!' he replied, 'je me méfie de ces gens de l'église lorsqu'il s'agit de l'honneur.' If he had wished to define his personality in a phrase, he could not have done so more succinctly. I never saw him or spoke to him again, and three years later he was dead.

In the years following the death of Bernanos I was in fairly regular contact with Albert Béguin, whom he had appointed as his literary executor. I contributed to the volume of the *Cahiers du Rhône* which Béguin edited in his memory, and I organised a public reading of *Dialogues des Carmélites*, in translation, at the French Institute some time before this work was brought to wider notice by Francis Poulenc's opera. At the same time I accepted an offer to write a book about Bernanos, and Béguin kindly gave me access to all the papers then in his possession. Gradually, however, more urgent work of various kinds distracted me, and I came also to feel that English readers – they were not very numerous – who wanted to know about Bernanos would prefer to read about him in his own language. I let the project drop, without abandoning it altogether; Béguin died in 1959; the papers passed into the hands of Mgr Pézeril, who had attended Bernanos in his last illness; and it was not until the summer of 1969 that I allowed my interest in the subject to be kindled afresh. I was convinced, not only that Bernanos was a great writer – which I had never doubted – but that he was, in some sense, more than ever a necessity in the present condition of the world.

The claim is a large one, and to some it may appear inflated. To describe Bernanos as a typical Frenchman is a contradiction in terms; he typified no one but himself. At the same time he cannot be understood without reference to the history and destiny – more

exactly, perhaps, the vocation – of France. There has never been a
writer to whom the idea of vocation is more applicable. He felt
himself *called* to be a Christian, to be a Frenchman and to be a writer.
These vocations were inseparable; one cannot be understood without
the others. Bernanos must be taken, though not necessarily accepted,
en bloc or not at all. This rootedness in a certain soil and in a certain
tradition should do nothing, for the intelligent reader, to diminish
his significance for those who are rooted elsewhere. Shakespeare is
the most quintessentially English of English writers; and *King Lear*
is for that reason a more universal work than *Paradise Lost*. In so
far as certain instincts and ideas are common to Western civilisation
(or to what remains of it), Bernanos speaks with an incomparable
eloquence to all of us who belong to that tradition. To those who
believe it to be a fabrication of myth he speaks with an irony and an
invective which occasionally defeat their object. But if Bernanos, in
his polemical writings, seems too insistently to be raising his voice,
it is because he is addressing an audience which is deaf although,
alas! it was never dumb.

It is natural, and to some extent necessary, to consider the polemic
and the fiction of Bernanos in distinct categories; but here, again, a
too arbitrary separation can mislead. He is integral in both. Rarely
introspective, he is none the less the most unmistakably personal of
writers. Nor should his apparent spontaneity – the jets of flame that
illuminate or cauterise from the printed page – deceive one into
thinking that he wrote *au courant de la plume;* his manuscripts, with
their careful corrections and erasures, attest the contrary. But he
wrote according to an internal logic, which was not the logic of
ratiocination. He does not balance one argument against another,
giving credit where credit (perhaps) is due. His adversaries will look
in vain for allowances; only on his death-bed will he extend forgiveness to Maurras or to Pétain. Each had been the spokesman of, and had
subsequently betrayed ideas in which Bernanos had believed. Just
as his characters come to us, fully bodied, out of the night of their
creation without previous biography, so do his arguments – or more
precisely his insights – come to us ready made from the heat of an
interior vision, without explanation or apology. Thus, in a book
like *Les Grands Cimetières sous la lune*, there is discontinuity which
should not be confused with disorder, variety but not irrelevance.
Where another man will write as he thinks, Bernanos writes as he

feels – not because he is the slave of sentiment or emotion but because, with him, thought and feeling are one.

The reader will look in vain in Bernanos for the sense of proportion – the famous *mesure* – which is commonly supposed to be a mark of the French intelligence.

By an extraordinary abuse of language, which would have stupefied the ancient Greeks, the sense of proportion is today confused with the prudence of imbeciles – as if there were any other sense of proportion for a man than to give himself without limit to values which infinitely transcend the scope of his own life.[1]

Bernanos is alternately violent and tender. His characters exist at the extremes of human experience – whether for good or evil. His saints, generally subject to the vertigo of despair which was his own besetting temptation, do something to redeem his sinners; only in the economy of grace can he be said to balance his accounts, with the risk of bankruptcy always round the corner – the Christian risk which alone made life for him worth the living. He is not a moralist, but a metaphysician; his universe is a battlefield of good and evil, not of right and wrong. His characters are not psychologically explained; they work out their salvation or their doom with a truth which is beyond analysis, and in a dimension of belief which the reader may not possess. This does not – or need not – forbid the imaginative acceptance that we give to the characters of Dostoevsky, with whom Bernanos has been so often, and so justly, compared.

If he belongs to the romantics by the verve and richness of his style, and also by a certain nostalgia which colours his political vision, he is a realist in the courage of his confrontations and in the vivid accuracy of his physical detail. A thesis might be written on the analogies he draws from the animal world. His descriptive powers are formidable; the picture of the Brazilian jungle in *Les Enfants humiliés* is a masterpiece of evocative prose, dense in atmosphere and clear in outline. But his reserves of strength and suggestion are such that he can afford what a contemporary French critic[2] has called *la force de l'implicite*. The phrase was used in connection with Henry James, and a personality more different from Bernanos could hardly be conceived; different, yet not altogether opposed – for

---

[1] *Lettre aux Anglais* (Atlantica Editora, 1942), p. 82
[2] Diane Fernandez

there is in Bernanos the apprehension of evil that one finds in James, just as there is the instinct of honour that one finds in Conrad. Bernanos read surprisingly little, once he had digested *La Comédie humaine;* but if he had been capable of reading English, one is tempted to guess that Conrad would have ranked among his favourite authors. If they had ever met, one is pretty sure that Conrad would have ranked among his favourite men.

There is a word which vanishes into irrelevance when you think of either; and that is the word 'class'. Each was as unconscious of class as he was aware of lineage; each was a royalist who knew that revolutions are sometimes necessary; each spoke with the accent of an aristocracy – exclusive to be sure – but claiming its certificate from the spiritual aristocracy of mankind. Each has his niche in the Pantheon of literature, and each comes to us from a world beyond the world of letters. Conrad would agonise for days over the right order of words in a sentence to end a story; the conscience of Bernanos was equally acute. There came a time when Conrad seemed to be losing his appeal because the drama of individual destiny no longer appeared in its original significance beside the revolt and reaction of the masses; and so, as if he felt the need to enlarge his canvas, he moved on to *Nostromo* and *Under Western Eyes.* In his notable comment on the loss of the *Titanic*[1] he for once treated directly of contemporary affairs. Bernanos was just as obsessed with individual destiny, but he too moved beyond it, reserving for his polemic the perspectives for which he could find no place in his fiction. An imaginary conversation between Conrad and Bernanos in the 'heart' of the Brazilian 'darkness', when Poland was enduring her crucifixion between two thieves, is a tempting invitation to pastiche.

Here, then, is abundant matter for literary criticism; but I had other motives in mind when I undertook to write this book. It was a significant coincidence that, on the only occasion when I set eyes on Georges Bernanos, another Frenchman should have been speaking about Charles Péguy. For Bernanos was of the same race of writers. True, there were differences. Péguy was the greatest and the purest of the Dreyfusards, whereas Bernanos could never quite rid himself of the anti-Semitic poison imbibed from Drumont and the Action Française. Péguy was a republican where Bernanos was a

[1] *Notes and Letters*

royalist. Private circumstances prevented Péguy from fully practising the religion to which he had returned; Bernanos declared that
he could not survive for five minutes outside the Church whose
ministers he castigated. Both were men of the north, but where
Péguy boasted never to have seen the sea, Bernanos could not have
enough of it – viewed from a Mediterranean shore. He reserved the
Pas-de-Calais for his fiction. But both men were possessed by the
daimon of prophecy, in the sense that each had a message that he
must deliver or die – and the message was the same. Both were
solitaries who assumed the conscience of the community, never
speaking more truly than when they were *minoritaires*. Both were
polemicists of genius, never mendacious in their pursuit of truth but
often unjust in their pursuit of justice. And when they looked for an
exemplar of the values they cherished, they found it in the martyrdom of Jeanne d'Arc.

For Bernanos, Jeanne d'Arc was the spirit of childhood, for lack
of which the twentieth century was perishing. She was the prototype
of the *enfants humiliés*. Hers, too, was the interior life against which
the world was in permanent conspiracy. Hers, again, was the
freedom to distinguish between canonists and casuists in league with
English and Burgundian invaders, and the Church that lost little
time in attesting the authenticity of the voices on which she had
relied. Hers, supremely, was the courage to assert her freedom.
Péguy and Bernanos met her at each cross-roads of their turbulent
itinerary; for both of them, as for Charles de Gaulle, she was a
certaine idée de la France. French nationalism dies hard – I remember
a little girl, not ten years old, saying to me one day: 'I despise you
because you burnt Jeanne d'Arc' – and this self-sufficiency, based
upon the belief that France is not only a country but an idea necessary
to civilisation, makes Bernanos not always accessible, or sympathetic, to the English reader. He tends to assume that one knows
what he is talking about – which is not invariably the case. The
parallel with de Gaulle is as striking as the parallel with Péguy. It is
disappointing to record that on the first occasion when they met
Bernanos did all the talking. No doubt a *déjeuner* was too short a
time for two great men to conclude a treaty of conversational
equality, particularly when one of them was as apt to listen as he
was to speak.

It so happens that a long acquaintance with France and with the

French people has made it easy for me to understand, and sometimes to excuse, an attitude of mind which others might criticise as chauvinistic. Of course, I think it important to know what a great French writer felt about the vocation of his country, not least because what happens to France matters a great deal to the rest of us. Recent experience has taught us this, if nothing else. But although France is very largely the context of Bernanos' writing, it is something less than its total content. Beyond 'a certain idea of France', Bernanos is inhabited by a certain idea of man. There was nothing original in the idea, although much originality in its imaginative or polemical exposition. Bernanos found everything he wanted in the Penny Catechism, and he might well have wondered what the Dutch were doing with a catechism of their own. Orthodoxy is more than intricate theological structure: orthodoxy is an instinct, and Bernanos possessed it, as another man will possess an ear for music. If he had been told, as a friend of mine was recently told by a group of Catholic students in the United States, that the Resurrection of Jesus Christ was a 'non-question', or by a respected theological journal that it was 'a happening, but not an event', he would have greeted these enormities with derisive and volcanic laughter. Perhaps, indeed, he foresaw that an apostasy, already fashionable in his lifetime, was paving the way for them – and for the shout of theological triumph that God was dead.

A novelist who found it difficult to keep his principal characters out of the presbytery could hardly escape the label of 'Catholic novelist'. Bernanos is a Catholic novelist in the sense that Dante is a Catholic poet; neither can be understood without a certain knowledge of Roman Catholicism. Dostoevsky writes in a similar context of belief, buttressed by strong dogmatic definitions. There is a parallel between Dostoevsky's rootedness in a certain idea of Russia and Bernanos' rootedness in a certain idea of France. They are the least cosmopolitan of writers. Bernanos avoided the contagion of the literary salons, although he compared his own vocation to write with another man's vocation to the priesthood. Each was a minister of the word, and for Bernanos the word was a species of sacrament. It was, pre-eminently, a means of salvation; and Bernanos was desperately concerned that the word, and himself with it, should be saved. You may write him down as a pessimist because he did not believe in progress, and as a reactionary because he did not believe in democracy – until you discover that the labels will not stick. The cotton-brokers of Manchester, with the opportunist dictators and theologians, are the villains of his piece; with such targets as these, it was hardly worth while to singe Karl Marx's beard. The hope that he retained in despite of all appearances was the reverse of a complacent optimism. It is not too much to say that from his earliest years he lived and wrote in the shadow of the Cross, and his hope was one that only the Resurrection could justify. He had seen too many victories thrown away to believe in any other victory but this.

It may be that not many more people, at least in the English-speaking world, will be interested in Bernanos today than would have been the case twenty years ago. In no sense of the word is he easy to translate; his climate is not ours. Between those who believe that man was made for God and those who believe that he 'happened' for the satisfaction of his own appetites; between those who believe, with Pascal, that he must possess himself in solitude and in silence before he can be of any use to society, and those who believe that he was created in the image of the ant-heap; between those who cannot live without the music of the spheres and those who cannot live without the blare of the loud-speaker and the screech of the motor-car – there is a gulf fixed, far wider than the gap between the generations. For the acolytes of the permissive society the man who liked to proclaim himself *le dernier des hommes libres* may well appear as a rhetorical anachronism. Nevertheless he was a catalyst of the times through which we all have lived, and of other times before either he or we were born. In trying to understand him – and he is not always easy to understand – we shall have gone some way towards understanding ourselves; what we were, and what we are, and what we are likely to become.

The Cities of the Plain have acquired a new look since Lot's wife turned her head in the wrong direction, and Marcel Proust subjected them to his microscope. There are more of them than there used to be. Around any ancient town, of Roman or medieval origin, the blocks of staring brick and obstinate cement lift their shapeless storeys to the sky, like an empty boast. They have been described as 'machines for men to live in', which is exactly what a human dwelling ought not to be. Below them and a little apart is a huddle of houses –

perhaps of slums – and a maze of narrow, twisting streets. There is
a town hall, often of classical proportions. There are public gardens
and a central square; and right in the middle of the town there is a
church, not much frequented. On the periphery there are one or two
factories, and in the road outside there may be a group of men on
strike because their wages are inadequate for the families in the
'machines that were made to live in'. Elsewhere, on the pavements,
a number of young people may be sitting down because they object
to the manufacture of a bomb which threatens to destroy them, or
to a war which is being waged at the other end of the earth. Georges
Bernanos would have shared their objections, and he would have
agreed that, if men made in the image of God were compelled to
live by the grace of machines and in dwellings that looked like
machines, they should at least be paid for their purgatory. But you
will not find him standing around with the strikers or protesting on
the pavement, although you might, it is true, find him manufactur-
ing his own bombshell, as he sits writing at the table of a café.
Indeed one of the insurgent students from the Sorbonne was
speaking to the point when he said that 'the youth of 1968 needs to
hear once again a voice like the voice of Bernanos'; and Bernanos
himself declared it to be 'a good thing that we should have socialists,
communists, royalists and anarchists amongst us, so long as they are
sincere – provided we have done with the conservatives'.[1] So you
might, after all, discover him behind the barricades; and it is wholly
appropriate that one of the streets leading into the 'Boul Mich'
should recently have been named 'Avenue Georges-Bernanos'. For
always in the front of his mind, and very often upon his lips, was
the same longing that de Gaulle expressed to Malraux: 'Si seulement
je pourrais avant de mourir revoir une jeunesse française . . .' In the
end, however, you will find him on his knees in the empty church –
just as a well-known photograph depicted him when he was not
more than ten years old: *le petit garçon que je fus.*

The following pages make no claim to exhaust their subject,
either as a writer or a man. They should not be read as 'definitive'
biography, nor as literary criticism 'in depth'. Of the latter there is
a great deal available in French, for which I refer the reader to the
bibliography. My intention has been to situate the work of Bernanos
in relation to his life, and to introduce him to a public which knows

[1] *Le Lendemain – c'est vous*

less of him than he deserves. England had meant little to Bernanos; nevertheless his *Lettre aux Anglais*, written from Brazil during the Second World War, was inspired by an example which England had given to the world. This book may be read as a reply to it.

CHAPTER I

FATHER TO THE MAN

I

THE landscape of Artois does not seduce the traveller. In spring the wide pastures, bisected by a rare stream or canal and by the long straight roads, stretch like an undulating desert, gold and ochre shading off into chalky white, and contrasted, here and there, with a livid green. Few hedges divide them; few trees relieve their monotony; and the villages are plain when they are not ugly. Here and there a château, faced in the raw red brick of Flanders, stands shuttered and secret among its trees, withdrawn a little from the road. Here, you would say, is a land designed for the march and clash of armies, the grandeur and the servitude of war; an uneventful landscape, scarred, and in a measure sanctified, by great events. Indeed, what principally attracts – and appals – the motorist are the cemeteries that blend into the soil to which the ploughshare and the tractor have returned, and the grave memorials of battle. This country, like the Beauce, has the linear beauty of the absolute, but you would never describe it as picturesque.

Some fifty kilometres to the west of Arras, and just off the main road between Hesdin and Fruges, stands the village of Fressin, remarkable only for the ruins of an ancient fortress. This was destroyed by the English in one of their medieval campaigns – the field of Agincourt is only a mile or two away, and the 'boiled remains' of the Duke of York are said to have been buried at Fressin, though his bones were brought home to England. But the curved wall of the bastion and several sections of the ramparts still survive, with trees sprouting from the masonry. A little stream – the Planquette – runs through the village to join the Canche, which flows into the sea at Le Touquet. It was in a large white house at Fressin, looking on to the road behind its screen of rusty railings and untidy yews, that Georges Bernanos spent a great part of his childhood. His father had bought it as a country retreat, and this was how the landscape of Artois came to be imprinted on the mind of the boy,

and later to furnish the *mise-en-scène* of the novelist. The temperament of Bernanos was the reverse of Nordic, but it was appropriate
to his character that the chief battlefield of Europe should have
cradled him and that he was to know it in war as well as in peace.
To spend the happiest days of one's youth within a short afternoon's
walk of Agincourt is hardly calculated to turn the average French
boy into an Anglophil, although Bernanos was anything but
average. *Militia est vita hominis* sums up his destiny, even if he did not
assume it as his motto.

He was in fact born in Paris, on the 20th of February 1888, where
his father, Emile, ran an upholstery establishment in the rue Joubert,
and afterwards in the rue Vignon. The firm had been responsible for
the decoration of the Turkish Embassy. But Paris counted for little
in those early years; what Bernanos remembered was the birdsong
and rustling of leaves in the Bois de Fressin, the wild yellow primulas
and celandines among the crumbling stones of the château, and the
lazy meander of the Planquette. The church also he remembered,
with its high Gothic arches, short steeple, and dilapidated *bondieuserie*.
Here were the uncoloured plaster statues of the curé d'Ars and Joan
of Arc, already exerting their fascination over the rather dreamy boy
who was later to turn the curé d'Ars into the curé of Lumbres,[1]
and Chantal de Clergerie[2] into a twin sister of St Joan. Underneath
the statue of St Joan the visitor may read the following inscription:
Famille Bernanos-Talbert d'Arc. Voeux exaucés 1925 – evidently a
thankoffering for recovery from serious illness. Bernanos' future
wife was directly descended from a brother of Jeanne d'Arc. Here,
too, was the confessional with its elaborately carved door behind
which Antoine de Saint-Marin[3] might have discovered the curé
dead upon his last battlefield. Except for an early stone reredos, the
church at Fressin has little to offer the antiquarian, but for the reader
of Bernanos it is alive with memories and premonitions.

The family of Emile Bernanos had been settled in Lorraine since
the sixteenth century, and his wife, Marie-Clémence Moreau, came
from Pellevoisin in the Berri. She was of rather simpler antecedents.
Each spoke with the accent of their native province, and Bernanos'
grandmother on his father's side taught him his first prayers in

[1] *Sous le Soleil de Satan* (Plon, 1926)   [2] *La Joie* (Plon, 1929)
[3] *Sous le Soleil de Satan*

German, a language he subsequently forgot. Bernanos is, of course, a Spanish name, and there were stories of a remote Spanish ancestry. It was noticed that when Georges was at boarding school in Artois he was not very particular about washing in the winter months; and if this was remarked upon he replied that he preferred to keep his Spanish complexion. A certain Major Bernanos had played a notable part in capturing Santo Domingo for the French in 1694. He was a freelance adventurer, but although Bernanos enjoyed the record of his exploits and would, no doubt, have liked to emulate them, the connection is purely legendary between this picaresque d'Artagnan and the solid ancestry of coopers, lawyers, shoemakers, vignerons, and humble artisans from whom Bernanos was descended on both sides of his family. There was, however, a 'Major Bernanos' on one side of his character, and he was proud of him. Only two years before his death he was asking his nephew to delve into the naval archives for information about 'the mysterious Bernanos who died in 1699'.

His mother was a woman of strong personality, beautiful and imposing presence, and strict piety. Like so many Frenchmen of genius, Georges owed her everything, not least his unswerving religious faith. They had the same large, interrogating eyes; the same conscientious devotion to the work in hand. 'The mothers who brought us up,' he was to write many years later, 'were too good, too patient, and too brave. They worked so hard, and yet they were so gentle; tender-hearted, valiant, and inflexible.'[1] The tribute reads like a description of Bernanos himself, if one adds a volcanic force of temperament even more Spanish than French. Emile, with his portly mien, twirling moustaches, and serious expression, looked very much the paterfamilias of the period. He dispensed a generous hospitality, and was especially proud of the rum omelettes, which he would go into the kitchen to make himself, and of the *bons crus* in his cellar. He also had a passion for photography, which we have to thank for so rich a pictorial record of the Bernanosian hearth and home. Georges was the only son of his parents, but he had a sister, Marie-Catherine, five years older than himself. The social, and also the spiritual, ambience of the house at Fressin is conveyed in a passage from *Les Grands Cimetières sous la lune:*

[1] *Nous autres Français* (Gallimard, 1939)

Every Monday people came begging, sometimes from quite a distance, from other villages. But I knew nearly all of them by name. It was a very reliable clientèle. They were even helpful to one another – 'I've come for so-and-so, who's got the rheumatism.' When there were more than a hundred of them, my father would say: '*Sapristi!* business is looking up'.... All I wanted to make you understand was that I was brought up to respect old people, whether they possessed anything or not; and particularly old ladies – a prejudice which has survived the hideous and wanton septuagenarians of today. In those days I was made to talk to the elderly beggars, cap in hand, and they found that quite as natural as I did. It didn't impress them in the least. They were people of an older France; they knew how to live; and they smelt rather strongly of tobacco and snuff. They didn't stink of the shop, and they didn't look like shop-keepers, sacristans, or bailiffs; they didn't look as if they'd been born in a cellar. They looked much more like the Bourbons and the Valois, like Vauban and Turenne.[1]

The villagers remembered the boy already as rather different from the others, with an originality sometimes disconcerting. It was all very well to borrow a shot-gun from a farmer, but although poaching was a fairly respectable occupation, to choose the farmer's poultry for target practice was going a little far. They remembered the boy's charm, and his own awareness of it; he knew exactly how to get what he wanted. Sometimes they would watch him climb to the top of a pine tree, and there settle down to a book, chant the *Kyrie* or the *Sanctus* from the Mass, and preach interminably to a congregation of his own imagining. For among the litter of photographs in his father's desk there were many of priests – *curés de campagne* whose features remained in the boy's memory, and were afterwards, perhaps, to furnish the features of the curé d'Ambricourt or the curé de Torcy,[2] an abbé Donissan[3] or an abbé Chevance.[4] Among the things he acquired through his own sophisticated technique of begging (or of poaching) was the key to his father's library, the large room with its four windows, draped in brightly coloured *caramani* curtains, and the trees shading it on either side. Here he would lie on the carpet for hours reading through the whole of *La Comédie humaine*. Instinct led him straight to Balzac as the French

[1] *Les Grands Cimetières sous la lune* (Plon, 1938), pp. 44–5
[2] *Journal d'un Curé de campagne* (Plon, 1936)
[3] *Sous le Soleil de Satan*   [4] *L'Imposture* (Plon, 1927)

novelist whose genius was closest to his own. He was only thirteen years old when he made the great discovery, and a discovery made at that age lasts a lifetime. The two shelves with the complete edition had long attracted him behind their glass case, and what he gleaned from their contents was a secret which had little to do with the 'social realism' of the Restoration. It was a world besieged, like the world of his own fiction, by a visionary of genius, 'distilling the anguish of a lucid nightmare, assailing me from every side, without ever shaking my reason'.[1] He allowed Balzac to take him by the hand until he was exhausted by this tremendous companionship; and looking at himself in the mirror he was surprised to find himself only a little pale, but tremendously and vibratingly alive. In later years Dostoevsky, Corneille, Barbey d'Aurevilly, Baudelaire, Péguy, and Victor Hugo were to find their place beside Balzac, with – eventually and half-reluctantly – Racine.

A celebrated photograph shows the boy Bernanos kneeling alone in the parish church at Fressin; and under this the man had written: *le petit garçon que je fus.* Haunted to the end of his days by his childhood, he never wished to return to it, and still less to root himself in the scenes and places he had known.

I have not been back to see them, and there are others that I prefer. I am a thousand times more strongly and jealously attached to Provence. It is true, nevertheless, that after thirty years absence – or what we call by that name – the characters in my books find themselves in the places that I thought I had left behind me. Here,[2] or elsewhere, why should I indulge a nostalgia for what I possess in spite of myself, and that I cannot betray? Why should I evoke with melancholy the muddy water in the rutted track, the hedge whistling in the rain, since I am myself the hedge and the muddy water?[3]

Or again, to his friend, Dom Gordan:

Anything good in my books comes from very far back; from my youth, from my childhood and its magic springs.[4]

Bernanos was the reverse of a 'regional' novelist. The 'older France', to which his fidelity was absolute, he carried in his bones, present and active wherever he happened to be. His whole life was

[1] *Le Crépuscule des Vieux* (Gallimard, 1956), p. 64
[2] Bernanos was writing from Brazil
[3] *Les Enfants humiliés* (Gallimard, 1949), pp. 37–8
[4] March 1943: *Correspondance* II (Plon, 1971), p. 502

a sequence of new departures; and its symbol was not the village, but the road:

I have never loved anything but the roads. The road knows what it wants. The man who made it, inch by inch, with his own hands, dug down to its heart of stone, and then polished and caressed it, doesn't recognise it any more, but he believes in it. The great and supreme opportunity, the unique opportunity of his life, is there beneath his eyes and under his feet, a fabulous breach endlessly opening out in front of him, a miracle of solitude and escape, a sublime vault challenging the sky. He made it – a magnificent toy given as a present to himself, and as soon as he has set foot upon the amber trail, he forgets that his own calculations have already traced its inflexible itinerary. The man who has never seen the road in the light of the early morning, cool and living between its two rows of trees, does not know the meaning of hope.[1]

There is a distinction in French between *espoir* and *espérance*. The second is not only the lovelier word, but it carries a deeper meaning. When Bernanos is speaking of 'hope', he generally speaks of *espérance* rather than *espoir*. For one whose hopes were so frequently disappointed, the distinction was a useful one.

2

In 1897 Bernanos was sent to school at the college of the Immaculate Conception, 391 rue de Vaugirard. This was run by the Jesuits and it enjoyed a high reputation; among its 600 pupils there figured, four years later, the name of Charles de Gaulle. Bernanos lived at home, for the school was only a short walk from his parents' house, 82 rue de l'Abbé-Groult. Out of his class of thirty-nine, five were day boarders like himself, arriving at the college punctually at 7.25 a.m., in their blue uniform with its gold buttons. No doubt he gained more from the Jesuits than he realised or admitted, but his hostility towards the Society of Jesus remained an inexpungable prejudice for this most prejudiced of men. It was not himself alone, he thought, but the whole company of the faithful that the Jesuits were putting to school, substituting the docile pupil for the free man. The elaborate casuistry then in vogue particularly repelled him. He detested the ideal of the 'humanist priest, swarming with Latin verses like a corpse with maggots', for in Christian humanism

[1] *Monsieur Ouine* (Editions de la Pléiade: Gallimard, 1943), pp. 93–4

he detected a betrayal of the Gospel and a cowardly compromise with the spirit of the times. The discipline imposed by the Society was the discipline of the circus; and he was to look back with a horror almost physical on the 'dismal irony' of his professors and the servile atmosphere of the class, the greasy refectory and the pompous celebrations of the Mass, where boredom was the only emotion he could share with the God whom he had come to worship. The meadows of the Pas-de-Calais were not particularly inspiring, but they were a paradise of liberty beside the servitude of the rue de Vaugirard, calling him to order just when the illusion of freedom, fostered by the *grandes vacances*, was beginning to have the taste of reality.

Nevertheless, it was in the chapel of this inhospitable establishment that Bernanos made his first communion on the 11th of May 1899. The event, which for many is a pure formality and the excuse for a pretty dress and a lavish luncheon, was to have a decisive effect on his whole life. For this we have the testimony of Mgr Pézeril who was at his side when he had come to the end of it. Indeed he was too wrought up with emotion to approach the altar with the others, but received the sacrament afterwards by himself. How did he appear, then, this boy of eleven years old, as he went for the first time to the supreme encounter?

A lad, full of fire, particularly when he spoke, eager for argument, sympathetic on the whole, in spite of a rather graceless physique; a muddy complexion; hair bristling and vaguely standing up on end; the eyes slightly bulging, but eloquent.[1]

In 1901 the anti-clerical legislation, which was the nemesis earned by the prosecution and imprisonment of Dreyfus, compelled the Jesuits to close their colleges, and Bernanos was sent as a boarder to the *petit séminaire* of Notre Dame des Champs. Here he was even less happy than in the rue Vaugirard, and the tension between his teachers and a spirit always in revolt, became so acute that his parents decided to send him to the *petit séminaire* of Bourges. This was his mother's country, and it was at the suggestion of two friends of hers – professors at the Collège Saint-Célestin, then studying in Paris – that he left for the Berri in October 1903. He remained a difficult pupil, noisy, unpunctual and eccentric. He was untidily

[1] Louis Chaigne, *Georges Bernanos* (Editions Universitaires, 1960)

dressed, and never appeared to brush his hair. The youngest in a class of sixteen, he was weak in mathematics, hopeless at Greek, and failed in his oral examination for the *baccalauréat* in June. In October, 1904, he was no more successful, after declaring to the examiner in cosmography that the sun spots had an influence on the seasons and on the electricity of the earth. He had imbibed this heresy from the abbé Théodore Moreau, an astronomer in charge of the Bourges Observatory. Bernanos took his failure pretty badly; nevertheless he was beginning to show his paces in French, polishing his essays and pleading this as an excuse when he was late in sending them in. He waited in feverish impatience for the corrections which exempted no fault of style, although his imagination and verbal generosity – not to say prodigality – received their meed of praise. The abbé Lagrange remembered him with 'arms folded on the desk, chin between his hands, and eyes looking straight into the eyes of his teacher, and muttering "Snake" between his teeth.'[1]

The friendship of Lagrange, and the ardent companionship of two fellow-pupils – Yves and Maxence de Colleville – were the most valuable acquisitions that Bernanos took away from Bourges, and neither was exactly academic. Lagrange's study was the scene of at least one spectacular fight in which the professor's books were the chief casualties.

In June 1902 Bernanos had only the thirty-second place out of a class of thirty-five, although he came thirteenth in French narration. His teacher commented, not without irony, that 'Georges Bernanos is a flower or a bird, and all one asks of a flower is its perfume and of a bird its song. Did not Our Lord say of those exclusive clients of His Divine Providence that they "neither work nor spin"?' In the following year Georges was still only twenty-fifth out of twenty-eight, but in January he had jumped to the head of the class in French prose. Professor Batisse described him as 'the amateur pupil, of whom he has some of the qualities and practically all the defects and caprices, notably an incurable idleness'. Out of school hours we find him playing the title rôle in *Les Fourberies de Scapin*. At last the authorities advised his parents to direct their son into the paths of commerce; he should waste no more time over the classical studies for which he had shown so little aptitude.

They were too sensible to follow this advice, and after spending

[1] *Cahiers du Rhône*, p. 251

only two years at Bourges, Georges was sent, on the recommenda-
tion of the curé at Fressin, to the college of Sainte-Marie d'Aire-sur-
le-Lys, lodging with the family of the mayor, Abel Delbende. His
letters to Lagrange give an intimate glimpse of the ideas and emo-
tions now fermenting in the boy's mind and spirit. The tone is
familiar and even teasing. He addresses Lagrange as 'Monsieur le
Licencié', for Bernanos never showed much regard for academic
distinctions. All letters sent from the college were censored by an
unsympathetic superior, but Bernanos managed to evade his scrutiny,
warning his correspondent to be prudent in reply since letters
arriving at the college were censored also. The environment was
not congenial to a spirit at once nonconformist and self-questioning.
This was Flanders, and the Superior was Flemish in every respect,
except that he very easily lost his temper; and when he did so the
windows shook. Many of the other pupils were Flemish too, or
boys from the good families of Artois. Several, however, came from
elsewhere, for a regiment was stationed in the town, and the college
was convenient for the officers' sons. There was another Parisian in
the class with Georges Bernanos, and the two of them lost no
opportunity for teasing their stolid schoolfellows, whose dreaminess
– they well realised – did not reflect a preoccupation with higher
things.

Bernanos, too, had his dreams, and it was through his letters to
Lagrange – ironical, introspective, and severely self-questioning –
that he tried to articulate them. His health was not robust, and the
fear of death was beginning to haunt him. He was also divided
between a vocation to the priesthood – he had thought of becoming
a missionary – and the facility of a literary career. Not until later
did his writing appear invested with the responsibility of a *sacerdoce*.
He was nervous of his own sensibility and romanticism and saw
that, for him, the temptations of the dilettante – 'to write pretty
books for pretty eyes in a pretty house' – were more insidious than
the temptations of the debauchee.

Emile Bernanos wanted his son to go straight into business, but
although the boy would gladly have dispensed with another year
at school, he decided to proceed to his studies in law, since a knowledge of this would be necessary for so many practical purposes.
Business, however, was not one of them – for business, he told
Lagrange, might very easily lead to the worship of the golden calf.

Nor was he further drawn towards the priesthood. What he feared was a parsimonious employment of his life, economising for himself and others; what he longed for was to throw himself, heart and soul, into the mêlée. He can little have guessed the opportunities awaiting him. Meanwhile, on the advice of a wise and sympathetic confessor, he was reading the works of Ernest Hello – a pioneer of the Catholic revival in France. The thought of death and its inevitable corruption still made his hair stand on end, and he wondered why he still found it difficult to endure the slightest contradiction, particularly when it touched his vanity.

So the dialogue continued throughout this year of critical development; one part of the boy's mind dreaming of high adventure and noble causes; another part given up to literature – to the books that others had written and to those that he might write himself. He was, in fact, already contributing to an illustrated royalist review, *Le Panache*, which had been coming out six times a year since 1903. His own short stories – there were seven of them – appeared between February and December 1907. They reflected the title of the review, and were certainly, in their forthright romanticism, adapted to its readers. Here, in little snapshots of history, real or imagined, were *chevaliers sans reproche* dying in desperate campaigns where the French never seemed to be victorious. The obsession with death as the supreme necessity of life is already evident; the vigour and purity of style are already marked. And one of the stories, dealing with the imprisonment of the Dauphin, ends with a sentence which explains how a royalist like Bernanos – or a republican like Péguy – could still discover the essence of royalty in a republic that had no more use for the throne:

He understood that for a king human suffering is of small account, since royalty is assured of survival in the race, and that if the king can die, royalty lives on.[1]

But the deeper thoughts of Georges Bernanos always came back to the 'little hole' he dreaded, and then literature came to his aid. Here it was Balzac all the time, with small doses of Bourget and Zola – only the early, sentimental, and inoffensive Zola, he reassured Lagrange, who thought he was reading too much and whose replies to his introspection were sometimes a little austere, bravely

[1] *Bulletin*, no. 26, p. 10

Georges Bernanos with his mother

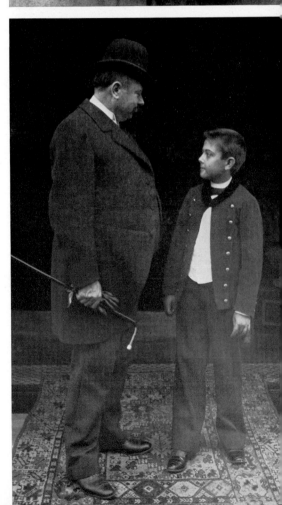

With his father

In the drawing room at Fressin with his father and sister

as he welcomed their austerity. It is hardly going too far to say that by October 1906 the ambitions of Bernanos were fixed, although his genius had not yet expressed itself; that the lines of his character were drawn, although they were susceptible to infinite modulation; and that his obsession with the shadow of death was now recognised as something he would have to live with, understand, and transfigure, both in his life and his work. To have done so is not the least of his achievements.

3

After another year at Aire-sur-le-Lys Bernanos said goodbye to secondary education, and Lagrange was invited to Fressin for the *grandes vacances*. The two friends walked and talked endlessly together. They visited the neighbouring curés, and Georges – haunted as ever by the mystery of the priesthood – was quick to observe their psychology and the way they discharged their duties. If he did not like them, he had no hesitation in saying so. In the library he lay on the thick carpet devouring Balzac, while Lagrange sat in an armchair reading his breviary. The religious ardours of adolescence had cooled a little, and the young Bernanos no longer had a taste for prayer. 'The heart is rusting', he wrote to Lagrange, 'clean it up for me'.[1]

In the autumn of 1907 he left for Paris, living first with his married sister, Mme Paul Hattu, at 74 rue des Archives, and then occupying a *pied à terre* at 196 rue de Javel, which his parents had acquired after their retirement to Fressin. He subsequently moved for six months to a mezzanine floor at 6 Boulevard Arago. These addresses were all within easy reach of the Sorbonne, where he obtained a degree in literature and in law. But his main interests were political. He was already a passionate adherent of the Action Française, sending Lagrange the brochures of Maurras in whom the Catholics of France, dispossessed of their schools, had found a useful, though dangerous, ally. It is not easy for the English reader, and no longer very easy for the French, to appreciate the influence of the Action Française in these early years of the twentieth century. The forerunner of many similar movements, loosely grouped under the name of Fascism, it was at once radical and reactionary; in spite of

[1] 23rd October 1906: *Cahiers du Rhône*, p. 26

its dogmatic anti-romanticism, it was also romantic. A distant
parallel to it in English politics might be found in the Young
Englanders of the 1840s, celebrated – if not quite immortalised – by
Disraeli in *Coningsby*. The parallel would not have been appreciated,
since anti-Semitism was among the principal articles in the *credo* of
the Action Française. Like all movements that aim at displacing – if
necessary by violence – the existing order, it could not do without
its enemies. These were the Protestants, the Freemasons, and the
Jews, alien intruders and corrupting influences in the pure citadel of
the French state and society. To these were added Liberals of every
kind, in politics or religion. In defending the rights and honouring
the prestige of the Church the Action Française stopped short of any
official adherence to Christianity. Of its two founders Léon Daudet
was a practising Catholic, whose erotic novels were an occasion of
scandal to the pious reader; already, at the Lycée Louis le Grand, he
had formed the habit of annotating his notebooks with sketches
of naked females. Charles Maurras was an agnostic positivist, and a
disciple of Auguste Comte. Both were journalists of unscrupulous
genius, and Maurras was a man of powerful intellect and ascetic
personal life. Each had a charismatic influence upon those who fell
under their sway. What they admired in Catholicism was set out
plainly in the first number of the *Action Française*:

its supreme wisdom and attenuated Christianity, filtered through the
happy genius of France . . . its practical sense, and its ability to treat man
as he really is, contrasted with the spirit of Protestantism, Freemasonry,
and Israel.[1]

The Action Française was more than a political movement; it was
a *Weltanschauung*, a package deal of opinions on every subject under
the sun. Its 'classicism' was more than a recall to order; it sounded a
retreat to the *grand siècle*. Its ultramontane and anti-modernist
Catholicism was a weapon, politically opportune, to beat the
Parliamentarians who were bent on the secularisation of French
society. Its royalism was calculated to appeal to all those who
remembered the greatness of France under the monarchy and
despaired of its mediocrity under the Third Republic – the régime,
as Thiers had argued, which divided Frenchmen the least, but still
looked like dividing them disastrously. Neither Maurras nor Daudet

[1] Henri Vaugeois, 10th July 1899

had the faintest understanding of English affairs – indeed the Protestant and liberal temper of English life, and the sting of party rivalries would have been grist to their prejudice – but there was something analogous to the Action Française in the anti-Semitism of Belloc and the two Chestertons, and their attacks upon the party system. All three were acquainted with the teaching of Maurras, although they did not know him personally; and the *Action Française* was read by many who disagreed with its views precisely because it was so readable.

Here then was a counter-revolutionary movement of the Right, making up in prestige what it lacked in numbers, and intellectually far more respectable than any of the derivatives to which it gave birth, directly or indirectly, in other countries. The Caesarism of Mussolini was a caricature of Maurras' *romanità;* and although the *camelots du roi* were always ready to man the barricades – a permanent temptation to the French – it is not easy to imagine them storming into the Sorbonne, as Franco's Falangists stormed into Unamuno's university at Salamanca, with their cry of *Abaja l'intelligencia*. Whatever their complaints about the Sorbonne – and these were many – *A bas l'intelligence* is not a cry that comes readily to French lips, whether they are cheering for the Right or for the Left. In any case, a counter-revolutionary movement of the Right was more appealing to a young man of inflammable imagination than a constitutional movement of the Left, and this was the only other option in sight. Marc Sangnier's Sillon was an attempt to use the Church to further the cause of social democracy, as the Action Française was an attempt to use it to further the establishment of a corporative state and the restoration of the monarchy. The young François Mauriac was among its early adherents. Each movement, in its different way, was anti-capitalist; but the capitalists, like the reigning Pontiff, Pius X, looked more kindly upon the Action Française. Each was eventually condemned by Rome; but the Sillon had not yet been proscribed when Lagrange expressed his surprise that Bernanos had not rallied to it. The boy shuddered with indignation: the salvation of France, in the spiritual as well as in the political order, depended on a traditional doctrine suited to the temperament of the race. The rosy-tinted abstractions of the Sillon were no substitute for a belief in original sin. Bernanos maintained that if you scratched a democrat you found a theologian. But it is only fair to point out in this connection that the ideology of the Action Française had its fair quota of abstractions, and that theologians were not wanting within its ranks.

Here spoke the musketeer of the Counter-Revolution, and what Jacques Maritain has called a *tempérament de droite*. Bernanos was never to go back on his original faith in the French monarchy, bitterly as he quarrelled with his former allies; and any attempt to 'democratise' his political beliefs is a vain, and indeed a ridiculous, exercise. He remained to the end of his days a *tempérament de droite* – although no one castigated the *droite* more ferociously than he. But these early years of the century were the honeymoon of the Action Française; its adherents dominated the Sorbonne; and the revolutionary wing of the movement were not ashamed to meet under the sign of Proudhon. It was to these groupings that Bernanos naturally belonged; he would have been ill at ease among the clerical generals, the bearded academicians and professors, and their attendant châtelaines.

The Ligue des Etudiants Patriotes was formed in 1905, changing its name a year later to the Union Nationale des Etudiants. Bernanos was among its members, leading a group which called themselves 'les Hommes de Guerre'. These young *camelots du roi* would sell *Action Française* outside the church doors on Sunday, mutilate the statues of Dreyfusard revisionists, and cause an uproar in the theatres where plays considered offensive to the Church were being performed. During the 'winter in the streets' of 1908 Bernanos was among the *camelots* arrested at the cemetery on Montparnasse after disturbing the ceremony organised in memory of Gabriel Sylveton. He was in the front rank of the students who chased from the podium a professor who had dared to insult the memory of Jeanne d'Arc, and afterwards gave him a sound thrashing. Bernanos was twice arrested in the course of this turbulent affair, and sentenced to ten days' detention. On the 16th and 17th of March 1909, his name figured on the roll of honour of the *camelots du roi* then under arrest at the Santé.

He was now fighting with his pen as well as with his fists. An article appeared under his name in *Soyons Libres*, one of those small weekly journals that spring up and then vanish overnight in the Latin Quarter. It was entitled *Les effets du préjugé démocratique dans le monde des lettres*, and was ostensibly devoted to an attack on Marcel Prévost. But its real target was a decadent romanticism which sought to exempt the writer from moral laws and social responsibility, and to deny the very springs of intellectual power – the classical traditions inherited from Greece and Rome. The Jacobin, by destroying the natural hierarchy of classes, had succeeded only in establishing the artificial competition of parties. As for Marcel Prévost –

One after another, the leaden phrases accompany the damp kisses: the bleating of vicious women mingle with the lachrymose groans of little good-for-nothings, with their soft cheeks, in a comedy that no one can believe in; the reflections of a pedantic philosophy and a vulgar science are reduced to the level of lavatory secrets – and all this adds up to the most infamous prostration before the democratic beast.[1]

The writer who was to employ language 'like a flamethrower' is already finding his style; hatred – *très belles haines* – is frankly exalted as a virtue. In the second part of his article Bernanos opposes the concentrated force of a great passion to the neurotic search for sensation.

The multiplication *ad infinitum* of diverse or contradictory sensations serves no purpose whatever. What matters is their powerful concentration around a great passion; we must raise to a higher level our capacity to feel. Woe betide the man who has never known the rough pleasure of sustaining, in the depths of his being, the shock of an insult, where every nerve jumps together to the rhythm of a unique hate! Disturbed as he may be by delicious and fugitive pleasures, he never tires of rallying the simple and strong convictions which sometimes reveal to us, like a clap of thunder, the unity of our inner selves.[2]

Quite as interesting, and indicative, as the tone of these articles is the address from which they were written; the *camelots du roi* were no strangers to the confinement of a prison cell.

Just as I write these lines (behind the walls of the Santé) a warder is struggling to bolt the door; let him get on with it. The useless and noisy gesture has filled my heart with a feeling, not of impotence, but of proud liberty. I am thankful for the conviction I have that all is so well ordered inside me, that each thing that happens to me impels me towards freedom, and that freedom impels me further towards the end I have in view. This

[1] *Bulletin*, no. 14, p. 5   [2] Ibid., p. 6

is the privilege of a well organised soul. The flock of rhetoricians may laugh at it; I can only wish all these writers, torn this way and that by their various desires, all these souls threatened with dissolution, the mental discipline of a *camelot du roi*.[1]

Here is clearly sounded the call to order, which was the watchword of the Action Française, and the exigence of liberty which was to drive Bernanos from its ranks. For the time being, however, the turbulent musketeer was happy with his chosen companions, Henri Tilliette and Maxence de Colleville, and asking a cousin in Holy Orders for the loan of a Lefaucheux rifle, which had formerly belonged to his father. We find them, with seven others, in the Café Napoléon at Arras where 300 socialist workers, mostly from the railway, had assembled to hear a certain Sebastian Faure lecture on the Blessed Virgin. Bernanos and his friends were careful to sit near the window, so that they could make good their escape, if necessary. Each had his half-pint of beer in a thick glass mug, to serve equally as a container or a projectile – for Bernanos was the last person to doubt that the honour of the Mother of God would have to be defended by force of arms. M. Faure's diatribes were rather too sophisticated for his audience of *cheminots*, and his challenge to any opponent in the room brought Bernanos, alone, to his feet – pale and thin beside the corpulent *conférencier*. The crowd started to boo, but were hushed by their leaders. There is no record of what Bernanos said, except that he presented a very different picture of the Blessed Virgin; and when a mining deputy mounted his chair in response to the excited appeals of the audience, it was to praise the courage – if not the opinions – of those who had opposed the speaker. This enabled them to leave without disturbance. The next day Bernanos remembered that they had forgotten to tip the waitress, and insisted that a suitable remuneration be sent to her by post.

In the neighbouring village of Sains-lès-Fressin a drama was enacted which might well have formed the scenario of a Bernanosian novel. The parish priest was a 'schismatic', and since he had control of the church, an orthodox and pious opponent was sent by the Bishop of Arras to challenge him. Excluded from both church and presbytery, he lodged in a farm and celebrated Mass in a barn. The

[1] *Bulletin*, no. 14, p. 6

sympathies of the parish were divided, but even the most virulent
anti-clericals went to one Mass or the other. One Sunday morning
Bernanos and his fellow-musketeers, each carrying a stick and a
pistol, having attended the orthodox Mass at Fressin, presented
themselves at the schismatic Mass near by. The preacher, sensing
hostility in the congregation, spotted Bernanos during the sermon
and fixed on him a pitiless stare, which was pitilessly returned. The
three musketeers were greeted with insults as they left the church,
but no blows were exchanged. Mme Bernanos, fearing a scandal,
had begged Tilliette – the least impetuous of the three – to make
sure that they returned in time for luncheon.

The Action Française never claimed to be a religious organisation
– in fact there were a number of freethinkers among its members –
but it was ardent in defence of religious orthodoxy. It became
increasingly cerebral as the years went by, but in these early days it
was always prepared to justify its name and to excuse its disturbance
of public order by a convenient distinction between *le pays réel* and
le pays légal. But the young Bernanos had no need of any such
casuistry to climb on to the stage of the theatre at Arras and interrupt
the speaker, Ferdinand Buisson, who was expounding the doctrines
of radical socialism. At the same time he was prosecuted for selling
the *Action Française* without a licence, and for shouting aloud the
headline which announced the withdrawal of a play by Henri
Bernstein, a confectioner of well-made melodramas who was then
the darling of the boulevards. The affair was settled after an enquiry
by a police official who knew the Bernanos family, and was indulgent
towards Georges' escapades.

For whatever reason Bernstein's play may have been withdrawn,
his name would have been enough for Bernanos to hiss it off the
stage. Here we are faced, straightaway, with a principle which was
always to linger as a prejudice; and there is no other name for it but
anti-Semitism. He had imbibed the poison, not from Maurras,
but from Drumont, and he had drunk it at his father's knee, for
Emile Bernanos would read aloud, every morning, from *La Libre
Parole*:

Did I really understand my poor father's explanations? Certainly I was
not of an age to understand them, or what they explained. Still that was
the time when I learnt everything, and not at school. The curés served up
to us a very different provender. But what is the use of a childhood that

cannot run its risks? The child that has never sensed the ambush will never be anything but blind or cowardly. If he has not faced the misery of the world with the clear vision of a fifteen-year-old, he will never be altogether fit to die, no matter if he lives to be a hundred.[1]

In fact Bernanos was only thirteen when he discovered *La France Juive*, a book as prolix as it was prejudiced, and as unreadable as it was widely read. But it fed the nationalist sentiment humiliated by the defeat of 1870, and the vindication of Dreyfus, and only too ready to fasten on a scapegoat with a Jewish profile acting as the agent of a German policy. That the scapegoat was largely an invention mattered little to a public thirsting for the return of the lost provinces. Nor was the vision of a fifteen-year-old necessarily clearer than that of his elders who, in this respect, were certainly not his betters.

There was more to Drumont than anti-Semitism, as we shall see in due course. What Bernanos owed to him was a vision of recent French history upon which he was never to go back, and when he wrote *La Grande Peur des Bien-Pensants* in 1929, he knew better what he was talking about than when he announced to the *trottoirs* that a play by Henri Bernstein had been withdrawn from the boulevards. Nevertheless, the seeds of his anti-Semitism had been truly sown. Charles Maurras and Léon Daudet were, of course, piping to the same tune in the *Action Française*, but it was principally from Drumont that Bernanos had picked up the refrain, and he went on humming it for a good time to come. Looking around him at the world of thought and letters, he saw the philosophers at the feet of Henri Bergson and the *littérateurs* at the feet of Marcel Proust. But there were other figures just as concerned as Georges Bernanos to preserve the Christian liberties of their country, and they did not look to the positivism of Maurras and the very lightly baptised paganism of Daudet for their defence. There was Paul Claudel who held the doctrines of the Action Française in 'utter abomination'; and Charles Péguy, who had drawn his sword for Dreyfus and was now turning it against Jaurès with an equal violence. Bernanos responded, in those days, to the voluble lyricism of Claudel, but he had not yet encountered Péguy. Yet the transformation of *mystique*

[1] Michel Dard, 'Fragments d'un journal': *Cahiers du Rhône*, pp. 293-300

into *politique*, which was the theme of Péguy's inexhaustible polemic, was to become the *leitmotiv* of his own; and before long the two men were united, although unknown to one another, in what each believed to be France's 'finest hour', and marching to a battlefield which was not of words.

CHAPTER 2

INTO BATTLE

I

MADAME BERNANOS regretted her son's decision to pursue his legal studies at the Sorbonne. Her intuition was correct, for the very notion of Bernanos at the Bar is a paradoxical hypothesis. He was never to forget the role of the canonists in the burning of Jeanne d'Arc, and wherever two or three Frenchmen were gathered together under the banner of Jeanne d'Arc Bernanos was among them. Patriotism had its part in this fidelity, but deeper insights were already at work; and he was to express them many years later in th album of a young Brazilian girl who had asked him for a message:

Keep your faith in the poets, and keep your faith in the spirit of child-hood! Never become a grown-up person! You only have to read the Gospels to see that there is a conspiracy among the grown-ups against the spirit of childhood. God said to the cardinals and the theologians and the essayists and the historians and the novelists, to everyone in fact: 'Become like a little child'. And from one century to another, the cardinals, the theologians, the historians, the essayists, and the novelists, went on telling the spirit of childhood which they had betrayed: 'Become like us'.

When you read these lines in years to come, give a thought and a prayer to the old writer who is more and more convinced of the impotence of the Powerful, the ignorance of the Learned, the idiocy of the Machia-vellians, and the incurable frivolity of the Serious. Everything beautiful in the history of the world is due, without our knowing it, to the mysterious accord between the ardent and humble patience of men and the gentle Pity of God.[1]

Bernanos did not live to be the 'old writer' prefigured here, but when he was only a young and turbulent *camelot du roi*, and had hardly put pen to paper, the 'spirit of childhood' sanctified in Jeanne d'Arc was already whispering its secrets above the *fracas* of the Latin Quarter. He and his fellow 'musketeers' would meet, almost daily, in the Café d'Harcourt, plotting attacks on their political opponents

[1] *Bernanos par lui-même* (Editions du Seuil, 1952), p. 96

– the Socialists or the Sillonistes – and since these horizons were too limited, dreaming of adventures further afield. In 1912 the advance of the Action Française had slowed down a little, and Bernanos, with his friends, made contact with the legitimist faction in Portugal. A plan was set afoot for the seizure of the fleet at anchor in the bay of Lisbon, combined with a *coup d'état* in Angola. It was hardly surprising that this conspiracy came to nothing. Two of the conspirators then offered their services to the Serbian irredentists; the Serbs, however, had no need of them, and they returned disconsolate to Paris, where they joined Bernanos in his bachelor establishment on the Boulevard Arago. The days were spent in the Bibliothèque Nationale or at the various *facultés*, and in the evening there were adventures in the kitchen, if not in the streets. A chicken, which had not been dressed, exploded in the *marmite;* and in the early hours of the morning, after hurling a fusillade of insults through the open windows of a cinema or vaudeville, screened only by the drawn curtains, they would concoct a brew of inky black tea, more conducive to nausea than refreshment. Political activity was naturally encouraged by alcohol, and accompanied by blows. Escorting home a comrade who had been hurt, Guy de Bouteiller, Bernanos, perfectly at ease and apparently sober, explained to Guy's father in some detail that his son was not feeling very well – and then made straight for the glass cupboard, mistaking it for the door which it reflected. By 1911 all the disparate groups of Right-wing activists had been assimilated to the Action Française, but Bernanos was never quite at home with the theories of Maurras. As one of his friends was to write later:

Certainly the A.F. was not enough, and would never have been enough, to give us all we wanted; it lacked a good deal that we should have liked, and we all had our difficulties with a movement that was totalitarian, if it was anything. But all the same we owed to it, beyond everything else, the pleasures of a hard and healthy comradeship in the fray. Georges was well aware of its defects, but he was not insensitive to these allurements.[1]

There was a tiny question mark in Bernanos' attachment to the Action Française long before the question mark had turned into a declaration of war.

As for his legal studies, 'no man in his senses would have dared to

[1] Ernest de Malibran: *Cahiers du Rhône*, p. 263

predict for me a lucrative career as a lawyer. To come clean with
you, what I loved was noise – and what better excuse is there for
making a noise than journalism?'[1] Already he was forming the
habit of writing in a café. He was to remember the marble-topped
table in the Brasserie de l'Opéra where every Thursday he would
compose an article destined for some review as noisy as himself, and
the waiter who sympathised with him for having 'to work with his
brains'. Of those engaged in the same polemic, his admiration went –
as we have seen – to Drumont, but also, very particularly, to
Daudet. This Dumasian figure, with his 'intoxicated laugh', his
gargantuan appetite, his critical acumen and imaginative verve, his
full-blooded eroticism, his 'gay, lucid, and universal curiosity', and
his 'Shakespearian nature', presented a human counterpart to the
Maurrasian cerebrations. 'Like Dante and Shakespeare', Daudet
'infused the world of the sensible with fire and steel, not in order to
extract from it some accidental and sublime outcry, but to recognise
in sensible things the cry of nature, surprised in its elemental travail'.
This was a long way from the serene classicism of Charles Maurras.
Haunted as Daudet seemed to be by the shade of Tolstoy, the sense
of Catholic order and vitality saved him from the Tolstoyan neurosis;
and he resembled in himself the heroes of his own fiction 'fighting at
their side against all the calamities of race and destiny, for the
conquest of free will – the foundation stone of human conscience –
with the redemptive Faith in front of him, and behind him nothingness and despair.'[2] The words may stand equally for Georges
Bernanos, except that the moment was to come when liberty as he
understood it, and order as Daudet and Maurras understood it,
could no longer be reconciled. But that time was not yet.

2

Both legal studies and an occasional experience of the law's strong
arm had been interrupted in 1909 when Bernanos was called up for
military service. For a *camelot du roi* the cavalry was a natural option.
As *cavaliers* they were distinguished from the *soldats* – a term reserved
for the infantry. Bernanos and his friend, Maxence de Colleville,
were attached to the same 6th Regiment of Dragoons, stationed at

---

[1] Lecture at Rouen, 1927: *Bernanos par lui-même*, p. 100
[2] Undated article: *Bulletin* XIV, pp. 7–9

Evreux. The new recruits were never permitted to walk; every move had to be made at the double. They were known as the *bleus*, and each *bleu* had an *ancien* of some experience to teach him his paces. Bernanos was well liked by his *ancien*, a certain Duviollier, who could use his fists to good effect and was insatiably addicted to *vin blanc*. He had all the tricks of the training at his fingers' end; and his favours, which considerably softened the rigours of military service, could be bought at the standard price of five francs a week. Bernanos' immediate superiors were also sympathetic, and so was the non-commissioned officer in charge of his platoon. But the corporal, who supervised the barrack-room where Bernanos and de Colleville both slept, aroused their hostility and contempt; de Colleville described him as 'stupid, deceitful, timorous, ignorant, spiteful, envious, and despotic.'[1] And they liked the chief non-commissioned officer no better. Fortunately the quartermaster-sergeant was an effective ally; and in general Bernanos was more popular with his fellow-recruits in the cavalry than he had been with his fellow-pupils at school. No doubt the years had toughened him, and he got along well enough with these farmers' sons, mostly from Calvados; only their addiction to the liqueur of their country threw an occasional spanner into the wheels of personal relations.

Nevertheless, Bernanos was not so tough as all that. After a short time, his health, never robust, gave way and he was temporarily discharged. De Colleville joined him at Fressin whenever he could, and we find the two friends walking the twelve kilometres to Hesdin in order to play billards at a café, or improvising a cannon out of an iron pipe. When this exploded, scattering its débris within a range of thirty yards, the curé of the neighbouring parish informed the two young men that he had heard from afar off 'a powerful detonation, the cause of which he was unable to explain'. Mme Bernanos had also heard it, and was anxious about the fate of her son and of the guest he had brought to the house. Then there were the boxing matches in the loft – without benefit of gloves, since de Colleville had forgotten to bring them – and long evenings in the library, with Mme Bernanos on the chaise-longue which she rarely left, and Georges deep in the novels of Sir Walter Scott. *Woodstock* and *Peveril of the Peak* had long been special favourites; Cromwell and his psalm-singing Roundheads, he was to write many years later,

---

[1] *Cahiers du Rhône*, p. 256

'were a terror and an abomination to me when I was fifteen years old'.

In September 1913 Bernanos accepted the editorship of the *Avant-Garde de Normandie*, a royalist weekly dependent on the Action Française, with its offices at Rouen. The offer came to him through Léon Daudet, who hoped that the Bernanosian *brio* would reactivate a dying periodical; the former editor, Count Cappa, having rather drowsily conducted its affairs, had now taken on the editorship of the *Univers*. Bernanos, with Ernest de Malibran as his secretary, intensified the polemic of the paper with more invective than argument, and brought a new life to its literary columns. He had discovered Villiers de l'Isle Adam through Daudet, and Barbey d'Aurevilly was beginning to exert a predictable influence. There was more than a touch of the dandy in Bernanos at this period, and he found the prince of 'dandyism' very much to his liking. He preferred the disciplined prosody of Mistral to the theatrical verbosity of Verhaeren; and he admired the Barrès of *Les Déracinés* because it exposed the hypocrisy of a liberal bourgeoisie, which in reality hated the poor it purported to succour.

Bernanos contributed three short stories to the paper. Two of these registered a considerable advance in depth from his previous essays in the same genre. In *La Tombe Refermée* he treated of an academician, dead to the life of the senses and the mind, a 'burnt-out case', whose whole existence had become an imposture. This looked forward, unconsciously maybe, to the abbé Cénabre of *L'Imposture*, over whom the tomb also closed to all intents and purposes. The influence of Barbey was evident in *La mort avantageuse du chevalier de Lorges*, where death held not only its familiar terrors but its 'precious secret'. For Bernanos death had long been something to face; it was now something to explore.

But of course his main contributions were polemical, all guns firing to port and starboard. There was Marc Sangnier – the *Roi du Sillon* – whose conciliatory moves towards the Left seemed to him a base compromise with liberalism. Sangnier was an ex-officer, and like Maurras he invited non-believers into the ranks of his movement. *Le Sillon* grew from a weekly into a daily newspaper, and it counted many of the younger clergy among its adherents. In certain Departments they were more numerous than the adherents of the Action Française. Sangnier's doctrinal deviations – if indeed they were deviations at all – were certainly no more dangerous than the Maurrasian *nationalisme intégral* and its totalitarian corollary; but they were offensive to the rigid conservatism of Pius X and Cardinal Merry del Val, his Secretary of State. The movement was condemned, and Sangnier submitted to the decree. All this was meat and drink to the Action Française. Bernanos never held democracy in greater contempt than when it assumed 'Christian' as a prefix; and it is a fair criticism of his polemic, all through the years, that once he had broken with the monarchism of Maurras, he never found anything to replace it. His own royalism remained a principle; it ceased to be either a policy or a programme. For the moment, however, he saluted Maurras as the champion of the whole French tradition against hostile and foreign influence:

the clear imagery of our poets, the method of our philosophers, the policy of our kings, the religion which has formed our consciences. Behind him, with the heroes who have built and defended our nationhood, I see the soil of our fatherland, the hills harmonious against the clear and light blue sky, our towns and villages that an imbecile régime would hand over to the defiling grasp of the conqueror. This armed and vigilant thinking has served them better than our guns.[1]

Maurras was then on trial, and the opposition of the *Journal de Rouen* with its Jewish clientèle, gave Bernanos an opening which he was quick to seize:

To be sure, before we listened to the teaching of such a master, we belonged to France, by virtue of our origins, our deepest instincts, and a thousand fibres of our being, but he disciplined this love of ours, and our enthusiasm was redoubled, both in heart and mind. We were completely under his spell. Let the judges sentence him, and the servile press keep silent, he is now at one with eternal France and a share in her destiny will be his. The day will logically arrive when all those wishing to serve their country will rally to his doctrine, for it stands at the very heart of what the safety of the state requires. He does not appeal in vain to the dismayed jury of his spiritual family, and the youth will answer him. Our arms are raised to protect the brain of our country. You shall not touch it! Every one of us will have shed his blood before that voice is hushed or that light extinguished. Let your laws and your lackeys do their worst – we are his servants, and he is the first servant of the King.[2]

[1] 2nd November 1913: *Bulletin* 17–20, p. 2
[2] Georges Vaury: *Cahiers du Rhône*, pp. 268–9

A more serious adversary than the *Journal de Rouen* was equally near at hand. Alain was then teaching at the *lycée* in Rouen; and Alain was the philosopher of radical socialism. He was indeed the only intellectual in a party which had always appealed to the commercial interests of the country. The residuary legatee of a Jacobinism *embourgeoisé*, it lacked the idealism of either the Socialists or the Action Française. All it had in common with the former was its hatred of the Army and the Church. It stood, on every count, for the individual against the institution, for the citizen against the city. As Sir Denis Brogan has written:

The unending audacities of elected persons in betraying their electors moved him [Alain] less to the indignation of Whitman than to an ironical resignation, to a resolve to reduce, as far as possible, their power for evil, as it was impossible to increase their power for good. . . . The Radical was the man who wished to keep to the ideas and practices of 1789; to defend the Rights of Man as interpreted in the pre-machine age; and to ignore the fundamental difficulties of applying the methods of the age of diligences in the age of motor-cars.[1]

Bernanos had no more trust than Alain in 'the audacities of elected persons', but nothing ever moved him to ironical resignation. He believed, like his master Maurras, that the state must be strong, although he did not think that 'elected persons' would contribute materially to its strength. There was, however, this much to be said for 'elected persons'; they had recently brought in a law extending military service to three years – a law which Alain had vehemently opposed. A time would come when Bernanos himelf was to denounce conscription as a symbol of totalitarian tyranny, but caught up as he was in the nationalist fever of the time, he regarded any opposition to the new law as tantamount to treason. Alain had written:

France will have a professional army and a militia, if she wants to. She may be running a great risk; she may be risking everything. Well, a lot of people risked everything in 1870, and they did so with a light heart. And why? To preserve their privileges. When we risk as much for an integral democracy, isn't the game infinitely more worth the candle? Justice and liberty at any price. It's better to die than to live enslaved – that is what my idea finally adds up to; and despise it, if you can.[2]

[1] *The Development of Modern France* (1940)
[2] *Cahiers du Rhône*, p. 269

Georges Bernanos, 1898

Watching his masters play chess

This declaration gave Bernanos the cue he was waiting for:

Better to die than to live enslaved, you say? But the death of a people is nothing else than its enslavement. If one day we should be conquered, thanks to your stupidity and the stupidity of those like you, how much will be left of the liberty for which you are willing to die? It's not your idea that I despise, it's you yourself. We have all seen these idiotic pawns wandering about our barrack squares. You can tell them by their narrow, mulish foreheads behind their professional spectacles, by their eyes in which there is no spark of pride, by the awkward and shambling way they walk about. These semi-literate creatures, puffed up with a little civic morale, would not impress the most junior subaltern, just arrived, bottom of his class, from St Cyr. . . . The seeds of the truth that we are sowing will grow and will bear their fruit, and against that truth you are prepared to do everything, up to the limits of treason itself. To be sure, the national defence will lose little by your efforts, for it is not in the quarters you frequent that the country will go looking for its martyrs. . . . When the blood of young Frenchmen is flowing everywhere, it is not to an obscure sophist like yourself that the mothers will hold up their immolated sons. Nevertheless, on the evening of our defeat, your insignificant silhouette and the shadow of your asses' ears will overhang our sacred fields, and the dead that cover them. You will have pointed the cannon of Krupp straight at the heart of the country. The German schoolmaster is none other but yourself.[1]

Alain had also insulted the memory of Paul Déroulède, who had died shortly before the war broke out, which for him, as for so many other Frenchmen, was to have been the war of revenge for the lost provinces. 'One can be sorry for him', Alain had written, 'but he ought to be shut up' – and now the wish was granted. It was only too true, Bernanos bitterly retorted, that he would never leave the narrow grave where hundreds of Parisians had laid their flowers, but his example would live on to inspire the cause in which he had believed – and in fact the first frontier post torn up from the crest of the Vosges in a premature offensive was to serve as his memorial.

A corrupt régime will always throw up its scandals, very much as a diseased body will produce its ulcers, and a succession of these had marked the chequered history of the Third Republic. The latest of them exploded on the 16th of March 1914, and it offered Bernanos fresh ammunition. M. Calmette, editor of Le Figaro, assisted by

[1] *Cahiers du Rhône*, pp. 269–70

Forain's deadly illustrations, had been waging a virulent campaign against Caillaux, the Radical-Socialist Minister of Finance. He had published letters written by Caillaux to the second Mme Caillaux (when she had not yet acquired that name) and the first Mme Caillaux had stolen them. Thereupon the second Mme Caillaux walked into Calmette's office and shot him dead. It is hardly necessary to add that she was subsequently acquitted, the *République de Rouen* saluting her as a 'Roman heroine' and 'an image of marital fidelity'. Bernanos stormed into the fray:

A man has died. We shall know whether his death will be avenged. We shall discover – yes or no – whether that vain little head, with its pretty hat, has been placed above the law by the authority of a former minister who betrayed his office. But what am I saying? We already know: she is now beyond the reach of justice. The audacity of some and the cowardice of others have preserved the guilty woman in those high places, where tyranny evades not only the law, but the judgment of the public itself. The dishonour of these two persons would seem to contaminate everything around them. I know this, and I am no longer capable of indignation. There is something in these infamies which would seem to put them beyond the judgment of an honest man. It sickens my heart to read, day by day, the articles in the Paris press. What is this malaise, and why are we stifling in it? The conscience is revolted before the mind has been able to discover from what putrid well the air is coming up to poison us. Of course, it is disgusting – but what is it that disgusts? How far has the treason gone? How much of the crime was due to pride, ambition, self-interest, or debauch? Here are a man and woman, the very sight of whom is enough to turn one's stomach – figures of monstrous vanity, cruelty and insignificance. I see them, and in seeing them I can read their crime. . . . They will be crowned, I have no doubt, with the highest honours the republic can bestow; but no matter what dress or decorations they may wear, the wretched couple will always bear along with them, I can promise you that, the stench of cold sweat and of blood.[1]

This was the last contribution of Bernanos to the *Avant-Garde de Normandie*. It was dated the 1st of August 1914. The Caillaux affair was an exception to the 'imposthume of much wealth and peace that inward breaks and shows no cause without why the man dies'. At the same time, we must remember, Péguy was attacking Jaurès with an equal violence; and before many days had gone by Jaurès was to

[1] *Cahiers du Rhône*, pp. 272–3

die from an assassin's bullet. There was more in all this than the virtuosities of invective. Violence was invoking an apocalypse much closer than most people then suspected, for already, when Bernanos had delivered his last broadside from Rouen, a shot had been fired at Sarajevo.

3

Bernanos would speak of those months at Rouen as 'the loveliest months, the only radiant months, of my life'. The reason was to be sought not alone in the daily exercise of a pen that was enjoying its polemic. There were passionate discussions with Ernest de Malibran at the Café Paul, where the set-up of the paper was organised, and long nights at the printers, and short trips to Paris, with heads nodding on the return journey and fears that they might not wake up at Rouen. Even more significant were the hospitable evenings with M. and Mme Talbert d'Arc, who lived only a few doors away from their lodging in the rue des Carmélites. Mme d'Arc, President of the Dames de l'Action Française at Rouen, was directly descended from a brother of Jeanne d'Arc. One of her daughters was also called Jeanne, and Bernanos quickly became attached to her. Other things being equal, their engagement was almost inevitable. To have met and fallen in love with a descendant of Jeanne d'Arc, and bearing the name of Jeanne d'Arc, in the place where Jeanne had been burnt at the stake was among the neater contrivances of Providence.

Another friendship was also beginning to ripen. On the 1st of February 1914 Bernanos reviewed *Les religions laïques* (*Un romantisme religieux*) by Dom Besse, a Benedictine monk from Ligugé. Besse was among the recognised theologians of the Action Française, and Bernanos, deeply impressed by his book, was quick to establish personal relations with him. His formidable influence now replaced that of abbé Lagrange, who did not share Bernanos' belief in *gesta Dei per Maurras*. What Bernanos admired in Dom Besse was 'a nature vigorous and even inflexible; a nature that the most burning conviction animates, but does not disturb'; a thought which 'nourishes enthusiasm and hatred at the same time... that kills without shedding blood.'[1] The spirit of this 'calm and terrible monk', as Bernanos called him, was the spirit of medieval Christen-

[1] Article of 6th June 1914

dom, and when the Action Française was under the threat of Papal condemnation, Bernanos was quick to pay tribute to the man who had done so much to confirm him in the essential tenets of its doctrine. While he was rejoicing in this fiery companionship, older but not necessarily wiser than himself, Maxence de Colleville and Guy de Bouteiller, in despair of finding in Europe the excitement they craved, had left for Paraguay where they were hoping to found a society more consonant with their ideals. In March Ernest de Malibran left to join them. But it was not long before Europe proved more exciting than Paraguay, and the three musketeers came scurrying home as fast as the merchant marine could carry them.

Albert Béguin would always say – he said so often to the present writer – that the 1914–18 war was the decisive experience in the life of Georges Bernanos. He came out of it, not changed but deepened, not cynical but disillusioned. He had seen the worst that men could do to each other on the field of battle – and behind it. The dandy who could stand before the doors of St Sulpice and exclaim to a companion: 'how do you imagine that the great Condé went to Mass?' and then enter the church twirling his cane, had shed none of his principles but a good deal of his panache. More exactly, perhaps, he kept his panache for his pen, and his pen had not rusted during the years that he was unable to exercise it. It was merely stained with blood and sweat, and with the tears of what was hardly distinguishable from despair. Where a lesser man will wrestle with the temptation of debauch, Bernanos wrestled with the demon of despair. Here, meeting him at every corner of the way, was the adversary that lurked in ambush for his *curés de campagne*. He was to know, only too well, what he was writing about; and in this sense it is true to say of him, as of any great writer, that his biography is in his books.

At the end of August 1914 he rejoined the second squadron of the second troop of the 6th Regiment of Dragoons, and eight days later was sent to act as a liaison cyclist with a brigade of *Spahis*. He quickly fell ill and after a period of convalescence returned to the Dragoons at the end of December. Future novels were burgeoning in his head and the first draft of a play was committed to paper; and when he was no longer capable of manipulating his 'dear phantoms' – so he told his fiancée – life would not be worth living. It was not greatly worth living, as it was, for he was missing her sorely and

offending on her account 'all the holy virtues of obedience, resignation, humility, and hope'.[1] He described the poor country church
where he had attended Mass in the early morning, the crudely
painted wooden altar, the cemetery white under the frost, and the
odour of dead leaves coming up to him through the mist. He had
prayed for the gift of peace, but it had not been given him.

Bernanos was not at home in the army, and he was not, it seems, a
particularly efficient soldier. Although he was wounded several
times and received a number of citations, he was not promoted
beyond the rank of corporal. At the end of February 1915, he was
sent back to the depot at Vincennes where he followed various
courses with fresh and incompetent recruits, ignorant of how best to
secure the 'benevolent indifference' of his superiors, a precious asset
for the cavalryman on active service. It was not enough apparently
to sit up all night arguing with an officer, whose views on Bonaparte
were different from his own – for Bonaparte had no place in the
hagiography of the Action Française. Bernanos confessed himself
'incapable of folding a greatcoat or packing a saddle-bag . . . but
full of illusions about civil and amateur equitation', which earned
him the contempt both of his horse and his warrant-officer. He was
beginning right at the bottom in fact, 'with a respect for nothing but
the job well done, unable to do my own properly, and forced in
consequence to spoil other people's.'[2] In 1917 he was attached for a
time to the aviation, flying forty-six hours on the early, broken-
winded Farman machines which had their rudders in front. And he
was later to experience the monotony of trench warfare, the illusion
of a victory that vanished like a mirage in a desert of mortal ennui,
and that when it was achieved in face of a courageous enemy was
betrayed by a corrupt régime.

The war was not important, then, or even interesting, for any
part he played in it; but it was crucial for the part it played in him.
He had never shared the euphoria of the *union sacrée*. Where other
camelots du roi were prepared to lay aside their differences with the
parliamentary democracy of the Third Republic, Bernanos could
only see a cabal of politicians masking a disorder of the state which
was really a disorder of the soul. Firm as ever in his convictions, he
was gradually becoming independent in his attachments. He felt no
particular sympathy for the dogmatic anti-Germanism which

[1] *Cahiers du Rhône*, p. 28   [2] *Les Enfants humiliés*, p. 50

Maurras was preaching from a rostrum safer than the parapet of a trench. The war only intensified and embittered his introspection. Where a Teilhard de Chardin, no less actively engaged, had seen in the carnage of Verdun the matrix of a new world, and the challenge to an heroic optimism, it brought Bernanos to the foot of the Cross, where he could do no more than echo the *Eloi, eloi, lama sabachtani* of his Master. To begin with, however, what he experienced was the tedium rather than the tragedy of war.

I had dreamt of writing to you with my knee pressed against my saddle-bag, my right arm in the strap of my lance, firmly seated on the saddle, and my ears turned towards the noise reaching me from the honourable enemy, and within easy range of his rifle fire. But there is no enemy, no cannon, no trenches, and hardly any dead. . . . I don't give a damn for the newspapers who make good people believe that this is a place where honour can be won. What sort of honour? The risk runs away from you like water.

I can hear the cannon, or something like it, but there is not the slightest sign of a shell. . . . This is a deceptive century we live in, my good fellow, and the glory of the olden times has lied to us. I don't know what I am defending, or for what I run the risk of death. The stupidity of it all is astonishing. . . . I have decided that my epitaph shall consist of the following two lines: *Here lies the man who fought and died for his personal satisfaction, and to enrage those who are unwilling either to fight or die.*[1]

The irony grew less playful as the months dragged on, and by March 1917, when the Allied fortunes were at their lowest and it seemed that only a German victory could break the *impasse* on the Western front, Bernanos was reminding the same friend that the burial of the human race was not a noiseless operation; and that while the world was disputing its future 'between blind force and an idiotic liberalism', their own place was in neither camp, but on the battlefield where God was waiting for them.[2] Looking back on the patient endurance of his comrades, Bernanos was to write:

They will admit, I daresay, that there were days when they didn't care a damn for anything – didn't care whether they lived or died. But I think they sometimes deserved that God should smile upon them, for, without realising it, they were living, at the bottom of their muddy holes, a life of brotherhood. It wasn't that they behaved irreproachably to one another;

[1] September 1915 to Jean-Marie Maitre: *Cahiers du Rhône*, pp. 30–1
[2] March 1917: *Cahiers du Rhône*, p. 32

they didn't call each other 'brother', like men in a monastery. A word of three letters, which I daren't repeat, was generally enough to express their cordiality. It's not a small thing to take over the guard of a tired comrade when the shells of the trench-mortar shoot up into the evening sky. They would do that, and many other things besides. They shared their last crust of bread, and drank in common the last can of stinking coffee. The sweat of their brow trickled on the gaping stomach of a friend, while their coarse and clumsy hands stuffed it with a whole packet of dressing. And that wasn't a little thing either, when the machine-gun bullets were whistling no higher than their shoulders.[1]

Writing from a little copse, where 140 horses lay buried, he finds reason and feeling both affronted by the squalor and violence of war; an offence, it seemed, against the sixth[2] rather than the seventh commandment. Only the rosary and the Magnificat murmured in the darkness, and the daily recital of the psalms and the office of a Benedictine Oblate, will do something to purge its infection. The despair engendered by material squalor in the trenches and moral squalor behind them was a more dangerous enemy than the Kaiser's levies then massing for their supreme assault.

4

Paul Valéry wrote of Degas that, for him, France was 'the blue on the mantle of St Louis'. Much the same thing might have been said of Georges Bernanos; and among 'the virtues of the antique world' chivalry wore a special halo in his eyes, because the essence of chivalry is doing battle against something for the protection of something else. For Bernanos that something else was France, but it was also, in magical microcosm, the girl he hoped to marry. As the years go by, it is easy to lose sight of her in the dust and heat of controversy. She was a self-effacing character, and it is through the high, clear, romantic dedication of her *preux chevalier* that her presence can be felt, even when she is neither seen nor heard. Bernanos liked to compare her to a lily, tall and straight and immaculate; her action and influence in his life did not belie the description.

He wrote to her with such regularity as the movement and mono-

---

[1] *Les Grands Cimetières sous la lune*
[2] In the Catholic Catechism the sixth commandment is the commandment not to commit adultery.

tony of war allowed, generally at nightfall, by the light of a single candle, when the needs of his horse had been attended to. He sent her extracts from the play he was working on, and told her of his battle 'with words and images', each page costing him 'a world'. He compared the heart of the country, which was sound, with the ludicrous debates of the *derrière*. He recorded how a sudden and spontaneous *Vive le roi*! had won him a certain popularity with the colonel; and how a shell from the Austrian 150 field-gun had exploded in the trench a yard away from him, removing him a considerable distance 'under an avalanche of smoking earth'. He wrote with particular relief from reserve billets in a weathered manor, elegant and discreet, with an Andalusian curve to the roof, redolent of the France he loved.

It was not that Bernanos disbelieved in the grand causes for which the war was ostensibly being fought. 'The grand abstractions are my friends.'[1] But it seemed more like 'a dance of savages' than any conflict in which chivalry could win its spurs. Nevertheless it was something to be a cavalier with a horse for one's master – the silent and dignified companion of whom one never tired – and there were moments when Bernanos' exuberant fantasy was able to transform the landscape of the western front into an illustration from *Les petites heures du Duc de Berri*. But these moods were rare. In the summer of 1916 Bernanos wonders whether he will be able to spend the next Christmas with Jeanne; whether they will be kneeling together at the midnight Mass, and looking further ahead to a rather noisy nursery. M. and Mme Talbert d'Arc were unwilling for the young couple to be married before the end of the war, but Dom Besse overruled their objections. The wedding took place at Vincennes on the 11th of May 1917. Dom Besse performed the ceremony, with Léon Daudet as witness. In April 1918, a daughter, Chantal, was born to Jeanne Bernanos. Georges, on compassionate leave for a day or two, had barely time to notice the colour of her eyes before rejoining his regiment. Although Ludendorff's offensive had spent itself, the Allied recovery had yet to gather its momentum, and in the meantime the rhodomontade of the politicians was 'troubling the peace of the cemeteries'.[2] By May 1918, the 6th Dragoons were in the thick of the fight. They had retreated in good order, at odds of

[1] *Correspondance* I, p. 113
[2] Letter to Jean-Marie Maitre, 30th April 1918: *Correspondance* I, p. 137

ten to one against them, just as if they were practising a manoeuvre
in the comparative safety of Vincennes. Bernanos was acting as
liaison between his troop and his squadron, going from one to the
other across a wood and plain raked with bullets, carrying his
orders at a walking pace, his rifle slung over his shoulder. His part in
this action won him a citation from the captain of his squadron and
the lieutenant in charge of his troop, but shortly afterwards he was
wounded, spending two months in hospital, and a further blessed
month of convalescence with his wife and child at Vernonnet in the
Eure. Chantal, he now registered, had eyes of a shaded blue, and a
Pre-Raphaelite forehead. From Vernonnet he wrote to Dom Besse
with a vehemence encouraged, no doubt, by a reading of Léon Bloy.
He was to remember how he had rolled in the meadows on the
banks of the Seine, literally weeping with rage, for Bloy's anger was
as contagious, and disproportionate, as his style. The future would be
disputed between anarchy and order; the city must be rebuilt upon
the ruins of a discredited romanticism. If only Renan were alive to
record the conversations between Bergson and Woodrow Wilson!

Bernanos had, in fact, been reading a good deal of philosophy,
asking Jeanne to procure for him Kant's *Critique of Pure Reason*,
Leibniz' *Monadologie*, Spinoza's *Ethics*, and Descartes' *Discours de la
méthode*. This systematic study was quite untypical of his normal
habits. On the 24th of August he rejoined his regiment, and on the
17th of September, when the strategy of Foch was still being put to
the test, he was at the end of his spiritual tether. Writing to a friend
that the feeling of God's absence was the only sign left of His
existence, he asked his correspondent not to tear up his letter, but
either to keep or burn it. Fortunately for our knowledge of his
mood within two months of the Armistice, the letter was kept. It
showed how little he expected from the victory, and how much he
feared it.

CHAPTER 3

THE ABORIGINAL CALAMITY

I

THE years immediately following the 1914–18 war were a period of literary and, above all, of spiritual gestation. It was also a time when Bernanos was obliged to earn his living and to provide for his growing family. We can best trace his spiritual itinerary – for upon this both his creative and polemical writings would depend – by taking up his correspondence with Dom Besse from the moment of his return from the front in August 1918. He writes very much as he had written to Jean-Marie Maitre in the letter mentioned at the end of the last chapter. The example of St Louis, asking God for the 'gift of tears'; the unsatisfying nourishment of a Stoic philosophy; the distrust of an Ignatian spirituality, whose methods seemed to him too external; the intention to place himself under the protection of Pius X, whose condemnation of Modernism and condonation of Maurras would have commanded an equal sympathy – all these illustrate the way his mind was moving. A Dominican friar was chaplain to the regiment, and Bernanos had the idea of asking him to direct a small group of men anxious to keep their foothold in the Faith at a time when it, as well as they, was coming under heavy fire. But the chaplain was moved to another unit, and Bernanos could no longer depend upon the daily reception of the sacraments. He seems to have been reading Newman, but he wrote to Besse that 'with these intuitionists one never knows where one is going'. Notwithstanding his suspicion of a mind which he criticised as 'brilliant and fluid', he did, however, cling to Newman's dying words: 'I have never sinned against the light', just as he clung to the words of the *Imitation:* 'I shall not cease to pray, and I shall persevere to the end, until your Grace returns to me, and you purify my inward being.'

Once he was demobilised, Bernanos was able to attend Mass and receive Holy Communion daily. He and his wife settled down in Paris at 3 rue de l'Université, where a son, Yves Philippe, was born to them in August 1919 – the second child within twenty-eight months of their marriage. Bernanos prided himself on a defiance of 'wise calculations'. It was at this point that he severed his active connection with the Action Française, the first and the last political party he ever belonged to. Ideology and sentiment had drawn him to it, but he now feared that the little army of militants would become a larger army of bureaucrats, and Bernanos had no taste for bureaucracy. History showed what happened when men set about to organise their conquests. The Action Française had not won political power, and was not likely to; but it enjoyed a considerable measure of prestige, because France had emerged victorious from a war which the leaders of the movement had foreseen, and for which they had prepared the country with a skilful and implacable propaganda. But it was a propaganda nourished on hate, and if there was one sentiment totally absent from the introspection of Bernanos during those four decisive years, it was the sentiment of hate. His thought, as we have seen, ran deeper than the dialectic of history, the cabals of politics, or the dubious satisfactions of revenge. He was to come back to politics in the end and, as we shall show, he was faithful to his old masters in the hour of their tribulation. But by then he had become a different and deeper person; indeed he was a different person already.

In Paris there was, once again, the *Bal des Quat' z' Arts*, which the outraged *camelots du roi* had broken up in those turbulent days before the war. But the men returning from the front had no appetite for violence. Instead of the expected slap in the face, the dancers and debauchees of the *derrière* received only 'a smile of false gaiety, of false complacency, and they never forgave us that smile because they never understood it. And they never forgave us, either, the humiliation of having to let themselves go and take off their shirts in our presence – for we stood for the dead. It was too late to call off the party, but we had spoilt it for them. By a perfectly legitimate reaction on the part of those who had promised to make beasts of themselves to their drunken hearts' content, they probably took their revenge on us by behaving a thousand times more disgustingly than their programme for the *Bal des Quat' z' Arts* had envisaged. And by another reaction, just as legitimate, the more disgustingly they behaved, the less desire we had to behave disgustingly ourselves.'[1]

[1] Journal, 1940: *Bernanos par lui-même*, p. 109

The chasm of incomprehension between the 'front' and the *derrière*, of which Bernanos was to write in *Les Enfants humiliés*, yawned wider than ever when the war was over.

In the summer of 1919 he was staying with his sister at Berck and already at work on the last section of the novel which was to become *Sous le Soleil de Satan*, for he had the climax clearly in his mind before he had fully developed the beginning. In July of the following year Dom Besse died at Namur, and it was many years before Bernanos found a spiritual adviser on whom he could rely so implicitly. When the crisis of the Action Française came to a head six years later, he must often have wondered how Dom Besse would have reacted to it. He spent his time between Paris and Fressin, earning what he could by his pen, until in the summer of 1923 he fell seriously ill. At the same time the health of Jeanne Bernanos was causing serious anxiety, and in July both she and her husband made a pilgrimage to Lourdes.

Turning his back on journalism for the time being, Bernanos could not escape the clear vocation of a writer. He was not in the least attracted by the career of an *homme de lettres;* writing, he had told Dom Besse, was simply the only way that he could live. But 'living' in this sense was rather different from earning a living for himself and those dependent on him. Moreover, the birth of a second son, Michel, in February 1923, and of a second daughter, Claude, in January 1924, with the cost of his operation, had greatly added to his expenses. He accepted, therefore, a post as inspector for the National Insurance Company, and on the 5th of January 1924, left Fressin to take up his duties. His district was the eastern departments, and he made his headquarters in Paris or at Fressin, and later at Bar-le-Duc. It was a life of constant travel from one town to another. The fall of Poincaré had terrified the provincial bourgeoisie, and business was bad. We find Bernanos in a dirty café at Rethel, with a slatternly waitress wandering between the tables, and a commercial traveller from Paris pinching her behind. In the square, beyond, a squirrel had come to rest on the branch of a lime tree, stoned to death by the inhabitants who had nothing better to do. Everywhere he goes, Bernanos carried the burden of his pessimism, even shifting it on to the beds in the hotels – one so like another – and tempted to spit out his spleen on to their coarse sheets. The century, whose scourge and catalyst he was to become, seems to him more like the 'bedroom of some beautiful sinner, who has just died repentant and pardoned. A cloud of incense, of the Holy Oils, and of another solemn odour still lingers among the familiar perfumes.'[1] With advancing years – although they had not advanced very far – he feels no increase of peace or security; only a 'grim lucidity', which reflects as much of Hell as of Heaven. Dom Besse is no longer at hand to succour him: 'I am between the Angel of light and the Angel of darkness, looking at them each in turn with the same enraged hunger for the absolute.'[2]

Fortunately he had found time to write, and here he was lucky in his friendship with Robert Vallery-Radot, himself a *littérateur* of taste and talent. They had first met in the courtyard of the Institut Catholique in Paris, after a rather pompous Mass of the Holy Ghost, surrounded by bishops and canons and academicians, company in which the young Bernanos, with his bowler hat cockily tilted to one side, was not naturally at home. Dom Besse had encouraged him to write to Vallery-Radot, and Bernanos had done so, enclosing an article for the *Univers*. Later they would meet, every Sunday, at Vallery-Radot's house in Versailles, with its spacious garden echoing to the laughter of his five children; and it was thanks to his good offices that *Madame Dargent* – a short story of considerable power – was published in the *Revue hebdomadaire* in 1922. Rather significantly, Bernanos placed as epigraph to this a quotation from Péguy, an indication that as the influence of Maurras receded, that of Péguy and Bloy was beginning to make itself felt. The lines may be taken as defining the whole aim of Bernanos' literary endeavour.

A poet, known, understood, classified and catalogued, who lies printed on the shelves of the sterile library at the Ecole Normale, and who would never be anywhere else, and would never light a fire in any heart, is a dead poet.[3]

Péguy had died on the battlefield of the Marne – an astonishing fulfilment of his destiny – but in another sense he was more alive than ever; and the day would come, during the Second World War, when Bernanos was at eloquent pains to rescue him from friends whom he would certainly not have welcomed.

In *Madame Dargent* a woman is on her death-bed – an essential

---

[1] 20th March 1925: *Bernanos par lui-même*, p. 112
[2] 17th January 1926: Ibid   [3] Editions de la Pléiade, p. 1

constituent of the Bernanosian *mise-en-scène*. Summoning her husband, she reveals her knowledge that the baby they had adopted was his natural son, and that it was she who had murdered both the child and her husband's mistress. In a last spasm of energy she goes to her escritoire and throws at his feet the necklace of pearls she had taken from the dead woman. Her husband then strangles her and the world has no difficulty in believing that Madame Dargent, in a fit of furious delirium, had died in her husband's arms. Charles Dargent is an eminent novelist, looking forward to Antoine de Saint-Marin in *Sous le Soleil de Satan* and Ganse in *Un Mauvais Rêve*. The type always fascinated Bernanos. These creatures, empty in themselves, and living only in the puppets they manipulated for the reader's casual enjoyment, represented the temptation of *littérature* from which he could only be delivered by creating them himself – for he, too, was the prisoner of his dreams. 'What you have dreamt, I have done,' Madame Dargent reminded her husband; and he could no longer escape responsibility for the deed. For Bernanos there was a communion of sinners analogous to the communion of saints, a reversibility of sins as well as of merits. For Bernanos, too, there was no separation between life and literature, whatever *littérature* might pretend to the contrary. Nevertheless, when Madame Dargent was no more,

The eminent master resumed his race for honours and fame with a robust optimism. What indeed had he to fear? Not twice in a lifetime does an author find himself face to face with a creature of flesh and blood who resembles, like a sister, the elegant and perverted dreams which divert both himself and the reader, his accomplice . . . But who knows? More than one image of murder, which the writer gets off his chest, is still found stirring ten centuries later in a book.[1]

The long hours lying on the carpet and poring over the *Comédie humaine* had not been wasted. Balzac's power of exact description, and at the same time his ability to make a scene transcend its setting, are here in the physical details of Madame Dargent's death chamber, with the nursing sister quietly going about her business, and the clock of St Thomas d'Aquin – close to Bernanos' own apartment in the rue de l'Université – striking the small hours as the 'great shadows of the inner catastrophe pass to and fro' across the face of

[1] Editions de la Pléiade, p. 14

the dying woman, and the 'beautiful tenor of contemporary literature' tries to escape her regard. Bernanos was never afraid of melodrama, because he realised, with Chesterton, that 'the essence of melodrama is that it appeals to the moral sense in a highly simplified state, just as farce appeals to the sense of humour in a highly simplified state.'[1] So the story moves swiftly to its climax, never bogged down by a distracting realism, and tightly held to a dimension which was metaphysical for all its melodrama, even if it is not specifically religious – as it was very shortly to become. The romantic essays of Bernanos' apprentice years had always come to an edifying full-stop, but here there was no place for edification. Madame Dargent's confession was inspired by rancour rather than contrition and no absolution was expected to follow it. Yet here, too, the perceptive reader could have seen, as Bernanos had seen in Balzac and in Barbey, a visionary at work.

It seems likely that the second story, *Une Nuit*, was written about the same time, although it was not published till later. It is twice the length of *Madame Dargent*. Ever since Bernanos' three fellow-musketeers had set out to discover, or to create, an earthly paradise in Paraguay, the country had haunted his imagination. Small love as he had for the Jesuits, he may well have read the story of their benevolent régime among the Indians, and its insane suppression. For this, or another, reason, the action of *Une Nuit* is set in the Paraguayan bush, 100 miles from Asunción, where a French commercial adventurer is on his way to make a fortune out of maté. He stumbles on the lightly-buried corpse of a man, recently murdered by an Indian girl, who surprises him at the moment of his discovery and leads him to the hut where she is living with a half-caste, also dying from the poison she had administered to him. The son of a French father – a former convict – and an Indian mother, he is obsessed with the nationality he had never known, and whose only relic is a trivial brochure – *Mille et une blagues à faire en société*. He asks his unknown visitor for a word of consolation, but the visitor has himself forgotten the words which might have brought him comfort. 'Is that the last message,' he asks himself, 'that I can bring to this lost child from the country he has so long been searching for? I have none better to offer him.' Nevertheless, as he tries to give him with his presence what he cannot give him with his prayers, he

[1] *Charles Dickens* (1906)

clings to the belief that 'the mercy of some god would burst over him like a thunderbolt'. Beside the dead body, with the silly book clasped in its hands, the girl – who was a baptised Christian and could perhaps have spoken the necessary word – lay dead also, killed accidentally in a scuffle with their midnight visitor.

The story is poignant with a deep and anguished humanity, and it shows, now for the first time, the power of Bernanos to establish a correspondence between the characters of his fiction and the world of nature that surrounds them. There is the night itself, immense and tropical, clasping the lonely traveller in its clammy embrace. There is the wild cat, half stripped of its skin, dangling over the door of the hut, and casting a macabre shadow across the threshold. There are the branches cracking overhead, and the girl's breath smelling of cinnamon. All these images are disciplined to a purpose, not to flatter the senses of the reader but to conduct him far beyond them. It would be an abuse of language to describe Bernanos as a sensual writer; he merely used his senses, and used them with all the prodigality of the romantic school to which he temperamentally belonged, in order to convey what was in his mind. But this mastery of mood, appearances, and situation demanded an ampler stage for its deployment. The 'unknown god' whose mercy scarcely lightened the gloom of the Paraguayan night was shortly to step out into the arena where his eternal adversary was in wait to challenge him.

2

One day in the hot summer of 1923, less than a year after the publication of *Madame Dargent*, Bernanos drew Vallery-Radot aside to the edge of a wood, and read aloud to him the first 100 pages of a full-length novel on which he had been at work since the Armistice. This was *Sous le Soleil de Satan*. His friend was encouraging but dissatisfied, and Bernanos revised the book in the light of his criticism, equally grateful for his 'strong and sensitive arguments' and the warmth of feeling which inspired them – 'the passionate impulse in the delicate frame'.[1] It was not until 1925 that the revisions were

---

[1] *Le Crépuscule des Vieux*, p. 67. Anyone who was privileged to meet Robert Vallery-Radot in the person of Père Irénée of the Cistercian Order will recognise the truth of Bernanos' description, and will sympathise with his admiration for one who was at this time his closest friend.

complete. Vallery-Radot then showed the manuscript to Henri Massis; and Massis, in turn, showed it to Jacques Maritain and Stanislas Fumet, who were then editing the *Roseau d'Or* series for Plon. Maritain had certain reservations of a theological order, and Bernanos made a number of corrections to please him, although he thought his scruples exaggerated. If the book scandalised one or two 'womanish souls', that could not be helped. He had yet to learn the 'polite way' to his salvation.[1] Once the novel had been published in 1926, Maritain was afraid that Bernanos ran some risk of condemnation in Rome. He asked Massis to communicate to Père Garrigou-Lagrange, a theologian whose word carried weight in those quarters, the opinion of Père Gillet, the Master-General of the Dominicans, that any censuring of the novel would have a deplorable effect. 'I have the feeling,' wrote Massis, 'that we ought to mistrust the liberal clan, who would like to get their own back on us through Bernanos. So don't let us go to sleep.' In the event, there was no trouble and Bernanos' fame was established overnight. A glowing review by Léon Daudet in the *Action Française* secured an immediate sale; the novel was translated into several languages; and Bernanos was able to leave his insurance company and live henceforward – though not always comfortably – on his pen.

The book was not only a success; it was a scandal. Here was a writer of indisputable genius, an analyst of human passion challenging the psychological realists on their own ground, a master of style and construction, who not only believed in the Devil but had actually introduced him into a novel. The Satan of Bernanos was not, as Matthew Arnold might have put it, 'a power not ourselves making for unrighteousness'; he was a person – tangible, visible, incarnate. Chesterton, one suspects, knew less about evil than Bernanos; yet he had written that it 'may be inhuman, but it must not be impersonal, which is, almost exactly, the position occupied by Satan in the theological scheme.'[2] Bernanos knew all about the scheme – not because he was a theologian, but because he had theology in his bones. He had no wish, in spite of his obsession with the priesthood, to become a 'Catholic novelist' in the confessional sense of the term. There is no such thing as the 'Catholic novel'. But the novelist who writes about good and evil is in a stronger position, *qua* novelist, than the novelist who merely writes about right and wrong; and in

[1] *Maurras et notre temps* I (Plon, 1951)   [2] *Charles Dickens*

G.B.—E

a far stronger position than the novelist who thinks that there are no such things as good and evil, or right and wrong, at all.

The book was born of the 1914 war, inspired by the feeling of overwhelming disgust at what the war had left behind it, a vast moral and intellectual confusion, a spiritual void which was itself a theological image of hell, and one had no need to be a theologian to feel it. The *patrie* had turned into a divinity, before which the thurifers of every confession, or of none, offered up their undiscriminating homage; and the coming of the kingdom of God was confused with the advent of universal democracy. The war memorials, with their *poilus* clasped to the breasts of bronze in a rhetorical allegory of sacrifice, were an insult to the living rather than a tribute to the dead. Equivocal and empty, they found a reflection in much contemporary literature. André Gide, whose influence was then at its height, was the very image of equivocation, sabotaging truth with sincerity and soliciting for vice with charm. The puritan *à rebours*, it was no doubt of him that Bernanos was thinking when he spoke of 'puritan idealism' being 'evacuated' into the sewers of a sterile aestheticism, whose understanding of man was stultified by its indifference to God. To be sure, Bernanos could not ignore the colossal genius of Proust. The characters of Proust, however, were no more than 'reasoning and lubricious animals, complicated and polished like surgical instruments, for whom Christ had died in vain'.[1] For Proust 'the intellectual state of grace would be a total indifference to good and evil'.[2] This attitude could be sustained only if the moral law were imposed on us from without; but for Bernanos it was part and parcel of our being. The novelist had everything to lose by leaving God and the Devil out of the picture, and Bernanos acknowledged that the influence of Proust might be regarded as beneficent 'by reason of the anxiety which lies at the root of the immense intellectual pleasure that he gives to us. He has awakened the desire to search. He has opened the field to us. But I wonder why the Catholic novelist should allow anyone to precede him in this descent into the abyss, since he carries a torch in his hand.'[3] To which the critic might reply that the torch was all very well, but the illumination of the abyss would depend on the hand that held it.

The character of Antoine Saint-Marin in *Sous le Soleil de Satan*

[1] *Le Crépuscule des Vieux*, p. 79   [2] Ibid   [3] Ibid, p. 87

was obviously inspired by Anatole France, a derivation that Bernanos did not deny. It was described as 'hateful':

To turn the hopes of men into a game is to cheat the hunger and thirst of the poor. Somewhere, perhaps, in the world today there is a wretched creature made for the satisfactions of certitude and dying in despair because the author of *Thaïs* was a witty man and knew how to write. That is the absolute and essential crime; that is the irredeemable sin. Even hatred gives way to a kind of sacred horror at the thought that this consumption of hope has only served, for more than fifty years, to procure for a cruel old man the felicities of a free-thinking professor. No, I don't hate him any longer. I should only like to borrow from the Gospel its most mysterious malediction and apply it to him: it were a good thing if this man had never been born.[1]

In the same interview with Frédéric Lefèvre, Bernanos pays tribute to those whom he called his 'masters': Balzac, of course, who had understood the notion of Catholic order with his mind, although it had not penetrated the deeper strata of his work, who had gone as far as analysis could take him, but had found the supreme effort of synthesis beyond him; Jacques Maritain 'in whose eyes the under-carrying patience and celestial obstinacy were like the reflection of another world'; Léon Daudet 'more truly human than any other man of our time'; the visionaries of the nineteenth century, Barbey and Villiers de l'Isle Adam; Léon Bloy, too prodigal of his anger for one who was so prodigal of his love; Vallery-Radot, who was among the first to realise what the war had to teach the Catholics of France; Henri Massis, who had so brilliantly exposed the equivoca-tion of Gide and the superficiality of Barrès in a critique 'essential, elliptical and tense, striking with incomparable force'. There was Paul Claudel with 'his voice of bronze', who had not altogether escaped the clutches of a *bienpensant* public, but had given neverthe-less to a whole generation what he claimed to have received himself from Rimbaud – 'the living and almost physical impression of the supernatural'. These were all, technically, *hommes de lettres*, but the catalogue was not the tribute of a man of letters. Alive or dead, known personally or only through their writings, they were the men whom Bernanos would have embraced on both cheeks if he had met them. They were his brothers-in-arms against the evil which in his first great novel he had set out to explore. They had

[1] Ibid, pp. 75–6

gone before him, but he was to go further than any of them. Maritain he came to know through correspondence, but before they met personally Bernanos expressed certain misgivings which cast a light on future disagreements. He had felt the steel, as well as the sweetness, in Maritain, and the moment would come when his own steel would clash with it. The hardness in Maritain was a philosophical intransigence, allied to a clarity of spiritual insight, which feared that in *Sous le Soleil de Satan* Bernanos was giving the Devil more than his due. To this the novelist could only oppose the dictates of a creative imagination working at white heat, and also a knowledge of the world to which the philosopher could not pretend. Maritain was a convert and, as such, rather more sensitive to the feelings of the *bienpensants;* Bernanos, to excuse the violence of his dialectic, argued that Christ was not the hospital nurse of the human soul, but even, in a certain sense, its executioner.

He was too steeped in a Catholicism that did not question its title deeds to follow with any interest the path of painful reasoning which had taken Newman to Rome; but when Newman spoke of a 'terrible, aboriginal calamity' that clamoured for redemption and explained a great many things otherwise inexplicable, even if it could not itself be satisfactorily explained, he met Bernanos at the point where every novel by Bernanos begins.

Here you have this child in its cradle, all grace and innocence, fresh and clear as a running brook, new like the spring, and sincere as the light of morning. Its little life leaps on its way, with such purity and candour. Who is it then – who, I ask you – that works away inside it with so sinister a care and clairvoyance, with the precision of a surgeon who knows where to put his scissors and forceps in order to reach the most delicate nerves, day by day and hour by hour, until twenty or thirty years later you find this radiant little creature transformed into an anxious and solitary animal – envious, jealous, or avaricious – eaten up alive by the absurd hatred of itself, and choosing the terrible and sterile pleasure that destroys it in preference to joy and freedom and all the good things of the earth?[1]

If it was silly to dismiss the Devil as a fantasy, it was risky to dismiss him as a fool. Claudel had written to Bernanos that the Devil was more stupid than people generally supposed; nevertheless humanity had paid dearly for its confidence in a 'partner that had so

[1] *Le Crépuscule des Vieux*, pp. 43–4

many trumps' and had recently claimed 'nine million human lives'. This, of course, was putting it rhetorically. No one imagined – and Bernanos least of all – that the lives lost in the 1914–18 war were lost to Satan. He merely saw its atrocious carnage as in some sense a victory for evil, and its aftermath a greater victory still. No doubt this was what Maritain had in mind when he detected in *Sous le Soleil de Satan* the traces of Manichaean heresy; a tendency to see the world of souls disputed by two equal and positive powers. Theologically speaking, Satan is not a principle; he is the negation of a principle. But the novelist, like the dramatist, is obliged to impersonate. It was not enough for the immediate purposes of Bernanos to show the forces of evil at work in this person or in that. They had to be concentrated – for *Sous le Soleil de Satan* is not only a drama; it is a duel. The reader must decide for himself whether the nocturnal encounter between the horse-dealer and the haunted abbé is reality or hallucination, and whether in a novel so packed with realism it is artistically justified. It was certainly a courageous defiance of literary convention, and a stumbling-block to those who had relegated the Devil to the lumber-room of medieval folklore. By the time he came to write his last great novel, *Monsieur Ouine*, Bernanos had found a much more subtle actor for his principal part; but in *Monsieur Ouine* the Devil has an altogether easier time of it. The history of the intervening years will tell us why.

I quite understand, [Bernanos explained to an audience in Brussels] that Satan is a subject that frightens the lady of the house more than any other. If you state the problem of Satan, you state the problem of evil – and that is one of those problems that you can't hope to resolve without upsetting a great many people. But what is one to say of the novelists who evade it, while they exercise their talent in a minute description and analysis of human passion? . . .[1] The war has left me dumbfounded, like everyone else, by the vast disproportion between the enormity of the *sacrifice* and the wretched ideology proposed to us by the governments and the press. . . . The religion of Progress for which they politely asked us to die is in fact a gigantic swindling of our hopes.[2]

Such was the mood in which Bernanos set to work on this extraordinary book. He wrote the first pages while staying with his sister at Berck, while his brother-in-law, Paul Hattu, bought the *langoustes*. Later he set to work in cafés and station-buffets from Belfort to

[1] Ibid, p. 39   [2] *Cahiers de l'Herne*, pp. 175–6

Bar-le-Duc and from Strasbourg to Rheims. It was at Rheims that he finished it on the 25th of February 1925, wrenched out of him, line by line and during odd moments of leisure. There were not enough of them, he told Frédéric Lefèvre, for him 'to strike an attitude in front of the mirror'; the circumstances of its composition guaranteed the book's sincerity. Except for personal friends like Vallery-Radot and Henri Massis, both intellectuals of the Counter-Revolution, his contacts with the literary world were minimal. He was alone with his obsession. But a mood is not the same thing as an impulse. It is a thousand pities that no manuscript of *Sous le Soleil de Satan* exists, because Bernanos was an extremely careful writer and his corrections are instructive. One would particularly like to know the nature of the revisions suggested by Vallery-Radot. He did, however, talk a good deal about the novel in interviews and lectures shortly after its publication. It was constructed in three distinct parts, respectively entitled *Histoire de Mouchette*, *La Tentation du Désespoir*, and *Le Saint de Lumbres*. Certain critics complained that the first part had too slight an organic relation to the other two, but Bernanos explained that without Mouchette – the girl from the café who murdered the aristocrat from the château – there would have been no Donissan to redeem her. It was Mouchette who gave the book its initial impulse, and Bernanos tells us how:

I can still see myself, one September evening, with the window open to a great twilit sky. I was thinking about the clever P.-J. Toulet, and his lively young daughter, about his charming poems sometimes going on wings and sometimes rather lamely, charged with a secret bitterness. And it was then that the little Mouchette rose up before me – from some corner of my consciousness, maybe – and made a sign to me with her avid and anxious glance. How slight and furtive and difficult to describe it is, the origin of a sincere book! I saw the mysterious little girl between her mother and her father, who was a brewer. Little by little I imagined her story. I walked behind her, I let her go on. And then the picture of her crime vaguely and gradually took shape around her, like a shadow on the wall. The first steps had been taken, and she was free.

But free for what? No matter what I did, in proportion as, one by one, the links of family and society that make each one of us a sort of disciplined animal, right up to the last degree but one of our degradation, were broken behind her, I realised that my unfortunate heroine was gradually sinking into a lie a thousand times stricter and fiercer than any discipline. No way and no escape was open to the unhappy and rebellious child.

Death or nothingness was the only possible end to this frenzied dash towards an illusory deliverance. . . . Once the problem had been stated there was no other possible solution. Once the human soul has reached a certain degree of abasement and sacrilegious dissipation, the notion of redemption is forced upon the mind. Not of a reformation or a return, but of a redemption. And so the abbé Donissan did not appear by accident: Mouchette's wild cry of despair called to him, and made him indispensable.[1]

In a letter to Bernanos, Claudel had seized the point. So far from finding the story of Mouchette external to the main drama of the novel, he saw that it was the necessary point of its departure. 'The whole of your book moves towards the succouring of this crushed little soul.'[2]

The rescue was not easy; nor was it effected beyond the last shadow of doubt. Mouchette is dead by her own hand when Donissan reaches her; unable to have saved her body, he can only trust that his prayers will have saved her soul. Nothing is absolutely certain in *Sous le Soleil de Satan*, not even the sanctity of the 'saint of Lumbres'; for mathematical certainty reduces hope to irrelevance, and Bernanos, as surely as any man, lived 'by admiration, hope, and love'. The Christian risk was inseparable from the Christian hope, and Donissan ran it to the limits of an almost superhuman energy. If Mouchette illustrated all the power of unassisted nature to destroy itself, nothing but the supernatural undiluted by the least alloy of humanism would suffice to save her. This explains both the character and the rôle of Donissan. Bernanos does not prejudge an issue which was beyond his competence:

My curé of Lumbres is no doubt a kind of saint, but it is his temptations and his despair that bring him close to us. The sensible experience of divine love is beyond the scope of the novel. But if I can force the reader to go down into the depths of his own conscience, if I show him with incontrovertible evidence, that human weakness does not explain every-thing – that it is maintained and exploited by a kind of dark and ferocious genius – what else can he do than throw himself on his knees and call upon God, if not in love, then at least in fear? . . . The Catholic novel is not the novel which only nourishes us with nice sentiments; it is the novel where the life of faith is at grips with the passions. Everything

[1] *Le Crépuscule des Vieux*, pp. 56–8
[2] *Cahiers du Rhône*, p. 64

possible must be done to make the reader feel the tragic mystery of salvation.[1]

And so it is that Mouchette disappears from the story until Donissan discovers her almost – if not absolutely – too late, and the great duel is fought, implacably, between the Devil and a prey worthy, at last, of his poison. Donissan, when we first meet him, is a young priest so unsuccessful and so uninstructed as hardly to be worth employing. Even his extravagant mortifications are a treacherous path to sanctity, for there is no corner of the purgative way where the Devil is not in wait for him.

You who never knew anything of the world but its insubstantial colours and sounds – sensitive hearts and lyrical lips where the bitter truth would melt like a burnt almond – he is not for you. Your dabblings in evil are made to the measure of your fragile nerves and your niminy-piminy minds, and the Satan of your exotic rituals is only a deformation of yourselves, for the man who has given his devotion to the universe of the flesh is a Satan unto himself. The monster looks at you and laughs, but he has not gripped you with his claws. You will not find him in your gossipy books, or in your blasphemies and your ridiculous maledictions. He is not there in your greedy glances, your perfidious hands, or your ears which hold nothing but the wind. It is useless to look for him in that most secret corner of the flesh which excites but does not satisfy your desire, and if you bite your lip the blood that issues from it is colourless and pale. But he exists, all the same. You will find him in the prayer of the Solitary, in his fasting and penance, at the core of his deepest ecstasy, and in the silence of his heart. He poisons the holy water, burns in the consecrated wax, mixes his breath with the breath of virginity, tears into the flesh with the hair-shirt and the discipline – there is no way that he does not corrupt. His lies are on the lips opened to dispense the word of truth, and he pursues the just man, in the thunder and lightning of the Beatific rapture, right into the arms of God himself. Why should he trouble himself with all these people who crawl about the earth like beasts, when they will fall into his hands tomorrow – an unnoticeable crowd that will go by themselves to their destination? He keeps his hatred for the saints.[2]

Here it is the author speaking; later, when the horse-dealer meets Donissan on the road whose desperate monotony Bernanos knew so well, Satan speaks for himself:

[1] *Le Crépuscule des Vieux*, pp. 82–4   [2] Editions de la Pléiade, pp. 153–4

This is a friend who has kissed you . . . I have filled you with myself, you silly little fool – tabernacle of Jesus Christ! Don't be frightened – it's nothing very much. I've kissed many other people besides yourself. Shall I tell you – I kiss you all, living or dead, sleeping or awake. That's the truth. I love to be with you, curious little god-man; curious, curious, creatures that you are! To be frank with you, I rarely leave your side. You carry me with you in the most hidden recesses of your flesh – in the triple recesses of your guts . . . I count you, and not one of you escapes me. There is not a single member of my flock that I should not recognise by his smell.[1]

The strength and weakness of the novel are illustrated by these two quotations. The first has more than a taint of Manichaean morbidity, but it forcibly translates the vertigo under which the book was written. The second is a *cliché* of conventional demonology. Absolute evil is as ineffable as absolute good; each can be reflected in human personality; neither can be directly personified.

In the third and last section of the book Donissan, now in charge of a country parish, has acquired the celebrity of a curé d'Ars, his confessional besieged and his charisma the subject of widespread curiosity and comment. The action turns on Donissan's failure – a failure which for a split second looked like a success – to bring back to life a dead child; and on the visit of Antoine de Saint-Marin – alias Anatole France – to the church and presbytery of Lumbres. These pages of blistering and disciplined irony are certainly among the most powerful that Bernanos ever wrote. We see the eminent writer in conversation with a neighbouring curé; 'the fine features wore at that moment the dull expression, the sly grin, and the frightful immobility of vice that you find on the face of an old man.' The author of *Le Cierge Pascal* is in a mood of dilettante despair; he has 'so many readers but not a single friend'. Alone in the church, where the 'distant lamp in the sanctuary burns like a ship's lantern on a solitary lake', he is an exile from his books and the prisoner of his memories.

Back and forth, across the limits traced by the calendar, the years and the days and hours call and answer to each other. A bright morning in the holidays, when you heard the jolly clanking of the copper pot in which they made the jam; an evening when the water was flowing, cold and clear, under the still foliage; the quick glance of a fair-haired cousin

[1] Ibid, p. 174

across the family table, and the heaving of her young breasts – and then, all of a sudden, fifty years have gone by – the first wrinkles of old age – a rendezvous that has not been kept – the great love, jealously guarded, defended inch by inch, disputed up to the last moment, when the lips of the aging lover press a mobile and furtive mouth which will have become ferocious by tomorrow. That is all that his past life still preserves of form and shape; the rest of it, his work and his fame, are nothing. The effort of fifty years, his illustrious career, thirty celebrated books – do they count for so little? And yet the idiots go on shouting that art . . . what art? The marvellous conjuror knows nothing about art but its servitude . . . and the decimated youth which saw Péguy lying in the stubble, with his face to God, draws away in disgust from the divan where the super-critic is polishing his nails.[1]

Yet there remained a flicker of curiosity to stimulate a last ambition. What if he too in the autumn of his age and fame should withdraw into the security of some rural retreat? Perhaps this priest, whom he had come to see and of whom he had heard so much, was not such a fool after all. He had withdrawn from life before life had withdrawn from him, and he was praying to be delivered from what other men were afraid to lose. Was it too late to imitate him?

A mystical peasant, brought up on old books and taught by crude masters, can gradually acquire the serenity of a sage, but his experience is brief, his methods naïve and sometimes ridiculous, complicated by useless superstitions. The methods of an illustrious writer, at the end of his career but in full possession of his genius, have a different efficacy. He can borrow from the saint whatever is lovable; recover without rigidity the peace of childhood; make his soul in the solitude and serenity of the fields; study the art of forgetfulness rather than of regret; observe, within reason and with due sense of proportion, the ancient precepts of abstinence and chastity, which are certainly not to be despised; enjoy his old age as one enjoys the autumn or the twilight; gradually accustom himself to the idea of death . . . this will be my last work, concluded the eminent master, and I shall write it for myself alone – actor and audience, in turn.[2]

Antoine de Saint-Marin little knew what he dreamt of imitating. He had already been shown the truckle-bed on which the 'saint of Lumbres' spent his sleepless nights; but how much more interesting to visit the confessional where so many sins were absolved – some

[1] Editions de la Pléiade, p. 297   [2] Ibid, pp. 302–3

of them, perhaps, as sophisticated as his own. He had already been shown the thick boots in which the 'saint' tramped the roads of Picardy, and now, as he approached the confessional, he perceived a similar pair projecting beyond the curtain, the fold of a soutane, a long leg in its woollen sock – quite stiff – and then, terrible and thunderstruck, the white face. Bernanos puts into his own incomparable language the prayer which the abbé Donissan might confusedly have uttered before death surprised him: 'Every life that is finely lived witnesses for you, O Lord; but the witness of the saint is wrenched out of him with the force of iron'; and to Antoine de Saint-Marin his message is unambiguous: 'You wanted my peace; come and take it.'

Such, then, is the book whose massive structure Claudel compared to a succession of great movements in Beethoven, and which he and many others have mentioned in the same breath with Dostoevsky. The range of Bernanos is narrower and his canvas more restricted, and as time went on he would purge his style of rhetorical excess. His theology of evil would be articulated with a greater subtlety. Yet the writing of the book had not been easy. Sometimes he would sit for a whole day in front of a blank page sooner than follow a false trail; and to those who complained that he had written a 'diabolical novel', he replied that what he had tried to depict was not a saint, but rather a hero of the spiritual life. Against the wiles of the devil heroism was not enough. But since Donissan was innocent of pride, it was reasonable that sinners should be saved through his sufferings.

CHAPTER 4

THE CRISIS OF THE
ACTION FRANÇAISE[1]

I

BERNANOS' attachment to his native landscape was visceral rather than voluntary, and emboldened by the success of *Sous le Soleil de Satan* and the publicity attending it, he moved in the summer of 1926 to Ciboure in the Basses-Pyrénées, and then in September to Bagnères-de-Bigorre, 11 allée des Coustous, where his parents joined him. His own weak health, and that of his wife, demanded a warmer climate. For some time he had been at work on a new novel, afterwards to be known as *L'Imposture*, but at first entitled *Les Ténèbres*. The provisional title was well chosen, for the months that followed were a period of deep anxiety. His father was now suffering from an incurable cancer of the liver, and Bernanos felt, as he watched the progress of the disease, that he was attending a rehearsal of his own death-bed. This was an extraordinary premonition; twenty-two years later Bernanos was himself to die from the same disease as his father.

In the meanwhile, public events had still further deepened the shadows that were closing in on a life to which he owed so much. On the 27th of August 1926, there appeared in the *Aquitaine*, the official weekly organ of the archdiocese of Bordeaux, a letter from Cardinal Andrieu strongly attacking the Action Française. It was so full of loose generalisations and gross inaccuracies that it proved almost as embarrassing to those who were in sympathy with it as to those who were not. Right up to the end of the ensuing controversy it could be claimed that Rome had acted on information that was demonstrably false. This was not, of course, the first that Rome had heard of the Action Française. Rome knew perfectly well that Charles Maurras, the founder and teacher of the movement, was an unbeliever who found in certain principles of Catholicism – though

[1] For a detailed account of this, on which I have largely drawn, the reader is referred to *The Action Française Condemnation* by Denis Gwynn (1928).

not in the Gospel of Jesus Christ – a support for his own mystique of 'order'. Pius X had referred to him as 'a great defender of the Faith'; and although a condemnation of the movement had lain on his desk, it had been carefully tucked away in his drawers. If the Austrian veto had not prevented the election of Rampolla to the Papacy in 1903, the crisis which broke in 1926 might have arisen twenty years earlier.

For the Action Française, as we have already noted, was more than a political movement to secure the restoration of the French monarchy and the organisation of society on a corporative basis. It was a *Weltanschauung* embracing every side of life and field of thought. Maurras himself drew his inspiration from 'the glory that was Greece' and 'the grandeur that was Rome'. An extension of these he found in an ultramontane and immobilist Catholicism, and in the 'classical moment' of the *Roi Soleil*. The diamond-hard lines of his thought and style reflected the Provençal landscape which had bred him, with its clear light and saturating sun. By a strange irony it was the landscape in which Bernanos – who was later to speak with an ungenerous disparagement of Maurras' Mediterranean origins – was himself to feel most at home. For Maurras and the other doctrinaires of the Action Française, whether they were Catholics or unbelievers, the state was an absolute. If political interest demanded the condemnation of Dreyfus, his innocence was of no account. No libel was too gross, no insinuation too base, for the brilliant band of polemicists who filled, day by day, the columns of the *Action Française*. Nevertheless it enjoyed prominent ecclesiastical support. For Cardinal Charost it constituted 'the first counter-revolutionary movement on an organised scale that had arisen in France since the Encyclopaedists, who led to the Revolution and to the immeasurable destruction that it caused.' If one recalls the influence of Maurras on powerful minds like T. S. Eliot and T. E. Hulme, it is not too much to say that the Action Française made reaction intellectually respectable. At a time when romanticism was acting as a dissolvent in morality as well as in aesthetics, it gave a renewed charter to classicism. Eliot himself acknowledged that Maurras had brought him closer to Christianity, and that the condemnation of Maurras had estranged him from Roman Catholicism; but for all that, the ethos of the movement, although it enlisted much Catholic support, was incidentally, if not intrinsically, pagan.

The muddled and mendacious accusations of Cardinal Andrieu would not have mattered if they had only been the expression of a personal opinion, singularly ill-informed. Léon Daudet and other Catholic adherents of the movement replied to the criticism that it had unbelievers in its ranks by pointing out that in this it was not exceptional among the political parties of the Third Republic; and that the unbelievers associated with the Action Française respected the Church and protected it, whereas the freemasons and the anti-clericals did everything they could to undermine its influence. 'We believe,' declared Daudet, 'what the Church believes.' Maurras, on his side, relied on the support of other cardinals, more theologically qualified than Andrieu, and on the apparent complicity of Pius X, who was no longer alive to confirm or contradict it. But the subsequent intervention of Pius XI, who wrote a letter to Andrieu in warm endorsement of his charges, raised the controversy to a much more serious level. This appeared in the *Osservatore Romano* on the 5th of September, and it was based, the Pope explicitly declared, on a personal study of the question. How far he was motivated by democratic influences in France and by pro-German influences in Rome was a matter of pure conjecture. As the head of a universal Church, he was naturally eager to reduce the animosity between France and Germany, which the Action Française had never ceased to foster; but the acceptance of Fascism in Italy, which owed to Maurras so many of its ideas, was not too heavy a price to pay for the settlement of the Roman Question, and the protection of the same Catholic interests which Maurras now invoked in his claim for Catholic support.

Cardinal Andrieu published a second letter on the 24th of September comparing the doctrines of the Action Française to the modernism defined by Pius X as 'the meeting-place of all the heresies', and concentrating his attack on Maurras himself. This was followed by other episcopal statements, and by further admonitions from Rome, until a position was reached where a formal condemnation could probably have been avoided if Maurras had resigned as nominal leader of the movement. But he was the last man to do so, even if his disciples had been willing to accept his abdication. Instead, a counter-attack was in preparation. Rome had not, as yet, called upon French Catholics formally to leave the movement – only to withdraw from such influences within it judged prejudicial to the security of their faith. Every pressure was therefore brought upon the bishops to prevent the condemnation which clearly lay ahead. A request, accompanied by profuse expressions of loyalty, was then sent to Rome for theologians to assist in the teaching given by the Action Française in its study circles and its daily newspapers. The third line of attack was to produce a copious dossier of evidence, most of it unproved or manufactured, to show that the Pope had been misled by his Germanophil entourage. An appeal was made from the Pope 'ill informed' – Pius XI – to the Pope 'well informed' – Pius X. This argument was to ricochet on its authors' heads.

The bishops' response was disappointing; only three out of 120 refused to sign a declaration of unqualified sympathy to the Pope. One of these, the aged Bishop of Montauban, exercised remarkable casuistry in interpreting the Papal intervention in a sense ultimately favourable to the Action Française. A warning, he declared, was not tantamount to a condemnation. This gloss earned a severe reprimand from the *Osservatore Romano*. Another encouragement for the leaders of the movement was a note from Cardinal Billot, the eminent Jesuit theologian, written to Léon Daudet after the publication of Cardinal Andrieu's letter and before the Pope's endorsement of it. The note was subsequently repudiated, and the Cardinal's resignation of his title was widely interpreted as a result of his indiscretion. Billot was known to be a supporter of the movement, and to have persuaded Pius X to withhold his condemnation of it. Moreover Rome – under cover of the *Osservatore* – now directed its attack on Daudet, whose novels were described as offensive to pious ears. Here they were certainly in good company, judging from the *Osservatore's* usual literary criteria. Equally damaging was the calling in question of Pius X's famous tribute to Maurras. The words so frequently quoted – *un beau défenseur de la foi* – were nowhere to be found among his papers. In what context had they been spoken, and to whom?

Nevertheless, the Action Française was able to count on yet one more significant advocate in the person of Cardinal Charost, the Archbishop of Rennes and Primate of Britanny. This had long been a royalist stronghold and the movement had many supporters not only among the older but also among the younger clergy, who might well have been influenced by the virulent campaign directed against it by the *Ouest Eclair*. The Cardinal did not deny the dangers arising from a movement whose leader was an agnostic and the majority of its members Catholics. He emphasised and explained the Papal warnings. But he made clear to everyone why Maurras had enjoyed the confidence of those who professed the faith which Maurras could not share. His words deserve quotation because they illustrate the agony of conflicting loyalties in which Bernanos and his friends were now caught up.

No one has placed in a stronger light the fertile beauty of the notion of order; no one has shown more pointedly that the authority of the State must encroach less in what it undertakes, while at the same time it must, within a better defined field, be made stronger for the realisation of the common good. No one has said better things about that tradition which preserves in a nation its spirit, its taste, its good manners, all the features of its spiritual physiognomy, all the alertness that it has acquired in every direction, through the inheritance of previous generations. No one has fought a stouter fight against the anarchy of the intellect, which breeds all other anarchies, and against that abstract liberalism which destroys liberty and real safeguards. No one has done better work in flagellating the spurious dignity of romantic love, which is represented as being sufficient in itself, however unworthy its object or pernicious its ravages – that anti-social thesis which has led to the destruction of the family by legislation, to an extent that we watch with dismay. We are certainly not exaggerating such services which have been rendered to causes which are dear to us, and which concern both the country and the Church.[1]

Maurras was the only political figure in France of whom these things could have been said without absurdity.

Any effect that Cardinal Charost's words might have had was neutralised by the defiant attitude of Maurras and Daudet; and if any Catholics were in doubt as to what was expected of them, the Pope spelt it out for them in a Consistorial address on the 20th of December. They were forbidden 'to be connected with the activities or, in any way, with the school of those who place the interest of parties above religion, and seek to make the latter subservient to the former.' The *Action Française* published the speech, and at the same time threw down the gauntlet with its famous *Non possumus*. On the 22nd of December the Vatican authorities at last laid hands on the documents relating to the previous – but never promulgated – condemnation by Pius X. These were published a few days later.

---

[1] Trans. by Denis Gwynn (*The Action Française Condemnation*)

On the 29th of December a number of books by Maurras, and the *Action Française* itself – 'while it remains such as it is at present' – were placed on the Index, 'without prejudice to future inquiries or condemnations' concerning the works of Maurras and Daudet. The ban remained in force throughout the Pontificate of Pius XI. It was lifted by Pius XII in the summer of 1939, when the paper was presumably considered to be other than what it once had been. It had certainly become much less readable, and there appeared to be no detectable change in its opinions. Meanwhile the leaders of the movement pursued their vendetta against the Roman officials of the Church which they still nominally supported. They were remarkably well informed. When a prominent Cardinal unwisely lent his motor-car to a nephew, and the nephew left it outside a house of ill-fame, a photographer was on the spot.

2

Papal intervention in French affairs has generally been disastrous; the suppression of the Sillon and the Worker Priests are other cases in point. If the Pope had contented himself with a solemn warning, and the appointment of theological advisers to the study circles of the Action Française – for these had been asked for – many thousands of French Catholics would have been spared a painful crisis of conscience. They were now called upon to deny the teachings of their master and to disown the benefits, so freely acknowledged by Charost, Billot, and other eminent authorities, which those teachings, for all their totalitarian implications, had brought to the country and to the Church. Maurras himself admitted that not everything he had written was designed to please the Catholic members of his movement. But now they were forbidden, on pain of excommunication, either to belong to it or even to read its newspaper. It may be argued that in the long run the Church in France gained from the condemnation of the Action Française, and that Pius XI should be thanked for his foresight. That he was acting within his rights there can be no doubt; that he was acting judiciously is more open to question; that his action, objectively speaking, was unjust has been held by many who agreed with it.

What is also quite certain was the catastrophic effect of the condemnation on Georges Bernanos. Here we can rely on the evidence of his letters to Henri Massis, with whom he was very close at that time. Albert Béguin, who came to know Bernanos only in the very last years of his life, referred to this as an 'ephemeral intimacy'.[1] It was not as ephemeral as all that. 'I love you in God,' Bernanos wrote, 'as the brother I have chosen.'[2] As we have seen, he deeply admired Massis' critical judgment, and it was only later that politics divided them. As Albert Thibaudet wrote, Massis was an 'esprit profondément et totalement *certitudien*', and in this he was not unlike Bernanos. He moved in the mirage of the Maurrasian *pays réel*. In his *Défense de l'Occident*, published in English with a preface by G. K. Chesterton, he confessed that he was less concerned 'to enlarge the waters of the Christian stream than to strengthen the dykes of western wisdom, which safeguarded both the purity of these waters and their harmonious *élan* towards the sea'. This was the *élan* of Maurras' *Musique Intérieure*, whose classical purity even an opponent can admire; and Massis was soothed by it. He was to be not less soothed by the tramp of Mussolini's legions and General Franco's Moors. But the many pages devoted to Bernanos in Massis' *Maurras et notre temps*[3] are indispensable for an understanding of how Bernanos reacted to the condemnation of the Action Française. Béguin was no doubt right in seeing the 1914 war as the central crisis of his life – and this Massis did not deny – but he was surely wrong in dismissing the events of 1926 as a passing quarrel which subsequent events of more general import put out of his mind. Bernanos may have professed for Maurras no more than an *admiration sans tendresse*, but his fidelities were too adhesive, even when they had turned sour, for him ever to get Maurras out of his system. Béguin was right in declaring that Bernanos 'belongs to nobody'; there was a time, however, when he had belonged to the Action Française. Béguin, when he came before the world as the official interpreter of Bernanos, had moved very far to the Left, and the Action Française had had its day. Those whom Massis described as the *nouveaux Bernanosiens* now had a monopoly of interpretation.

Like Massis, Vallery-Radot, and many other friends, Bernanos was torn between the alternatives of disobedience and dishonour. For a man whose watchword was fidelity, there was no question of 'fidelity' to a Pontiff whom he regarded as prejudiced and misin-

---

[1] *Esprit* (1951)   [2] September 1926: *Correspondance* I, p. 263
[3] Vol. I, pp. 178–249

formed. Bernanos held that the attitude of the Action Française was altogether too deferential towards the Roman authorities, for he saw the crisis not as a quarrel between royalists and republicans, but between those who manned the front line of Catholicism in France and those who were only too anxious to sabotage it. Where others were eager to save the peace, Bernanos was spoiling for a fight. Cardinal Andrieu's broadside had caught him just as he was on the point of moving to Bagnères-de-Bigorre and recovering from a severe illness of the kidney. He declared himself 'extremely tired, both in mind and body'.

Nevertheless he immediately wrote to Maurras a letter, subsequently published, with Maurras' permission, in *La Gazette Française*. It has been written before the Pope's endorsement of Cardinal Andrieu's charges, but that was no reason to withhold it from those eager to know where the celebrated author of *Sous le Soleil de Satan* now stood. It will be observed that it was first of all in the name of religious orthodoxy that he gave his support to Maurras.

We owe it to one of our greatest Popes, who honoured you with his paternal friendship, that we saw thrown out of doors or reduced to impotence those unfortunate priests or laymen, who dreamt of a reconciliation between religion and science in accord with their primary conceptions, their democratic envy, and their sentimental feelings. While that great voice, which was hushed too soon, cut them off from the living Church, and annulled their activity, you contributed your witness from outside, and sat in judgment on their revolting anarchy in the name of order and reason. If I may for once employ their inept vocabulary, these reformers imagined that they were 'advanced'. It was you yourself who found the word for them – the most backward party of the lot; and they will never forgive you for it.

After this summary and *simpliste* execution of modernism, Bernanos touched Maurras more closely:

Your work remains and a few blasphemies, which we disavow with all the strength at our command, will not efface the good that it has done. There is not an enemy of the Church who will not honour you with his hate. That will serve you well, Maurras, in the face of God; that hatred will bravely escort you when you appear before Him. . . . No one wishes more ardently than I, and no one would more gladly sacrifice his own miserable life, to restore you to the divine all-embracing Truth. I know of some who have made this sacrifice on your behalf, and who now stand before the adorable Face from which you avert your eyes in vain. But the Spirit blows where it listeth, and chooses the hour of its visitation.[1]

Meanwhile another voice had entered the debate, to which Bernanos and Massis were both obliged to listen. In the autumn of 1926 Jacques Maritain published his *Une Opinion sur Charles Maurras et le devoir des Catholiques*.[2] Maritain was not himself a member of the Action Française, and he had only a slight acquaintance with Maurras. But he was a close friend of Massis, collaborating with him in *La Revue universelle*, where many Maurrasian ideas were presented at greater length and with a greater sophistication than was possible in the daily columns of the *Action Française*. In having subscribed to the latter, Maritain was acting – as in so much else – under the influence of Père Clérissac, OP, who was among its warm supporters. Whatever reservations he may have had about Maurras, his attidude was not wanting in sympathy.

He saw in him 'one of those true Republicans, whose type was formed in the little cities of Greece or in the municipalities of the Renaissance'; a natural pagan, by reason 'of a certain preference for, and delight in, the finite – in the perfectly created thing'; a political theorist, whose ideas had much in common with Bossuet and Joseph de Maistre; an agnostic whose approach to the Christian religion might be described as 'a grave and ardent regret, not far removed from desire'; a disciple of Auguste Comte, who nevertheless had wondered what would become of Comte's agnosticism; not a political philosopher in the strict sense of the word, since he reached his conclusions inductively, but a thinker, nevertheless, who had deserved well for his tribute to Cardinal Mercier's promotion of Thomism. Mercier – Maurras had written – was 'the servant and interpreter of a certain philosophy, whose constant rôle was to place, or to restore, ideas and objects where they properly belonged.' As for Maurras' anti-Germanism, Maritain knew more about Germany than Maurras, having studied there; but he could recognise the existence of 'an inhuman Germanism which still troubles the world and will continue to do so until we start once again to civilise our Europe with the teaching of Aristotle and St Thomas.'

Maurras had been criticised for his watchword – *politique d'abord*.

[1] *Bulletin* 17–20, p. 8   [2] Published by Plon

Maritain conceded that if *d'abord* was taken as referring 'not to the end in view and to the priority of intentions, but to the conditions envisaged for the execution of it, then it was a truth plain to common sense.' Whatever might be said for the ideals of the French Revolution, as an historical fact it was 'animated by a spiritual principle and by a profound *intentio* which is the enemy of humanity, because it envisages the creation of a humanity which dispenses with God. That is why Joseph de Maistre described the Revolution as *Satanic.*' Maritain distinguished between three forms of democracy: social democracy, as outlined in various Papal Encyclicals; political democracy, as defined by Aristotle and St Thomas; and Rousseauist democracy, as set out in the *Contrat Social.* Only the third was unacceptable, since it was based on a perfectionist view of man. In all this Maurras would have agreed with him.

But the immediate question was the duty of Catholics in face of the attacks upon a movement to which so many of them adhered. Their first business was to

construct a truly Catholic synthesis – that is to say a universal synthesis – to build it up and integrate it, insisting above all on the positive elements it contained; and with this end in view to reconcile first of all in their minds, in the indispensable light of theological wisdom (for without this there is nothing to be hoped for) aspects which have been separated for too long, and which are really complementary – doctrinal absolutes and evangelical daring, fidelity to the purity of truth and pity for the sickness of souls, tradition and revolution where each is necessary.

Without subscribing to all the ideas and political directives of the Action Française, they should recognise 'what, in my opinion, is the most important aspect of its work – its critique of the liberal ideology and the revolutionary dogmas.' While he admitted that 'some of the most generously supernatural hearts that I have known were among the most fervent disciples of Maurras', he warned his readers against attaching themselves to the Church for the sake of its temporal benefits, reminding them that it could never be 'really at home in the kingdoms of the earth'; and that it had 'suffered almost as much in defending its independence against the Christian kings, as it had from the anti-Christian governments in defending its existence'; that the human condition was not 'a purely natural state, but a state of nature fallen and repaired, and the line of conduct for the individual and for society could not be divorced from supernatural considerations'; and that 'the political ideas of Maurras took no account of a doctrine concerning the last end of man'. The present situation was 'abnormal, but not unreasonable' and it required a '*supernatural* obedience'. Père Clérissac – and no one was more sympathetic to the ordeal of those seeking his advice – had defined this as 'the most delicate discernment between the degrees and kinds of authority and submission, for what is in question is a free and living docility of the practical judgment, not a servile and mechanical execution of it'. The Christian could not say 'To Hell with the Pope', and then do as the Pope told him. He must be prepared to suffer 'not only for the Church, but at the Church's hands'.

Bernanos was neither a philosopher nor a theologian, and the refinements of Maritain's reasoning left him cold. He found it difficult to draw the line between submission and evasion, and a merely negative obedience would fall below the level of events. He distrusted the project for the study circles, with theology muzzling politics from one day to another. In November, therefore, he sent a further letter in support of Maurras to the *Revue Fédéraliste*. His position was all the stronger inasmuch as he was not himself a member of the Action Française, and it will again be noticed that the grounds of his support were spiritual rather than political. He was writing from Fressin, and from his father's bed of sickness.

None knows better than ourselves the power and range of your effort, whose splendid intellectual generosity led us to the very frontiers of the faith. But genius cannot escape the curse once laid upon our nature, and it too must be redeemed. We possessed what you had not. We were the leaven working from within, that made effective what the workman had produced. You gave us the genius; we brought you the indispensable, the divine Charity. But alas! once again, our work and our prayers and our love were insufficient. The benediction we besought for you and for the common task was no doubt implored in vain, because our hearts were wanting in courage. So now we are failing you at the critical moment. . . . We are answerable for you before God, Maurras, and we ask your forgiveness.[1]

Bernanos was well aware that the Action Française was 'deplorably lacking in interior life'. He was shocked that a young girl from the

[1] *Bulletin* 23, p. 15

'best' society, and a member of the movement, should be proclaiming her admiration for Anatole France in the salons of the Faubourg. Both Massis and Maritain were shocked that her admiration should be shared by Maurras himself; and Bernanos feared that 'under the pretext of reaction against a new romantic anarchy, the eighteenth century was attempting a come-back at the heels of this exhausted old man'.[1] Certain disciples of Maurras professed a similar admiration for Stendhal, whose genius Bernanos admired but whose chilly sensuality repelled him. He believed that the purification of the movement, for which Maritain had proposed the recipe, could only be realised by rallying behind Maurras, not by deserting him. Beneath all the slogans of 'Christian democracy' he saw the symptoms of a renascent modernism, and if the Papal intervention had the effect of mobilising opposition to this, it might still be recognised as providential. He remained firmly seated on the *Syllabus* of Pius IX, and he could easily imagine how the Sillonistes must be rejoicing at his present discomfiture. He saw the clergy infected with anarchism, and the day might come when he would be 'shot by Bolshevik priests with the cross on their chests, and the *Social Contract* in their pockets'.[2] Similar fears were expressed by the minority at the Second Vatican Council, and who knows but that Bernanos would have shared them?

Massis, on his side, addressed a long letter to Maritain in which he spoke for 'these young people, recently so confident and now so unhappy beneath their appearances of revolt'.[3] Would not Maritain's counsels of submission seem an impossibly negative solution to their dilemma? Would not the liberals and modernists of yesterday and today use their new-found argument of obedience to Papal authority in order to discredit the philosophical work in which Maritain was then engaged? Massis and Bernanos had both sought the advice of the eminent Jesuit, Léonce de Grandmaison, who was among the early protectors of Teilhard de Chardin. He had advised them to send the disconcerted *jeunesse* back to Joseph de Maistre and other Christian thinkers of the Counter-Revolution, to whom Maurras constantly referred. But what was the use, argued Massis, of asking the young *camelots du roi* to search in the dust of libraries for the

---

[1] *Maurras et notre temps* I
[2] October or November 1926: *Correspondance* I, pp. 277–8
[3] *Maurras et notre temps* I

texts to which Maurras, and he alone, had given the colour and the actuality of life?

Maritain was not insensitive to the pleas that Massis, as one more urgently concerned with what to do than with what to think, had put forward. But he could offer no better comfort than the hard truth as he saw it.

At the present moment I believe that the very essence of Christian life in our country is at stake; that the Action Française is purely and simply schismatic, and has destroyed in a few months all that it could have done for the cause of order; that the sum of what Maurras has accomplished will have been to assemble all that is most solid and traditional in France into a bloc, *insensitive* to the voice of the Church; that what the Church has struck at is a spirit of naturalism and national pharisaism just as liable to corrupt the virtue of charity as modernism was to destroy the virtue of faith. Such is for me the lesson, all too terribly evident, of what has happened during the past year.[1]

Bernanos reacted to this reply with the derisive and almost animal laughter which was so often the expression of his rage. The blood mounted to his eyes and the foam to his mouth. These fine theological distinctions were only too reminiscent of the casuistry which had condemned Jeanne d'Arc to the stake.

One thing is sure, my friend; it is not with their distinctions between the abstract and the concrete that these miserable creatures will recover any intellectual authority whatever. Wisdom, as you know, has never been my strong point. All the same, this is not how the wisdom of Catholicism has imposed itself on the world for fifteen hundred years. . . . I am a man of faith, in fact I am nothing else but a man of faith. I don't possess, as you do, the priceless gift of a critical mind, and I can leave Maritain to go to bed with the goddess of reason. But I ask myself under what curse and what disgrace the Catholic intelligence is suffering that in order to instruct its flock it has to seek its provender from the disciples of Bergson and Cocteau,[2] made up to look like Thomists? . . . I give Maritain this charitable warning of the fate in store for him. Whatever he does from now onward, he will only jump from the stove to fall into the fire. And I also predict that his turn will come, and that he too will be 'condemned', unless he changes his coat once again . . . Maurras is right to defend the temporal safety of this people and this race of Frenchmen. The temporal

---

[1] *Maurras et notre temps* I

[2] Maritain had once been a pupil of Bergson; and Cocteau, under Maritain's influence, had been converted to Catholicism.

is his business. When he reminds us of the laws of politics, he is serving in his own rank, but his rank is not ours. We are grateful for the respect with which he speaks of the Church and of France; but the French tradition, the French Christianity, which for us Catholics is the most precious part of our national heritage, this is what we should have stood in the front line to defend. That is our place. . . . We are failing Maurras and his work of salvation because in the first instance we failed ourselves and what charity demanded of us – for we possessed the thing that Maurras did not have. Now we are asked to condemn ourselves and to divorce obedience and honour. To what depths of meanness and servility do the ecclesiastics want to reduce us? I am ashamed of them, I am ashamed of myself, I am ashamed of our own helplessness as Catholics – in face of the great Maurras. 'Submit, submit,' whisper all the soutanes as they slink away, routed, to the door! Don't the unfortunate creatures see that *France is on the road to her destruction?*[1]

When the diatribe was over, with its characteristic blend of generosity and injustice – the reaction of a nervous system strained to breaking-point as well as the protest of a heart and mind – Bernanos, we are told, sank back exhausted. 'His eyes darkened, and their flame disappeared behind the swollen and sinking pupils. His features seemed deformed by a sudden puffiness; the circles round his eyes were darker beneath their heavy pouches; his face grew more bilious, his complexion more leaden, and under his straggling moustache his lips curled in a bitter sneer. Then, after a silence, and as if his heart were liberating a thought for too long held in check, his melancholy gushed forth in a raucous sigh: 'I have had enough! I have a very good mind to take myself off to America or elsewhere, as far away as possible from this part of myself which at present is no better than a corpse.'[2]

The time was to come when he would act upon this impulse, but for reasons which had nothing to do with the crisis of the Action Française.

[1] *Maurras et notre temps* I   [2] Ibid

CHAPTER 5

SACRED AND SECULAR

I

BERNANOS and his friends were in a cruel dilemma, from which only heroic resignation or desperate casuistry could deliver them. In those pre-conciliar days no one claimed that since the Papal condemnation was not infallible it might be disobeyed with impunity. Of course, it was widely disobeyed, and many adherents of the Action Française lived without the sacraments rather than desert their master. Bernanos, in whom docility and revolt were always at odds, enquired of Père Janvier, the eminent Dominican whose Lenten sermons drew all Paris to Notre Dame, whether he might continue to read the proscribed journal. 'You may read it,' came the astonishing answer, '*once a week*'. Albert Béguin informed the present writer that Bernanos 'submitted, but not immediately'. He certainly took his time, since we find him addressing adherents of the movement on several occasions during the following years – a movement, be it remembered, to which he no longer formally belonged. Where the trauma of the controversy shifted Maritain towards the Left in politics, it only consolidated Bernanos' *tempéra-ment de droite*. He was too impatient to enter into the arguments with which Maritain counselled resignation and Maurras justified defiance. A man to whom he and many thousands of Frenchmen owed their political faith was in trouble; that was enough for him. He could not help seeing in the condemnation a triumph of the democracy and the liberalism he detested. The barricades were up; it was not in his nature to abandon them.

Nor did the moment seem propitious to accept the decoration of the Légion d'Honneur, which was now offered to him, at a time when honour was so much in question. This was only the first of his refusals. On the 2nd of January 1927, Emile Bernanos died, and was provisionally buried at Bagnères-le-Bigorre. In the same month Massis, who was at work on *Défense de l'Occident*, came to stay; his presence brought much consolation. In March the body of Emile Bernanos was laid to rest in the cemetery at Pellevoisin where, twenty-one years later, his son was to lie beside him. Bernanos proceeded to Belgium on a lecture tour, followed by similar appearances at Strasbourg and Rouen. In July, restless as ever, he bought a house at Clermont-sur-l'Oise, 33 Place de l'Hôtel de Ville, and moved there shortly afterwards.

Meanwhile Maritain had published his definitive word on the crisis of the Action Française. *La Primauté du Spirituel*[1] was a first step towards *Integral Humanism*, and for Bernanos it was a further step in the wrong direction. In a crisis where Bernanos could see only the perplexities of conscience – an essentially human situation – Maritain was doing his best to resolve them in the light of unchanging truths. The author of *Anti-Moderne* could hardly be accused of modernism, but he was compelled to the detachment of a philosopher, where Bernanos was still in thrall to the passions of a partisan.

Maritain declined to accept Bernanos' new novel, *L'Imposture* for the *Roseau d'Or*, and again it was through the good offices of Massis that it was taken by Plon. He was no longer collaborating with Massis on the *Revue universelle*, and his relations with Bernanos became very strained. When Bernanos attacked him in the *Action Française*,[2] the rupture seemed to be complete; but it was healed two years later in circumstances that did credit to both parties.

Graham Greene has written that every great writer is in some degree a man obsessed. A notion of obsession that includes Jane Austen and Thackeray has to be considerably broadened – but let that pass. In the narrower sense of the word, Georges Bernanos was a *locus classicus* of obsession. It would be altogether too *simpliste* to describe him as a priest *manqué;* but he did feel an intimate relationship between the vocation of the priest and his own vocation as a writer. Each was a vocation to the proclamation of truth; truth was the only excuse for writing at all. And in so far as he detected the taint of theological liberalism in the clerical opponents of the Action Française, this undoubtedly coloured his conception of the abbé Cénabre in *L'Imposture*, the novel on which he had been intermittently at work over the last two years. Whether his suspicions were justified is not here to the point. He imagined with an implac-

---

[1] This appeared in English as *The Things that are not Caesar's* (1930)
[2] 15th November 1928

able insight the kind of humanist priest – erudite, desiccated, and prudently *avant-garde* – who would have rejoiced in Maurras' discomfiture. One knows the type, and the reader can fit the cap to any head that occurs to him. Many people thought that Bernanos had Henri Bremond in mind, although Bremond's slight physique and nervous manner had nothing in common with the solidity of Cénabre. Bremond himself certainly recognised the portrait, and protested to the publishers, who requested Bernanos to modify certain details which might have lent substance to Bremond's complaint. Bremond accused Maurras, with whom he was then in controversy, of inspiring Bernanos to a libellous caricature; but Bernanos needed no such persuasion. He admitted shortly before his death that the features of Cénabre had come to him after reading Bremond's history of religious thought in France; that Cénabre was born of Bremond's book, though not of Bremond himself. In Bremond, as in Cénabre, he would have sniffed 'the contradictions of Renan, his womanish sensibility, his coquetry and sly egotism, the sudden access of tenderness – all evidence of a soul evading the issue through a wilful dissipation'. For Bernanos, as for Claudel, Renan occupied a place of honour among the renegades of nineteenth-century Catholicism; his exquisite prose style only made the poison of his pen more palatable. Bremond had flirted with 'the Mystery of Newman'; Cénabre was engaged on a life of the German mystic, Tauler, whose orthodoxy had itself come under suspicion. At the beginning of *L'Imposture* Cénabre loses his faith; at the end of its sequel, *La Joie*, he recovers it – and then goes mad.

Opposed to Cénabre, and redeeming him from beyond the grave, is the abbé Chevance whom Cénabre summons at the crisis of his apostasy. There is here a certain reminiscence of the curé de Lumbres. Chevance is obscure where Cénabre is celebrated, diffident where Cénabre is decisive, simple where Cénabre is sophisticated, ailing where Cénabre is robust, humble where Cénabre is proud. But he is a gentler soul than Donissan, and he discovers his counterpart in Chantal de Clergerie,[1] whose spiritual director he becomes. Chantal is one of Bernanos' most attractive creations; her death at the hands of Fiodor, the mysterious Russian chauffeur, has a Sophoclean dignity and pathos. Here, and not for the last time, Bernanos plunges the reader into a kind of Dostoevskian darkness;

[1] *La Joie*

indeed the climate of these two novels is the antithesis between darkness and light, like a picture by Georges de La Tour. Their respective titles give the clue to it. François Mauriac used to say that if he had to keep one novel of Bernanos and lose the rest, he would choose the first hundred pages of *La Joie*. It was an intelligible option.

The middle ground, so to speak, is occupied by a number of characters, all of whom are variations on the central and obsessive theme of *imposture*. The book is far from being the best of Bernanos' novels – the satiric element is too intrusive, and the Balzacian technique of narration too clumsily adapted – but the title might be taken as the *leitmotiv* of everything he was to write in fiction or polemic, with the exception of the *Dialogues des Carmélites* and the *Journal d'un Curé de campagne*. For Bernanos the lie was the mark of the Beast, and he pursued it with the tenacity of a bloodhound. So, in these two novels we have a number of characters who are the sinister or derisive counterfeits of their profession. Each betrays his particular *sacerdoce*, whether of the Word or the word. In *La Joie* it is upon M. de Clergerie, another *homme de lettres*, that the novelist expends his ferocious irony. De Clergerie stands in the same relation to secular as Cénabre stands to ecclesiastical affairs. He, too, is an *imposteur*.

M. de Clergerie was a small man, with a dark and tragic complexion and a head like a rat. He had also a rat's anxiety, with his petty and precise gestures, and the rat's perpetual agitation. A dozen boring volumes were there to read on his narrow face, creased and wrinkled incessantly by a secret thought – assiduous and vigilant, and always the same at every stage of his life, and so intimately familiar that he no longer recognised it, and could no longer express it in intelligible language. Laborious and calculating, he ruminated over the misfortunes of his rivals, but without any expenditure of hatred. He simply weighed up his chances, for he had the honour of belonging to the Académie des Sciences morales, and he was aspiring to a seat in the Académie Française.[1]

In the central portion of *L'Imposture* the action revolves around a *petite chapelle* of literary and clerical intrigue, only lightly related to the drama of Cénabre and Chevance. At its centre is M. Guérou, a writer of professed agnosticism and scandalous private life. Beside him, nevertheless, we find the Bishop of Paumiers, Mgr Espelette,

[1] Editions de la Pléiade, p. 535

whom he had known as a student and treats with merited contempt.

The ideas of the Bishop of Paumiers, or at least what his conceit took for ideas, were those of a mentally impoverished professor. Incapable of deliberate treason, and with a childish faith that withstood all the fancies of his superficial mind, he cherished the insane ambition to be simply a 'priest in time', whereas in fact he was a priest for eternity. When he repeated: 'I am a man of my own time' he seemed to be bearing witness on his own behalf. He never took the precaution of realising that each time he did so he was denying the signature that marked him.[1]

There were many such that Bernanos may have had in mind on the morrow of the condemnation. He was to meet – and often to misjudge – them all through his life. He could have met many more of them today.

The Bishop of Paumiers believed in Progress, and his idea of Progress was suited to his own capacities. This professor, who wore his title so proudly, was able to enrich himself with ideas without delivering his intelligence from the tyranny of his feelings. He thought with the loves and hatreds, the desires and the rancours, of his adolescence, and anything he said which was quoted for its boldness and novelty was really no more than the abstract expression of some humiliation he had suffered in his youth of which he still felt the smart. The men in power laughed at this kind of servility. The unhappy creature solicited their friendship, only to be rewarded with a cordial contempt of which he was unaware – for parties in power generally detest the people who flatter them. He was liberal with his promises, and the letters he wrote made the headlines; he seized every opportunity to appear between a Protestant minister and a Jewish rabbi; and in so far as he challenged the position of these official functionaries, he did so with humility. But it was all in vain. His pride had never been hurt so bitterly, but he was at an age when the mistakes and vices of youth enter into the flesh and blood, and finish by being loved for themselves in proportion to the tears and disappointments they have caused.[2]

Other members of the Bernanosian *inferno* include a former colleague of President Combes; a ridiculous aristocrat who puts on democratic and Voltairean airs; a diplomat with a secret line to the Vatican; and his wife whose verses, like her character, are understood to be no better than they should be. In painting his *dramatis personae*, down to the last detail of their physical habits, Bernanos

[1] Editions de la Pléiade, p. 388   [2] Ibid, pp. 388-9

shows himself an implacable moralist, standing outside his characters more judicially than he would learn to do later on, passing with pitiless clarity from the particular instance to the general conclusion. 'In the long run,' he writes, 'nothing is less like a frank and intrepid vice than the same vice transformed by a necessary dissimulation and cultivated in depth.' There was something almost heroic in the hypocrisy of Cénabre, as he proceeded to base his life on the hypothesis of God – simply because it was a convenient way of living.

'If it is only God that I have lost,' he had repeated to himself a hundred times already, 'then I have lost nothing. But my life was built up in the light of such an hypothesis. This was its *raison d'être;* this made it seriously worth while. God is essential for my work and my habits and my position. I shall carry on as if he existed. And I shall make this decision once and for all.'[1]

When Bernanos had written to the abbé Lagrange about *vos petits employés du Sillon* he may well have had in mind just such a character as Pernichon, the journalist and editor of *La Vie Moderne,* who receives absolution from Cénabre only a few minutes before the 'power of the keys' becomes no more than a working hypothesis. Bernanos was always impatient with the ecclesiastical layman, indefatigably *affairé,* scuttling from one presbytery to another, editing this or that brochure, wistfully and timidly 'with it'. Such people, replete with good intentions and confused ideas, were of course the natural enemies of the Action Française, finding in its dilemma some consolation for the proscription of their own movement. The very name of Pernichon is in itself indicative; it rhymes with *pleurnichant,* and the unhappy Pernichon whimpers his way from the confessional to the *petite chapelle,* engulfed in the half-truth where Cénabre is engulfed in the total lie, confused where Cénabre is clear – until the treachery of his associates drives him at last to suicide.

The piety of the young editor of *La Vie Moderne* was not a pure hypocrisy. One might even call it sincere, for it sprang from the most hidden depths of his being, in the obscure fear of evil and the sly itch to attain it indirectly, with the minimum risk. The little he possessed of social or political doctrine was subordinate to the same pathetic need to surrender his soul to the enemy. What the idiots of his entourage described as boldness and

[1] Ibid, p. 457

independence was only the visible sign – albeit misunderstood – of his dismal nostalgia for total abandonment, for a definitive liquidation of himself. Every foe to the cause which he claimed to serve already had the key to his heart; every objection of his adversary awakened a complicity in his mind. When those of his own party were the victims of injustice, he was at once aroused not to revolt, nor even to a cowardly complacency. What he felt in the double-faced recesses of his womanish soul was the hatred of the oppressed, and the ignoble love for the oppressor.[1]

L'Imposture is the only one of Bernanos' novels in which there is not, so to speak, a breath of fresh air. With reason he had thought of entitling it *Les Ténèbres*. From first to last the scene is laid in Paris – a nocturnal Paris, wonderfully evoked, where the novelist, once again, passes from the particular to the general, so that we hear not alone 'the triple rumour of the place de Rennes', but the midnight hush and midnight murmur of any great city, scarred by the 'aboriginal catastrophe'.

How the cities call to one across the darkness, and with how deep a voice! How painfully their joy finds its breath . . . how it rattles! As soon as you have crossed the dazzling and crowded street, it follows you in the shadows with a fearful complaint, diminishing little by little, until another street, just as crowded and glaring, raises its harrowing voice to mingle with the first. And yet 'voice' is hardly the right word, for only the forest and the hill, the fire and the water, have voices and speak a language. We have lost the secret of it, although the memory of a sublime agreement, of the ineffable alliance between mind and matter, cannot be forgotten by the lowest of mankind. The voice that we no longer understand is still a friendly and fraternal voice, pacific and serene.

And then, irresistibly, Bernanos summons the figure of Anatole France to preside over the City of the Plain:

The poetaster, basest of his tribe, whom the modern world has honoured as a god, cherished the ridiculous belief that he had given it back to us. But all he had done was to rid nature of the dryads and wood-nymphs, and leave us his dismal sensualities in their place. . . . There is not a single meadow, glistening with the morning dew, where you will not find their traces, like a litter of dirty paper on the lawn, on a Monday morning. But for all that, if man can impose his presence upon nature, and the marks of his vulgarity, the interior rhythm and deep rumination of nature escape him. He may stifle her voice, but she will not answer. Her sublime

[1] Editions de la Pléiade, p. 315

chant goes on, as a vibrating chord chooses its harmonies among a thousand, and responds to them alone. . . . But this does not happen with the landscapes of rubble and girders and iron – with the cities.[1]

It is only in the last pages of *L'Imposture* that a ray of spiritual sunshine illuminates the darkness. Chevance is dying in poverty. He dreams that Cénabre has come to visit him – a figure, now, of Satanic pride, only regretting the occasion when he had thrown him to the ground, and linked, by very reason of this involuntary violence, 'to your detestable little person for all eternity'. Chevance had been his victim; would he therefore be his vanquisher? The affirmative answer is not given until the end of *La Joie*, and it is Chantal de Clergerie who gives it. Just as she has passed her own charisma to the dying Chevance – 'I want to give you what I have, and what you loved, so much – what I no longer need and what I shall never need any more – my joy' – so the charisma of Chevance has passed into her to rescue Cénabre at the terrible price of his sanity. She had achieved the 'transparency' of the saints, for she wished to be 'nothing more than a crystal, a drop of pure water, in which God was visible . . . or a little grain of impalpable dust suspended on the will of God'; and her fragility was the measure of her force. It was the first intention of Bernanos that Cénabre should die after receiving what was literally the *coup de grâce*, but on second thoughts he thought it more appropriate that God should strike his reason. Of the two novels – in reality a single work which the author always regretted not having published as such – *L'Imposture* was rather coolly received; but Bernanos treasured to his dying day a letter from Antonin Artaud, father of the Theatre of Cruelty. It was a strange source of compliment. Artaud had been deeply shaken by the death of the abbé Chevance, even if he had misunderstood it. In these pages, he wrote, the 'haunting power is nothing beside the perspiration of despair which trickles from them.'[2]

With Chantal de Clergerie, the Bernanosian *espérance* had survived the immolation of joy, but it remained the prisoner of the Passion. Nowhere is the author's spirituality more movingly and accurately conveyed.

He was thinking of the treason, and she was thinking of it too. It was over the treason that he wept; it was the execrable thought of the treason

[1] Ibid, p. 326   [2] *Cahiers du Rhône*, p. 63

that he tried vainly to put out of his mind, drop by drop, with the bloody sweat. He had loved, as a man will love, the simple inheritance of mankind – his hearth and his home, his bread and his wine, the grey roads gilded by the rain, the smoke rising from the villages, the little houses behind the hedge of thorn, the peace of evening, and the children playing on the doorstep. He had loved all that, as a man will love it, but in a way that no man had ever loved it before, or would ever love it again; loved it so purely and jealously, with the heart he created for that purpose with his own hands. The evening before, the disciples were discussing among themselves how far they should go the next day, where they should sleep and what they should eat – like soldiers before a night march. They were a little ashamed to let the Rabbi go up there, practically alone, and they were talking rather loudly, on purpose, with their thick peasant voices, slapping each other on the shoulder, like drovers or horse-copers. And all the while he was blessing the first-fruits of the death that was close at hand, just as, the same day, he had blessed the bread and the wine, consecrating for his own people – the sorrowing race of men and women – the Sacred Body, which was his own work, and offering it for all mankind. He raised it up before them with his holy and venerable hands, over the wide spaces of the sleeping earth, whose seasons he had loved so dearly. He offered it once and for all, while the brilliance and the strength of his youth were still with him, before resigning himself to Fear – face to face with the ugliness of Fear, all through that interminable night until the morning brought its abatement.

No doubt he offered it for all mankind, but it was of one man alone that he was thinking. The one man to whom that Body truly and humanly belonged, as the body of a slave belongs to its master. The man who had captured it by cunning, having already disposed of it like a legitimate possession by due process of sale and contract. The only man who was able to set mercy at defiance, enter on the same footing into despair, make of despair his habitation, cover himself with despair as the first murderer had sought the cover of the night. The only man who really possessed something, was really provided with something, since there was nothing else he could receive from anybody, for all eternity.[1]

Bernanos completed *La Joie* at the end of December 1928, writing the last pages 'as one makes the last kilometres on the road – in a kind of stupor';[2] ending it as he had begun it 'living with two lovely saints, true saints, and I do with them what I like.'[3] It might

[1] Editions de la Pléiade, p. 684   [2] To R. Vallery-Radot: *Correspondance* I, p. 335
[3] *Bernanos par lui-même*, p. 161

have been truer to say that Chantal de Clergerie did as she chose with Bernanos. In a copy of the book presented to Marie Vallery-Radot he had inscribed: 'I am rather good at death beds; I hope I shall not make a mess of my own.' *La Joie* appeared serially in the *Revue universelle* between October 1928 and January 1929; it was published by Plon in June; and in December was awarded the Prix Fémina. Re-reading it six years later Bernanos felt that he would find here 'the prefiguration of everything that is happening or will happen to me. And the skunks want me to write a novel like that once a year!'[1] It was an accurate premonition; some time would pass before he again turned his hand to fiction.

While the figure of Chantal de Clergerie was still haunting him, Bernanos looked back to her historical prototype. His short essay on the trial of Joan of Arc, *Jeanne – relapse et sainte*, was published by the *Revue hebdomadaire* in July 1929. This gave full scope for his irony at the expense of the canonists and the casuists; for the nostalgia which was also, as Emmanuel Mounier pointed out, a supernatural view of history; and for a triumphalism which boasted of nothing but the treasury of the saints. The writing has the disciplined eloquence, the masculine and moving sincerity, of Bernanos at his best, prefiguring in some respects the *Dialogues des Carmélites*.

She had loved the horses, the processions, and the parades; the nights of bivouac under the stars; the advance along the rutted track between two walls of grass; the deployment on to the plateau, and the rattling of a hundred banners, and the snorting of the beasts, and over there – the city, all blue, waiting to be captured . . . She had loved the same things that a soldier loves, and as he will love them, attached to nothing, ready to leave it all any day of the week and beg their daily bread from the hand of God.[2]

The last pages, with their refrain, 'Our Church is the Church of the saints', repeated eight times over, takes its place in any anthology of Bernanosian prose. It opens up for us the vision which was the author's viaticum against despair:

The man who approaches the Church with misgiving sees only the closed doors, the barriers, and the windows where you buy your ticket, a kind of spiritual constabulary. *But our Church is the Church of the saints.* To become a saint, what bishop would not give his mitre, his ring, and

[1] Ibid, p. 162   [2] *Jeanne – relapse et sainte* (Plon, 1934), pp. 48–9

his pectoral cross, what cardinal would not sacrifice his purple and what pontiff his white robe, his chamberlains, his Swiss guards, and all his temporal appurtenance? Who would not crave the strength to brave this marvellous adventure? For sanctity is an adventure; it is even the only adventure. Once you have understood this, you have entered into the heart of the Catholic faith; your mortal flesh will have trembled, no longer with the fear of death, but with a superhuman hope. . . .

God did not create the Church to ensure the prosperity of the saints, but in order that she should transmit their memory; . . . Our Catholic tradition carries them along, unhurt, in its universal rhythm. Saint Benedict and his raven, Saint Francis and his mandola and his Provençal verses, Joan and her sword, Vincent and his shabby soutane, and the latest arrival, so strange and secret . . . with her incomprehensible smile – Thérèse of the Child Jesus. They lived and suffered as we do. They were tempted as we are. The man who dares not yet accept what is sacred and divine in their example will at least learn from it the lesson of heroism and honour.

Not one of us who carry our load of responsibility – to our country, our family, or our profession – with our poor faces hollow with anxiety, our hands hardened with toil, the immense tedium of our daily life, with our daily bread to earn, and the honour of our homes to defend – not one of us will ever know enough theology even to become a canon. But we know enough to become a saint. Others can look after the spiritual side of things; others can argue and legislate; but we hold in our hands the temporal kingdom of God. Ours is the inheritance of the saints. For ever since the bread and the wine were blessed for us and the stones upon our doorstep and the roofs where the doves build their nest, the beds where we dream into oblivion, and the roads where the farm-carts go grinding past, our lads with their rough laughter and our girls who weep beside the spring – ever since God himself came to visit us, is there anything in this world that the saints have not taken upon themselves? Is there anything which is beyond their capacity to give?[1]

2

With the exception of a lecture tour which took him to Lyons, Grenoble, Avignon, Montpellier, Béziers, and then to Switzerland, Bernanos had spent most of 1928 at Clermont, writing *La Joie* at the Café Français in the village of Mouy near by. But in July we find him at the sanctuary of La Salette, celebrated by Léon Bloy in

---

[1] *Jeanne – relapse et sainte*, pp. 61–8, *passim*

Celle qui pleure. Here the Blessed Virgin was said to have prophesied fearful disasters to a world which had disowned her Son, and to have declared that only her intercession could stay His avenging arm. For Bloy, and also no doubt for Bernanos, the date of the prophecy was significant; on the 19th of September 1914 the shells of the German artillery had fallen on Rheims cathedral. The visions of La Salette have never been officially recognised, but the place has always drawn its quota of pilgrims. Bernanos remained there for a month, only embarrassed by the battalions of *dévots* whose appearance lent no reinforcement to a state of grace. Nevertheless the superb and lonely situation of the sanctuary was a rich consolation, and its penitential ambience so powerful that he resolved to give up smoking, burying all his pipes near by. The resolution was short-lived; he made a second pilgrimage to recover one of them! Later he was visiting the presbytery of the curé d'Ars. Here nothing disappointed him. 'I found the slippers of the abbé Donissan and the neck-bands of the abbé Chevance.'[1]

On the 1st of November a third daughter, Dominique, was born to Jeanne Bernanos; and on Armistice Day, the 11th of November, Bernanos was in Paris addressing the students of the Action Française in the Salle Bullier. This occupied a site in that part of the Avenue de l'Observatoire which now bears the name of the Avenue Georges-Bernanos. Already, on the 22nd of March 1927, the death of Marshal Foch and the funeral which Bernanos followed with the silent crowds, had inspired a disillusioned meditation on the victory which the strategy of Foch had done so much to achieve. Bernanos described it as the *victoire muette*,[2] because the men whom Foch had led were dumb spectators of their own betrayal. This mood was not, of course, in the least peculiar to Bernanos; it was shared by most survivors of the war that so signally failed its promise – to put an end to war for ever. It lay heavily upon all who stood beside the coffin, face to face with the tomb of the Unknown Soldier under the arch of the Etoile. It was a crowd, like so many Parisian crowds, sensitive either to enthusiasm or revolt, and its low murmur lingered in the ear with a reverberation of mourning and also of menace. It closed upon the remains of the dead Marshal, 'like a crumbling wall'; the men removing their hats, 'as they might have removed

[1] To Maurice Bourdel, August 1928: *Correspondance* I, p. 330
[2] *Le Crépuscule des Vieux*, pp. 248–53

them at the passing of Clovis or Turenne'. It was strange that after
making a great deal of noise through four years of desperate engagement, the people of France should now hear nothing but the hollow
rhetoric of the forum, and the whispered confabulations of those
who were preparing to sabotage the peace they were professing to
save. The sole guarantors of the *victoire muette* were those who would
open their mouths 'only to give up their souls to God'.

Bernanos had no hesitation in opening his. *La Grande Peur des
Bien-Pensants*, on which he was at work for the next eighteen
months, launched him as a pamphleteer in the great tradition. What
is immediately surprising about the book was its inspiration, not by
Daudet or Maurras, but by Drumont. Bernanos was faithful to the
lessons learnt at his father's knee. Drumont was neither a royalist nor
a proclaimed believer; call him a national socialist and you set him
at the head of a not very reputable lineage. But, as Bernanos pointed
out in the first paragraph of his book, he could claim a less controversial descent: 'of your lineage and mine, a sturdy Frenchman, a
little heavy in the shoulders, marching at a steady pace'.[1] He was the
kind of Frenchman Bernanos had known in the army, and Bernanos
saluted the man before he endorsed his opinions. He even gave an
unmerited salute to his prose style. 'Through nearly every line of his
writings – so powerful and dense, soberly and even a little awkwardly
constructed, with their background of serious melancholy – like a
fort on the summit of a hill against an autumn sky, gilded and bare,
and on enemy ground, a kind of heroic resignation, the deliberate
acceptance of death.' The last time Bernanos had seen him was the
day when Cardinal Richard was expelled from his palace by the
decree of an anti-clerical government. Drumont had suddenly
appeared on the steps of the palace, his beard now almost white,
and the last trace of irony vanished from his smile. He seemed to be a
man content henceforward to have neither friends nor enemies; to
be wrapped in a Stoic solitude. The crowd chanted the *Credo*, and
some women, brutally thrown back by the police, called out: '*Vive
Jésus!*' Drumont disappeared through the host of umbrellas, and
Bernanos never saw him again. The indefatigable journalist of *La
Libre Parole* would have liked to sit among the forty 'immortals' of
the Académie Française, but Marcel Prévost was elected instead.

[1] *La Grande Peur des Bien-Pensants* (Grasset, 1931), p. 7

Having written fifteen thick volumes of embittered polemic, and fought a duel with Clemenceau, he died not long afterwards. 'He waited, day after day, and year after year, for destiny's supreme act of treason, regulating in view of this decisive ordeal the vigorous beating of his heart.' It was to fail him an hour too soon; and after the long hours and days of dying, there was only 'the bitter laugh which finishes in the convulsion of disgust'.

La Grande Peur des Bien-Pensants is not a book on which the admirers of Bernanos now like to dwell, except for a few surviving voices on the extreme Right who regret his subsequent options. The truth is that he had not yet discovered his independence; he was still a passionate partisan. To the end of his days he found it difficult to admit the innocence of Dreyfus; all he would concede was the injustice of condemning him for political reasons. Even if we remember that people would speak about Jews in the days of their social and financial ascendancy as they would not dare to speak about them today, and even if we admit a measure of justice in their complaints, one cannot exculpate the Bernanos of those days from the charge of a very superficial, and essentially chauvinistic, anti-Semitism. Like so many Catholics of his time, he believed the Jews to be a menace; he could not see that they were also a mystery. His simplifications had nothing in common with the anxious exegesis of Claudel. Even if they were a nuisance in the temporal order, they were also a spiritual necessity. 'Spiritually we are Semites', Pius XI was presently to declare; but the voice of Pius XI was not, as we have seen, a voice to which Bernanos was invariably docile.

As he looked back, with Drumont at his elbow, he saw the Jews installed in the best positions, and it seemed

impossible to deny that for a moment, at least, the Republic believed that it had found in them the cadres of a new aristocracy, and also, no doubt, the artisans of a kind of artistic, literary and philosophical Renaissance, to which it had been able to give its name. Publicity did the rest, since the peaceful invaders were already seated in the editorial chairs and working to their mutual advantage. The benevolent murmur of the fashionable salons responded to the rumour of the boulevards, thanks to the numerous rich heiresses of Jewish blood, now duchesses and marchionesses, who dictated the tone of society. In short, for ten or fifteen years, the Jew was all the rage. The Jewish irony, his childish, desperate, and oriental melancholy . . . his heartrending cynicism – prophetic of a race at the end of its tether – his frightening apprehension of death – all this went to the heads of the French.[1]

Bernanos endorsed the judgment of Drumont, who had written of 'the irresistible attraction which pushes into the arms of the Jew those whom he is out to destroy'. He spoke of the 'long Patriarchate of the Rothschilds' and the racing colours of Baron Hirsch floating from the pavilion of the Jockey Club; of the strange men who 'gesticulated like apes, educated in the contempt of the past, profoundly indifferent to the traditions of their race, foreign masters importing a new mystique, excellently adapted to the mystique of Progress and to the Messianic modernism which expects nothing more of mankind than the revelation of a future god.' Nor did Bernanos fail to remind his readers that, only a few days after the arrest of Dreyfus, the Chief Rabbi, Zadoc-Kahn, had warned the Prefect of Police that 'the country would be split from top to bottom, all the Jews standing to arms, and war between the two camps'. It was an accurate prophecy; but Bernanos did not add that a great many Gentiles – and notably his 'cher Péguy' – would be standing beside the Jews.

The contempt of Bernanos for democracy, even in the later days when he had only democrats for his allies, was persistent and ingrained. Yet it was not irrational:

In putting man in the place of God, we have at the same time destroyed the notion of Law, and involved in its collapse those functions which derived from the Law, and from the Law alone, their sacred character. Henceforward they are condemned to triviality. There is nothing august about the laws of democracy. They express the will of the greatest number; in brief, they express a necessity.[2]

Nevertheless, in attacking the mystique of democracy, Bernanos was really attacking the mystique of material progress to which the classic democracies of the Western world had nailed their political colours. To assure the greatest degree of material comfort to the greatest number – what alternative could any party, not bent upon suicide, propose to its electorate? Bernanos was shocked by the complicity of the clergy in the cynical transformation of a world hitherto impregnated by Christian belief. Balzac – a surer guide than Drumont – had seen the progressive impoverishment of the

[1] *La Grande Peur des Bien-Pensants*, p. 201   [2] Ibid, p. 432

state by the anonymous forces of money, but here the curés could see only 'a venial avarice and an innocent greed'. All their homily was directed against the sins of the flesh – an obsession, Bernanos maintained, unknown to the Christian centuries. Nor was their crusade attended with much success; it rarely is. In this context Bernanos wrote very much as Eric Gill was writing at about the same time, and from a similar identification of democracy and Mammon. The Catholic priest was becoming like the Protestant pastor in the United States: 'well-dressed and well-nourished, with his bank account and his Buick, waiting for a better organisation of contraceptive services and mental hygiene to make his ministry superfluous.' To complaints that spirituality had retired from the field, the *Osservatore Romano* would no doubt reply that it was 'still living at the residence of the Apostolic Nuncio, 10 Place des Etats Unis, and that His Excellency had dined with a good appetite the previous evening at the table of the Duchess of Tralala.'

Bernanos did not delude himself that a programme of Franciscan poverty would win an election; but then he had his own ideas about elections. They were shared by other protagonists of the Counter-Revolution, which is not necessarily to be confused with what was soon to be known as Fascism. Bernanos was not in the least impressed by the brittle tramp of the March to Rome, and still less by the purring of the limousine which brought Signor Mussolini to join it. What he understood by the Counter-Revolution was a wide-ranging social reform, of which the Comte de Chambord had dreamt on his death-bed – 'the reconciliation of the people and the State, united against financial oppression'. Many a good democrat has cherished the same dream; but Bernanos did not believe that democracy could fulfil it. For him, as for Maurras, the only revolution was the revolution for order, preached by the founders of the Action Française in 1899, at a time when the Movement, like Drumont and Barrès, was still Republican. It was not only – or even primarily – the instinct for conservation which attracted Bernanos to the monarchy; it was the proved ability of the monarchy to initiate necessary reforms.

The *ancien régime*, traditional in principle, was in reality no doubt the least conservative of any. Even on the threshold of irreparable events, the policy of Louis XVI, with Necker or Turgot, was on the contrary imprudently reformist, as if for the last time, in the face of an unknown peril, our ancient and dying monarchy was trying to hurl itself into the van. Only the complicated stupidity of certain people on the Right could have invented the absurd epithet which would make an enemy of every Frenchman who showed signs of discontent – for where will you find a Frenchman who is not discontented, who does not dream of destroying or reforming something?[1]

The Counter-Revolution dreamt of destroying the power of the bourgeoisie which the previous revolution had established; but it was the paradox of the Action Française, and other movements akin to it, that it attracted most of its adherents from the class to which it was theoretically opposed. Neither the peasantry nor the proletariat in France flocked to its standard, dearly as Bernanos would have liked them to. The weakness of a radicalism of the Right is that it attracts so few radicals, and for all Bernanos' anathemas the democratic dream has persisted among those he hoped to convert, and who hated the same things as he did.

In a famous article, Julien Benda had shown that the *idées claires* of the Action Française were in fact a tissue of confusions. The young monarchist of good family to whom he addressed his 'Letters' was actuated by hatred of a régime, which he believed had robbed him of his privileges, forgetting that it was the monarchy itself which had begun this dispossession. The more conservative among the clergy hated it for its separation of civil and ecclesiastical power, forgetting that the monarchy had practised this separation without preaching it. The wealthy bourgeoisie hated it because it permitted the means by which the proletariat might climb to power. The *petite bourgeoisie* hated it because its parliamentary forms seemed to them a cloak for sinister and anonymous forces, which they wished to see displaced by a visible and personal authority. Certain intellectuals hated it for its drabness, and others, of little natural distinction, wished to become conspicuous by their disgust. It was the task of the Action Française to excite, and if possible to unify, these separate resentments.

Its main appeal was to patriotism, but it met the immediate obstacle of a nobility that had never been slow to emigrate, and a clergy tainted with ultramontanism. It was principally in the *petite bourgeoisie* that the Action Française found a solid core of patriotism, and it was probably to attract this tradition to itself that the move-

[1] *La Grande Peur des Bien-Pensants*, pp. 98–9

ment became so violently and vulgarly nationalist. In brief, a movement which appealed to many by the architecture of its doctrine was in fact flagrantly opportunist. Having discovered that the Republic was hated by a number of people for a variety of reasons, it attempted to express this hatred by certain rigid definitions. In spite of its logical appearances, the Action Française was romantic rather than rational, emotional rather than intellectualist.

It was royalist, because it claimed that France had been made by its kings. This was a loose manner of speaking, and the French people had a right to reply that they, too, had had a share in the business. If it were objected that France had grown great under its kings and declined under its republics, they could answer that the kings had had a thousand years and the republics little more than a century; that if the Most Christian Kings had comprehended the doctrine of the Rights of Man they would still be on the throne, where the French people had so desperately tried to keep them. If Maurras retorted that the kings had, after all, summoned the States-General, the Republican could answer that they had done so five times in 800 years. If he argued that the monarchy had respected provincial liberties, his opponent could reply that Louis XIV, the most Maurrasian of the French monarchs, had suppressed the States of Rouergue, Quercy, Périgord, Berry, Maine, Anjou, Touraine, Orléanais, and Auvergne. If he maintained that the kings, as distinct from the republics, had always entrusted the government to competent ministers, one was entitled to reply that both under Louis XV and Louis XVIII prefects of police had been made ministers of the marine. The French monarchy had been a great thing, and it was not difficult to argue that its disappearance was a national disaster. But before it could be restored it would have to be recovered; and before it could be recovered it would have to be recognised; and after it was recognised it would have to be reformed. The French people did not recognise it under the formulas of Maurras, and they were not convinced that he could reform it.

The Action Française extended the merits of the monarchy to the society it had crowned. The aesthete looked back to a Utopia of good taste. He forgot that the farces of Molière had been far more popular than Le Misanthrope, and that Bourdaloue had been preferred to Bossuet; that while all Paris rushed to see La Mariamne of Tristan l'Hermite, Racine retired from the theatre, discouraged by his lack of success; that while the *Timocrate* of Thomas Corneille had eighty consecutive performances, *Andromaque*, which was Racine's greatest triumph, had only twenty-seven. He forgot that in the following century the *Lettres Péruviennes* of Mme de Graffigny made almost as great a stir as *La Nouvelle Héloïse*, and that the early editions of Mme de Sévigné's 'Letters' nearly ruined her publisher. These caprices of opinion are common to every century, and they are not quoted in disparagement of the *grand siècle*. But M. Benda had reason to point out that the Third Republic had little to fear in comparison with them. It was Gide and Valéry, Bergson and Claudel, Poulenc and Picasso, Cocteau and Matisse, Mauriac and Proust, who were *à la mode* in its literary salons.

The failure of the Action Française was essentially a failure of hatred. Instead of seizing on the tremendous truths of 1789 and showing how they could be incorporated into a purified monarchy, Maurras pretended that the Revolution, and all the popular movements that succeeded it, had been the work of foreigners. He could not too directly insult the people he was trying to persuade; they became, therefore, the helpless dupes of the Protestants, the Freemasons, the Jews, or the *métèques*. Under a hereditary monarchy he imagined a 'Jewish province, with no territorial rights, but based on tradition, religion and race'; and this province would be guaranteed by laws 'which would favour the spirit of Judaic fidelity, and take into account its spirit of subversion'. There were certain exceptions to this discrimination. Occasionally a Jew became so far assimilated into the French society as to give his adherence to the Action Française; then he became a *Juif bien né*. But in the France of Pétain, where the ideas of Maurras were partially in vogue, Henri Bergson chose to share the proscription of his people while Henri Massis was preaching Péguy to the young. The refinement of irony could hardly have been carried farther.

It was a Jewish writer, Benjamin Crémieux, who remarked in the course of a controversy with Maurras that there is no demagogue so crude as the anti-democrat. This was in 1934, when the Ciceronian eloquence of Jaurès seemed the echo of aristocracy itself when it was compared with the ravings of Nuremberg. But Maurras and his disciples, for all their catchwords of power *par tous les moyens, même légaux*, were amateur revolutionaries. The *camelots du roi* could not organise a revolution; they could only organise a 'rag'. Maurras

had not the secret of mass-appeal; it was in vain that he presented
the monarch as the 'father of *all* his subjects' and the 'impartial
arbiter of the conflict between Capital and Labour'. The French
worker, who had the Commune in his blood, was not attracted to
the theory that 'the most solid guarantees of all the rights of the
humble are bound up with the security and well-being of the
powerful'; the French worker has an unerring nose for Tartuffe. He
was poor, often to the point of destitution, but he still retained his
patriotism; and he was not prepared to accept from the hands of
Maurras the one thing that he really could call his own. He might,
however, have listened to Maurras, if Maurras had understood the
conditions of monarchy in the modern world; that a monarchy
must grow from the people, that it cannot be imposed upon them.
The royalism of the Action Française was as irrelevant as the
Basilica of St Denis, described by Drieu la Rochelle, who had seen
it as a superb anachronism, standing gaunt and unregarded in the
middle of M. Doriot's[1] *faubourg*. The problem for a monarchist in
the twentieth century is to see how the principle of royalism – the
king as head of his people – and the principle of aristocracy –
quality, whether hereditary or acquired, must have the means to
preserve and to express itself – can be accommodated within a
democratic framework. The theorists of either political extreme
will say that the adjustment is impossible. But it is a great pity
that Charles Maurras came to England only to see the Elgin Mar-
bles.

At the time that he wrote *La Grande Peur des Bien-Pensants*
Bernanos was still the prisoner of certain deep-seated *partis pris*,
and some of them he was never able to expel. He did succeed,
however, as time went on, in distinguishing them from their official
proponents. From this separation resulted both his power and his
solitude; in this sense, at least, he had the right to describe himself
as *le dernier des hommes libres*. But he was not yet free from what
Drumont had taught him when he was only a boy, and Maurras
through the years of his early manhood. A case in point was the
ralliement – Leo XIII's appeal to the French Catholics to rally to the
Third Republic; to those who 'sow discord between Church and
State, and risk the rupture of the links which still unite them.' To

---

[1] Jacques Doriot, formerly the Communist mayor of St Denis; later an eminent
collaborator under the German occupation.

this appeal the Comte de Chambord had merely replied: 'I thought that the Church forbade suicide.' Bernanos maintained that 'the handful of sincere men who were preparing the *ralliement* realised too late that, so far from merging the Catholics in the mass of the population, their false manoeuvre had created a new party – the party of those without a party; the one party which the huge majority of Frenchmen will always violently reject; the clerical party. To escape the trap held out to it, all the Republic had to do was to exclude these neophytes from its regular formations, leaving them in opposition whether they liked it or not – an opposition deprived henceforward of any political significance; a purely religious opposition, simply carrying out the instructions of the hierarchy.'[1] It was not until 1945 that the Mouvement Républicain Populaire brought the Catholics into public life as a serious political force; and it was not long before the MRP betrayed the hopes reposed in it. The country could not be saved by any party, or coalition of parties. It needed a man without a party – such as Bernanos himself had by then long since become – to vindicate many, if not all, of those principles of monarchical government which Maurras had preached for half a century. And it was the ultimate paradox of the Action Française that Maurras should not have recognised him.

Having declared his war on the bourgeoisie, Bernanos is naturally on the side of the Commune in 1870. So long as it remained master of events, it was not responsible for a single execution. Only when Macmahon succeeded in gaining entrance for 70,000 soldiers into the city, did a Committee of Public Safety follow the example of its revolutionary forebears. Bernanos did not excuse the execution of six hostages – the Archbishop of Paris among them – nor the massacre of the Dominicans at Arceuil; and he did not deplore unduly the fate of insurgents killed at the barricades. He had seen too many men killed in circumstances not so very dissimilar to refuse nobility to a passionate and calculated risk. But there was no common measure between the fury of the insurrection and the ferocity of the repression which punished it. This had reason to be severe; but the repression which followed those *événements de mai* was not only severe; 'it was vile'.

The chief actors – or supernumeraries – of the Third Republic are

[1] *La Grande Peur des Bien-Pensants,* pp. 154-5

passed in review and consigned, more often than not, either to
obloquy or oblivion. President Félix Faure, 'dead between the arms
of a woman, no doubt too expert'; Clemenceau, 'with his cruelty
and magic, eaten up with contempt, among his ridiculous Chinese
trinkets';[1] Victor Hugo, 'the man with the belly of a demi-god,
drunk with all the dreams of adolescence, even on the threshold of
old age, pivoting between the grotesque and the sublime'. For
twenty years Hugo had become 'the lyrical conscience of a well-
intentioned crowd, thanks to the majesty of exile' – and the crowd
had 'harmonised its little tunes with the great organ notes of
Guernsey'. Bernanos compared the man whom André Gide was to
describe as 'the greatest French poet – *hélas!*' to 'an aged and grey-
haired Silenus, running from rock to rock in vengeance and hate';[2]
and while admitting that many verses in *Les Châtiments* were admirable, he confessed to a preference for others that were absurd.

He could hardly escape a comparison between Drumont and
Maurras. Where the destiny of Maurras presented a line of logical
development, maintained with an extraordinary courage and
consistency against all the odds, the destiny of Drumont was like a
blazing apparition between two zones of darkness. Where the
intellect of Maurras marched forward at a steady pace, always
master of itself, Drumont was a force of nature, 'suddenly finding
its expression, accomplishing its task, and then, almost immediately,
retiring into its dream to die there.' Drumont was the Jeremiah of
French nationalism. Where Maurras, 'with the patience of genius,
and even a kind of sanctity, had spent years in convincing a number
of disciples that a democratic and republican régime was powerless
to defend the secrets of the State, the sentences of justice, and the
superior interests of the army', Drumont was concerned only to
bring home to every Frenchman the fact of his fetters and his shame.
'My friends,' as he was fond of saying to those who worked with
him, 'put some fire into their stomachs.'[3]

Bernanos, in his preface, had promised Drumont *un livre vivant*.
These are old stories, even to a Frenchman of today; to a foreign
reader they may seem to rattle like old bones. But there can be no
question that Bernanos, with the force of his conviction, the flame
of his prophecy, and the *brio* of his style, had brought them to life.
What he wrote of Drumont's polemic applies equally well to *La*

---

[1] Ibid, p. 196   [2] Ibid, pp. 41–2   [3] Ibid, p. 356

Grande Peur des Bien-Pensants. This desperate retrospect on M. Thiers' republic risks also to be misunderstood if the reader

expects from it a direct teaching and a positive doctrine. He should try to view it as a whole, and to see in the rhythm and movement of its anxiety, like the record of a tragic experience, the sum total of disappointment inscribed in the heart of a Frenchman.

Bernanos had thought of dedicating the book to Maurras *qui n'a pas péché contre l'espérance;* but chose instead his old friend Maxence de Colleville 'in memory of the grand dreams of our youth which life has humiliated, but which our sons will perhaps avenge tomorrow'. He sent an inscribed copy to Marshal Lyautey, who replied that where the past was in question their views very often disagreed, but that he was at one with Bernanos in his analysis of the present, and his prophecies of the future. It may be said that with *Sous le Soleil de Satan* Bernanos had taken up the pen, and that with *La Grande Peur des Bien-Pensants* he had taken up the sword. Only towards the very end of his life was he to lay it down.

CHAPTER 6

THE PARTING OF FRIENDS

I

BERNANOS had passed the summer of 1929 in Le Crotoy, which he described as a 'sinister country', for the rains had turned it into a lake of mud. He had put up a table in the diminutive garden of a rented house, and sat there writing through the six weeks of the obligatory *grandes vacances*. On his return to Clermont he learnt that his mother had developed a renal tuberculosis, and she died six months later, on the 8th of March 1930. This was the occasion of a reconciliation – of heart, if not of mind – with the Maritains. Bernanos sent them a *faire-part* to which Raïssa Maritain, in the absence of her husband, replied with a card of sympathy. Bernanos wrote in much indignation that he could not understand how 'friends' could content themselves with sending a mere card when one of them had suffered a bereavement. Raïssa answered him with gentle reproaches, and Bernanos replied with a letter, unfortunately lost, which had the immediate effect of restoring friendly, though never intimate, relations between two men who stood, basically, for the same things, and whom future events were to bring together. But just as he was healing the breach with Maritain, Bernanos forfeited the friendship of Massis. A requiem for Mme Bernanos was being held at Clermont, and Bernanos was astonished that Massis did not arrive for it with other friends from Paris. The cause of the rupture was apparently some opinions Bernanos had expressed about a third person, which Massis was not prepared to tolerate. There was a logic in this separation, and the events of the next few years would make it plain.

A further bereavement was the death of a valued friend, the abbé Sudre, in a mountaineering accident. The friendship had withstood the abbé's defence of Maritain against Bernanos' diatribes, and although he was a man of more liberal temper than Dom Besse he had done a good deal to replace him. Bernanos himself was now suffering from heart trouble, and spent six weeks of the summer at

Divonne-les-Bains, in the Ain. Here he slaved away at *La Grande Peur des Bien-Pensants*, depressed by the hysterical women 'of a certain age' who were also taking the cure.

Once the book was off his chest, he rented a pretty little maisonette with a terrace, near the lake of Geneva, where he installed his wife and family. But the *midi* was once again calling him strongly, and having decided to sell the house at Clermont, he proceeded to Toulon with no very clear idea of accommodation. On arrival he found nothing to rent, and was forced to install his parents-in-law in a hotel, his Swiss maid in an attic, his cat with a florist, whose Maurrasian sympathies would have left her lodger indifferent, and his dogs with the *concierge* of the Lutheran temple. Eventually he found a tiny villa, shaded by huge trees, with a garden going down to the sea. It was cramped quarters for Bernanos, his wife and five children, his parents-in-law, the Swiss maid, four mastiffs, and a Siamese cat. When Michel Dard – a younger friend and fellow-novelist – arrived, there was a certain electricity in the air. The eldest child, Chantal, with a face that Renoir might have painted, leaped upon the visitor, exclaiming: 'Are you ready to defend me to the death?' Michel, eight years old, was hammering on a nail, grinding his teeth, and denouncing *Mort aux vaches*! Bernanos retired with his young friend into the garden, where they were presently disturbed by frantic cries. They found the children brandishing logs of wood and threatening their grandparents. Mme Talbert d'Arc, white as a sheet, had fainted; her husband, eye-glass askew and beard shaking, was mustering what dignity he could behind a shirt-collar which appeared to be strangling him; the mastiffs were biting each other and jumping on each others' backs; and Jeanne Bernanos, shrugging her shoulders, was placidly finishing her cigarette. Only a single word, 'Justice', could be distinguished above the clamour of explanations, and Bernanos proceeded to dispense it with a dog whip, long as a lasso, scattering the children to their rooms. Only the youngest, Dominique, aged three and a half, toddled from door to door, encouraging her brothers and sisters: 'Don't give way, I'll support you... naughty Papa, I protest' – while the astonished visitor could hear from beyond the erection of the barricades. Bernanos was, of course, secretly delighted that his children should make a revolution, although before and after meals the scene was very different. Then – never more paternally *père de famille* – he would recite the *Bénédicité*, a prayer for France, and the *De Profundis* in French, with the family gathered round him.[1]

Michel Dard and his wife had rented a villa next door. Sometimes he and Bernanos would practise shooting with revolvers on the beach, using as a target an iron stake at a distance of a hundred yards. One evening they dined with the painter, Maurice Denis. The talk was of current literature, where Bernanos was out of his depth. The conflicting claims of literature and religious belief, which tormented Mauriac, seemed to him to have no sense whatever. He thought that Catholic writers like Maritain and Charles Du Bos were cutting themselves off from Catholicity by confinement in a *petite chapelle*. In any case, he distrusted converts, and the vacillations of Jean Cocteau did nothing to edify him. He read, in fact, incredibly little – only in the morning while he dipped his chunks of bread in a bowl of coffee. What he enjoyed were the tales of explorers, adventures of war, some history, and lives of the saints. After breakfast he and Michel Dard would sit down together before their blank sheets of paper at a neighbouring café. Bernanos was always ready to waste time in conversation with the waiter, or the man at the next table who was also dipping his croissant in his coffee, or the man who came selling oysters. He would launch into staggering verbal caricatures of Briand, or Henri Bordeaux, a very *bienpensant* novelist, or Cardinal Andrieu, the villain of the piece for any faithful Maurrasian. And when he had done, his tremendous laughter would rise above the astonished silence of his audience. Michel Dard describes how he got to work, as he contemplated the writer's immense responsibility:

I sat opposite him at the other end of the big bay window that looked on to the sea. He opened his schoolboy's notebook, and held his bulging eye crushed between two fingers, as if to rectify his vision. He began to write, slowly and painfully, in his regular, round script, so different from his character. It was no longer the same man; he gave you the feeling of *submission*. He had a faraway look, and as the moisture thickened on the glazed glass of the window, the crowd went by in front of him, the great port humming with sailors and housewives and tourists. He was looking at the terrace, as it filled up with customers, at the motor-boats discharging their cargo of top-knots, at the girls in their calico frocks juicy with promises of pleasure. Was he absent, or was he really there? If he saw

[1] Michel Dard: *Cahiers du Rhône*

nothing, why that little shivering laugh? Why that pucker of the eye-brows? An old man was passing by; perhaps the face of a child had escaped from a face which life had treated hardly. Menou-Segrais[1] or Cénabre? Which saint had the keys to deliver that heart from its duplicity?[2]

Michel Dard was reminded of the peasant in one of Dostoevsky's novels, standing immobile in the middle of a birch forest, until he himself was indistinguishable from a tree. Then he woke up, made the sign of the cross, and set fire to his village. The café – any café where Bernanos habitually wrote – was a medley of faces and expressions, from which the touchwood of his imagination was always liable to catch fire.

The caravanserai moved, after a month or two, from the Villa Sainte-Victoire to the Villa des Algues, and the following Easter found Michel Dard and the children singing old French songs – many of them handed down from the Middle Ages. Bernanos, overhearing them, burst into the room in a fury. This was the occasion of a diatribe against the classical tradition which had imposed an alien mythology on a Christian people: 'Ganymede or a swan to make love to, Hecate for a midwife, and Saturn for a father. Which of you has ever set eyes on Jupiter?' Here was another prototype of *imposture* – the humanist priest of the Renais-sance, 'reading the Gospel with one eye, and Lucretius with the other.' Bernanos envied the Englishman who could see his own reflection in Shakespeare; what Frenchman could recognise himself in Racine? This invited the reply, from anyone bold enough to give it, that François Mauriac did so without difficulty; and that the *cher Péguy* would not have spoken thus of Lucretius. In the mean-while the children went on singing – though more softly now: '*Sur les marches du palais*' and '*Le roi a fait battre tambour.*'

There was a visit to a bull-fight at Arles, the first that Bernanos had ever seen. He entered into it with a child's enthusiasm, sensitive to the courage and the pathos of the matador, exposing himself to the limits of mortal risk and then charming away with a rhythm of body and arm the death he had solicited. There was also a flying visit to Clermont, where the house had been sold and the contents had to be put in store. The future was not bright. Debts were piling up, and writing was increasingly difficult. Bernanos had won a great

[1] *Sous le Soleil de Satan*   [2] *Cahiers du Rhône*, p. 296

reputation in Paris, but Paris had a short memory. How could he maintain himself and his family, and at the same time forego the material advantages of his fame? Paris always had the same question on its lips: '*Que est-ce que vous préparez?*' Bernanos did not expect to make a fortune out of *La Grande Peur des Bien-Pensants*. With some reason he had been called 'the Ezekiel of the Action Française'; and Michel Dard did not hesitate to put the last fifty pages of the book, with Péguy and Michelet, among 'the sacred books of the nation'. But the public and the press responded coolly. Why was Bernanos bothering about Drumont at this time of day? Why should he invite the label of an 'anti-Semitic writer'? For all the volcanic force of his temperament and his style, there was more smoke than fire in the volcano. How far could he rely upon the admirers of *Sous le Soleil de Satan* and *La Joie*? Sixty thousand readers were not to be sneezed at, but where were they? You did not see them in the cafés or the railway compartments. There was no doubt that Bernanos had a public, but it was not the *grand public; La Grande Peur des Bien-Pensants* had not added to it; and when he had seen the book through the press, he was not at all certain what he should 'prepare'.

In July he moved to the Villa Fenouillet at La Bayorre, further along the coast, two or three kilometres from Hyères. It stood on the side of a hill overlooking the road to Toulon, approached through a long avenue of palm trees, with a vineyard on either side, and a magnificent view of the sea. At night, the chirping of crickets accompanied the conversation, and the Mediterranean glistened under the stars 'like an answered prayer', Bernanos would talk of the expanding universe, and the first atom leaving its explosions in space, each essentially equivalent to the others, a veritable 'congregation of the Cross'. Thus understood, the 'salvation of the universe' had a meaning. And then he would add with a strange violence: 'What are these millions of stars to me beside the single pearl of a tear shed by a human being?' There was a private chapel attached to the villa, and a retired priest, the abbé Calendini, acted as tutor to the children.

The devotion of Bernanos to the 'revolution in the name of order' did not prevent anarchy from reigning in the house. The best he could find in the way of servants was a very young couple, respectively seventeen and sixteen years of age. The boy had come straight out of a seminary and was accustomed not only to kick his wife in the stomach or take her by the throat, but to invite the children to look on. They, for their part, literally took to the *maquis*, where their hiding-places were known to Michel Dard alone. The freedom of Bernanos' commentary on every subject under the sun – marriage, the Church, and the seven capital sins – recalled the realism of medieval imagery; and Dard wondered whether the open-eyed astonishment of the family would follow the paternal finger up to the summit of the pointed arch, 'whence the Divine pity would smile down upon them'? Bernanos was certainly happy in his family life, with an elder son who wanted to be an admiral, a younger who thought of going out to darkest Africa as a missionary, and a daughter – Chantal – who dreamt of becoming a Carmelite. It was small wonder that, *faute de mieux*, they were all taking to the *maquis*.

Bernanos was still suffering from occasional bouts of angina, and these were aggravated by the violence of his opinions. A young abbé, invited to prepare Yves and Michel for their first communion, had been requested not to excite him. He found Bernanos in bed with a high temperature, inflamed by a copy of *La Vie Catholique* – whose democratic views were always calculated to enrage him. The visit resolved itself into a monologue loud enough to fill a public hall, and ended with a charming – though exhausted – *au revoir*. By September Bernanos was without a penny. Only a tiny allowance from his parents-in-law was available to keep several bodies and souls together. Food that would normally have nourished two people had to serve for ten. The money realised from the sale of the house at Clermont had vanished – no one knew how. In these circumstances Bernanos thought of founding a review – without capital, editorial committee, or premises. Grasset would publish it, without imposing any conditions, and Bernanos would edit it, with Michel Dard, on their own responsibility – very much as Péguy had edited the *Cahiers de la Quinzaine*. It was to be a miscellany of commentary and correspondence; but the project came to nothing.

He started work instead on a new novel, which was later to become *Un Mauvais Rêve* – most of Bernanos' dreams at this period were bad dreams – and then abandoned it to write the first chapters of *La Paroisse Morte*. This eventually appeared as *Monsieur Ouine*. He was at the end of his tether, moving from one café, and from one book, to another. Neither made much progress, but in June 1931,

Réaction – a word which still preserved a semblance of respectability – devoted a special number to Bernanos; from a review parading that title *La Grande Peur des Bien-Pensants* had merited no less. In the same year he addressed and published what can only be described as a Christmas card to the Royal House of France.[1]

His passionate and romantic royalism had always been independent of his attachment to the Action Française, and it was to survive his breach with it. Henri, Duc de Guise, was in exile, living in a modest villa at Louvain. Bernanos had met him there – a frail silhouette, with head erect, and wearing an expression in which a certain shyness was mingled with pride and candour. He found nothing worth while to say to him – subjects are not usually communicative when they meet their sovereign for the first time; he merely felt that not only his own youth, but the youth and energy of an eternal France, was coming forward to meet him – the France of which Péguy, republican that he was, had written that it 'made glad the heart of God'. Here was Philip the Bold, and the unfortunate Dauphin in his prison cell, and even the Young Pretender whom Bernanos remembered from his reading of Walter Scott. In wishing a later Pretender the compliments of the season, he promised him the loyalty of all those who had inscribed the Marne and the Yser and the Somme in the legend from which royalty derived its title deeds. The crew-cut of the plodding *poilu* would put to shame the moustachios of the men who had fought at Rocroi. This was no time for modesty; modesty was not a military virtue. 'But up to now we have only made war; with you, and when you will, we shall make history.'

In November 1931 he began to contribute regular articles to *Le Figaro*, then under the direction of François Coty. It was not long before this association had consequences at once momentous and unforeseen.

2

Bernanos contributed thirteen articles to the paper between November 1931 and December 1932. But what should have been an agreeable and useful co-operation, keeping the author's name before the public, was disturbed by a violent polemic between François Coty, who owned both *Le Figaro* and the *Ami du Peuple*, and the

[1] *Noël à la Maison de France* included in *Le Crépuscule des Vieux*, pp. 105–12

directors of the Action Française. In October 1931 Coty had been active in the formation of the Union Nationale, and was now promoting it by the considerable means at his disposal. The very notion of a Union Nationale not committed to their own ideas was anathema to the Action Française. Bernanos was decisively involved in the dispute when Jacques Ditte, on the staff of *Le Figaro*, presented himself as a candidate for the Chambre des Députés in the 7th sector of Paris. Maurice Pujo, editor of the *Action Française*, initiated a violent campaign against him and, therefore, indirectly, against Coty himself. On the 15th of May Bernanos published, in reply to this, an open letter to Coty, which appeared in the *Ami du Peuple:*[1]

I shall not enquire what advantage either France or the monarchy can hope to gain from this ugly polemic. Its character of cold cruelty does not appear to have even the excuse of a calculated risk. At a time when the Action Française was anti-Semitic, the word 'plutocracy' was used to describe the reign of 'anonymous and vagabond finance' denounced in 1896 by a Pretender who was also a gentleman, with the true heart of a king. I cannot help writing today that it is really iniquitous – iniquitous and stupid, for the two words mean the same thing – to apply it to a man who had acquired the means to take his place among the anonymous masters of the world, but has chosen instead to put his whole existence at stake, to run the risk and take the consequences. I should add that it is impolitic, and in any event premature, since the Royal House has taken every opportunity to assure us that it will maintain people in the positions which they already hold. It invites us to cherish the dream of a monarchy established within a framework of republican administration. It is therefore, as I say, impolitic and premature to promise you a cell in the *Santé* – although it is true that I shall be there myself to keep you company.[2]

Several friends of Bernanos had begged him to hold his pen, even if he could not hold his peace. But he was now beyond caring whose susceptibilities he hurt; he was concerned only to defend the good name of a man who stood 'alone among these wolves and hyenas'.[3]

Coty replied gratefully to this letter on the 16th of May, also in the *Ami du Peuple;* and on the same day Maurras launched his excommunication of Bernanos. The feast day of Jeanne d'Arc, which the adherents of the Action Française celebrated with their

---

[1] All the material relevant to this dispute is contained in nos. 17–20 of the *Bulletin de la Société des Amis de Georges Bernanos*
[2] *Bulletin* 17–20, pp. 17–18   [3] Ibid

annual procession and customary rhetoric, lent a particular irony to
the riposte:

This was a matter between friends of yours – Pujo, Daudet, and myself –
with whom, not so long ago, you declared a total sympathy, both of
heart and mind. Yet you refrained from telling us of your disagreement.
It never entered your head to come to us and say: 'This or that is disturbing, or irritating, or displeasing me. What is it all about?' Had you
done so, memories and friendships and fidelities would have been saved –
it was your last chance to save them. But no – you chose to sacrifice all
that without appeal, as if you wished to derive some merit for yourself;
and if one examines a little more closely what you had in mind, it has a
look of heroic bravado.[1]

Maurras began his letter with *Bernanos, je vous dis adieu;* he ended
it with *Je vous dis adieu, Bernanos.*

It was not until the 21st of May that Bernanos replied to him in
Le Figaro and the *Ami du Peuple.* He wrote the letter eight times
before sending it off; the final version marked so critical a turning-
point in his life that it demands generous quotation. Addressing
Maurras as *Mon cher Maître,* Bernanos proceeds:

The idea of entering into polemic with you seems to me too absurd to be
thought of for a single moment. Whatever you may do or say, you
remain, in spite of yourself, far above our daily quarrels and agitations.
Already, in the prime of life, you belong to the history of my country. I
neither expect, nor ask, of you any kind of justice. At the point where we
now stand, I confess that I even prefer your harshness. It will be enough
for me to preserve henceforward, in the citadel of my soul, with the
memory of our dead, the lesson of grandeur with which you enraptured
our youth, and which we shall hand on to our sons ...

Let us speak plainly. Over a period of several weeks an evening newspaper has been dragging the director of *Le Figaro* and his collaborators in
the mud. The person responsible, whose name I refuse to mention,
boasted the other day that he was unburdening his conscience – probably
into the sink. You know who he is. What meaning, therefore, can I
ascribe to your neutrality? I cannot help regarding it as a sign, if not of
discreet approval, at least of secret jubilation. Thank you. Thank you in
my own name, and in that of your friends who are working at my side,
on the paper that you allow thus to be dishonoured.

For six months I have been well placed to observe the strange and

[1] Ibid, p. 20

disturbing unanimity created at the expense of a man whose only fault was the prodigious imprudence of putting immense sums of money at the disposal of a society absolutely incapable of making use of it; of poor fellows already three parts corrupted by lies, who will never forgive him for having spent so much for nothing – for France!... I reject categorically the permission you extend to others, as a mark of exceptional favour, tolerance and magnanimity, in allowing them to work on M. Coty's newspapers. I humbly submit that a French royalist can write for *Le Figaro* without being obliged daily to disown its director, or to plead the necessities of his family budget. Because I have publicly blamed an atrocious polemic... have I failed in loyalty, I will not say to the principles, but even to the friendship of the Action Française? By what right do you exclude me from the communion of the faithful? Must I go on to the end, from minor to major excommunication, and from one interdict to another? Everyone knows how well I am appreciated by people on the Left! And now *L'Imposture* and *La Grande Peur* have brought the *bienpensants* to my side. Today, it is your turn to expel me. With whom, then, should I go? – With such men as are free.

They exist everywhere, no doubt, but with you, I think, more than elsewhere. God forbid that I should divert from the Action Française the smallest part of its brave adherents – I know what I owe to my country. I would hardly dare to crave your permission to say to the best among your followers – as I meditate on the injustice you have done me – that they have the right to less strict and harsh a discipline – one more worthy of themselves, of us, and of our past.

Bernanos was sensitive to the reproach that he had not warned his friends of the line he was proposing to take. If he had not done so, it was because he knew they would have requested him to keep silent, and he did not think he would have had the courage to refuse them. 'What I had to say had to be said publicly, or it would have served no purpose whatever.' He concluded his reply as follows:

As for myself, let me now take you at your word – 'à Dieu'. Of course, for you it has not quite the same meaning that it has for me. But it is at once your honour and your misfortune to be one of those men who are today most burdened with supernatural responsibilities. Anyone who has understood you will speak of himself in a way that takes into account that mysterious vocation. We have given you everything, Maurras. Allow me to remind you of it after this summary execution, which in turn reminds me of other executions, served upon you from another quarter. *A Dieu, Maurras! A la douce pitié de Dieu.*[1]

[1] *Bulletin* 17–20, pp. 21–4

To a friend, whose name is lost to us, Bernanos summed up his personal feelings for the benefit of others whose considered approval he hoped to win:

Please remind them that all I did was publicly to acknowledge an unfortunate man, when he stood alone, whom, at this very moment, the régime is subjecting to an atrocious blackmail. He is risking the loss of everything he has – and I know perfectly well that he would not survive his ruin by forty-eight hours. In face of this tragedy the sneers of the men sitting in the rue Boccador[1] were really too much for me.

To what was only a warning Maurras replied with an Adieu. I answered him with another. I owe very little to Maurras. I was a royalist before I even heard his name. I have only *four* times set eyes upon him. And however disagreeable it may be to recall the fact, I do not consider that any French Catholic who has run the risk that you well know, on the sole guarantee of his word, his honour, and his intellectual probity, is any longer in debt to such a teacher for anything whatsoever.[2]

From now on Bernanos pursued Maurras with a virulence less worthy of his convictions than the gravity of that painful farewell. Very soon he was referring to him as 'that unfortunate Greek from Alexandria', with the clear implication that a Greek from Alexandria was inferior to a Greek from Athens – for it was to Athens that Maurras, like many other people, proclaimed his allegiance, conveniently forgetting that Athens was the cradle of democracy and that it also happened to be a republic. Bernanos lost no opportunity for a gibe at Maurras' Provençal origins, as if the shores of the Mediterranean, to which he was himself so attached, secreted some inescapable corruption. Here then was indeed a parting of friends, but not a recantation of ideas. Bernanos was moved, however, by an instinct that found no place in the psychology of the Action Française – or at least in that of its chief philosopher. 'When you see one man set upon by four,' admits the murderer of Becket in T. S. Eliot's play,[3] 'your sympathies are naturally with the underdog.' No more than Becket did François Coty fit the conventional picture of an underdog; but the sympathies of Bernanos were with him, and for the same reason.

[1] The street where the Action Française had its offices.
[2] May 1932: *Bulletin* 17–20, p. 26
[3] *Murder in the Cathedral*

3

These serious disputes had been heralded, earlier in the year, by a grotesque *contretemps*. A play of no consequence, *La Loi d'Amour*, was presented in Paris at the Théâtre Fontaine. Its author was Georges Bernanose-Rancio. This inconvenient *littérateur* had come before the public on the heels of *Sous le Soleil de Satan*, hoping to draw some credit from the similarity of his name to that of a best-selling novelist. Now he had dropped the hyphen, and several newspapers, in reviewing his play, had dropped the 'e'. *Le Petit Parisien* thought fit to recognise, here and there, the Bernanosian 'power of emotion'! Bernanos wrote with some irritation to Plon, asking them to give the widest publicity to the mistake.

It is a curious fact – though less surprising than might at first appear – that at the age of forty-three Bernanos had never left the mainland of the European continent. He had merely dreamt of going to Paraguay. The neurotic restlessness that was henceforward increasingly to mark his itinerary merely took him from one *plage* or provincial town to another. His world was France, and he knew little history or geography beyond its borders. Nevertheless, as he sent up his articles to *Le Figaro*, he was becoming conscious of a world elsewhere similar to the world of his own experience, and he was finding a voice to speak to it. To realise the solitude of modern man and the growing impoverishment of his interior life, he had no need to look further than the street beyond the windows of the café where he happened to be writing.

I have watched them all the summer long, three long months of a Provençal summer – strange creatures on the beaches swept by an eternal wind, hugging each other close, with arms and legs intermingled, like something spawned on to the shore by the purposeless pulverisation of the sea.[1]

It was here, at the bar, or on the dancing-floor, that they 'discovered the warmth and security of the herd'; and yet the contemporary itch for sociability did not conceal the poverty of communication:

The incapacity to break the monologue, the sly and mysterious timidity

[1] *Le Crépuscule des Vieux*, p. 272

which the exaggerations of language only serve to underline – the *inouï*, and the *colossal*, and the *formidable* – these are like hammers manufactured to crush the burgeoning idea ... to suppress any chance of contradiction, and eliminate the slightest intellectual risk.[1]

When he turned to politics, Bernanos was not encouraged by the 'vast reserves of humanitarian clichés' with which American idealism and ignorance were devaluing the exchange of international parley. Somebody had written, when he was still a young man, that democracy was 'sinking with all hands aboard'. True enough; it was certainly sinking; for there was always Aristide Briand 'with his bladder newly relieved, and a fresh hump on his shoulder'.[2] Bernanos wrote as the humour, playful or ferocious, took him and on any subject that came to hand.

On the 24th of June he informed Coty of his decision no longer to write for *Le Figaro*:

I shall astonish nobody when I say that the policy of Union Nationale, as proposed by *Le Figaro* on Sunday last, is not my own. I should add that the hypocritical formula which is already counting on the advantages of M. Tardieu's early return to power leaves me no better satisfied. The decision I have taken to cease from today my collaboration with the paper naturally in no way affects my personal feelings towards its director. I am honoured to remain his friend. He would give me tomorrow, as he gave me yesterday, an absolute freedom to say what I like, and it is not without regret that I take my leave.[3]

Coty replied:

We can only regret the decision of our eminent friend and collaborator Georges Bernanos. Although we are convinced that a misunderstanding is largely at the root of it, we cannot and we should not sit in judgment on a departure motivated by personal reasons, worthy of the highest respect.[4]

Bernanos did, however, return to the paper in October of the same year. For two months he shared an office with Vallery-Radot, trying to build up an aggressive opposition to the Action Française, for which *Le Figaro* appeared the designated focus. He did not question Coty's good will, only the accuracy of his vision and the validity of his methods. Coty was living out at Louveciennes, and

---

[1] Ibid, pp. 279–80 [2] Ibid, p. 281
[3] *Bulletin* 17–20 [4] Ibid

was rarely seen at the Rond-Point des Champs Elysées. Nor was his choice of subordinates always wise. Bernanos was anxious to enlist a literary *élite*, but he was given no idea of how much money he could spend on securing their collaboration, nor proper quarters in which to receive them. The several long letters[1] he wrote to Coty at this time show a remarkable flair for journalism. He put his finger on the difference between a daily newspaper and a weekly or monthly review. He complained that the front page of *Le Figaro* was generally 'too arid, too difficult, and too austere'. A newspaper depended for three-quarters of its popularity on its front page, and its worst enemy was the boredom of its readers. A pretty and intelligent woman should be able to read it from cover to cover. Once it had become 'the thing to read' in the world of Society and Letters, and once it had attracted the young, the moment would be ripe to launch an offensive against the Action Française. The easiest weapon was the exposure of a personal scandal, but Maurras was the last man to lay himself open to this form of attack. Bernanos realised, however, that the movement was slowly, though noisily, dying. Its period of greatest influence had been the early years of the century up to the end of the First World War. It had now become 'a little church jealously shutting its doors to any influences from outside'. The aim must be to detach it from the royal family which it claimed to serve but which for some time had been restive under the despotism of Maurras, and from what remained of its once considerable public. Bernanos believed that it would be possible, within a few months, to give to *Le Figaro* the prestige which the Action Française had enjoyed in its beginnings, enlarged to the measure of current events. Once this intellectual centre had been created at the Rond-Point des Champs Elysées, the Action Française would lose its *élite* and the greater part of its public. In the course of time, and for different reasons, this is what happened. It became like the ghost of the *grand siècle* contemplating the Seine, and shaking a spectral hand with the ghost of the Roman Empire contemplating the Tiber. Maurras' *mes idées sont au pouvoir* echoed among the ruins of the Third Republic; but they were not in power for very long.

Unfortunately Coty was not the man to give substance to Ber-

[1] *Correspondance* I, pp. 445–62

nanos' grand design, and Bernanos was not the man to enter at all easily into the equivocations of 'union nationale' – although he struck up a surprising friendship with Ramon Fernandez, a brilliant critic and editor of *Marianne*, who stood very far left of centre. Bernanos was a highly opinionated man, but he always cared more for men than for opinions. Having turned his back on Maurras, he could not without inconsistency now turn his face to Herriot. Meanwhile a rejuvenated Germany was on the march:

If it is true that I have myself added a few useless pages to the absurd mountain of paper which is now our only defence against the hatred, the contempt, and the rapacity of the world, I shall willingly – and very soon – receive my discharge at the hands of these young warriors, with a bullet in the stomach. Anything better than to read, in five, ten, or twenty years time, phrases about the left bank of the Rhine, supposing that the culmination and the paradox of French patriotism should then consist in occupying the left bank of the Oise.[1]

Charles Maurras, in whom the capacity for political hatred seemed to be reinforced by the austerity of his private life, was also on the march, and once again Bernanos met him on the way. The occasion was obscure and not particularly interesting. A certain Brenier-Gâtebois, on the staff of *Le Figaro*, was accused by the *Action Française* of complicity in the arrest of Paul Déroulède by the Waldeck-Rousseau government in 1901. This was looking a long way back, but the *Action Française* could never look back far enough to identify and pillory its victims. Coty's newspapers were once again under fire, and Bernanos – in a postscript to the article quoted from above – returned to the charge:

In resuming my place on this newspaper at a time when I should be ashamed to do otherwise, it is unfortunately difficult for me – much as I regret the necessity – not to refer, at least, to the note in which M. Maurras replied, six months ago, to a letter of farewell. Here I was at pains to express, as I was bound to do, what was due to him in gratitude, admiration, and respect. . . . Since I belong to no coterie, and have never written for anyone but a few friends – their number, it is true, was at one moment dangerously augmented, but I hope that the future will progressively reduce it – you will understand that certain exaggerated insults leave me absolutely unmoved. Let me say once and for all – and to have done with

[1] *Le Figaro: Bulletin* 17–20, p. 28

the matter – that M. Charles Maurras is sheltered by the memories of my youth; he could not have a safer or deeper refuge; and from there he is perfectly free to insult me without risk. I shall not tread upon my own past to strike at him, and I only hope with all my heart that as he grows older he will not prove an immense disappointment to my country.[1]

The fears which this hope concealed were realised, to the letter, in 1940. On the part of the Action Française the polemic took on a disagreeably personal tone. Bernanos was a 'deserter' from the movement; references to the 'memories of his childhood' made Maurras 'sick'; this was really a case of *imposture*. Bernanos replied in *Le Figaro* on the 10th of November:

The furious pastoral letters of M. Maurras describe me to his flock as a deserter. A deserter from what? M. Coty may be a republican, but at least he can boast of no decorations, which proves that he has fewer friends in the régime than M. Jacques Bainville.[2] As for myself, everyone knows that I am a royalist: even a royalist of the Action Française, if it is enough to know *Enquête sur la Monarchie*[3] pretty well by heart.... I merely wish to say that it is useless any longer to cradle young Frenchmen in the illusion that there is nothing greater or more heroic than to trace accurately, day after day, the curve of national humiliation. We expect something better for our country than a lucid and stoical deathbed. The true and only master of M. Charles Maurras is Lucretius. But after two thousand years of Christianity we have someone better than Lucretius; we have Pascal and we have Péguy.

My friends will be aware that what I am writing now, I could just as well have written in 1919. In any case M. Maurras himself has taken care to admit that his police had, long ago, kept him informed on the matter. I may say, in passing, that I am astonished to find myself the subject of this espionage. I have seen M. Maurras and M. Daudet five or six times in the course of my life. I have never held any official position in the Action Française. I left it of my own free will in 1920. This did not prevent me from being one of the few writers publicly to take its side in 1926 – an intervention which cost me infinitely more readers than the two generous articles of its director . . . had gained for me. During the following years, due no doubt to the prudent silence observed by my fellow-writers, the Action Française made the best use, as it had the right to do, of what M. Léon Daudet, with his habitual exaggeration, likes to

[1] *Bulletin* 17–20, p. 29
[2] The eminent historian, who was a member of the Académie Française.
[3] The book in which Maurras had stated the case for the monarchy.

call my fame. But I have never, since 1920, belonged to its regular formations, or even to its editorial board. Had I not the right to think that a scruple of independence – perhaps excessive – would allow me one day to hold an opinion about M. Coty different from that of M. Maurras, without being convicted of dishonour and spiritual suicide?[1]

It would be tedious to pursue the recriminations and the person-alities which answered each other, like an interminable rally on the ping pong table, all through the autumn of 1932. Bernanos himself was disgusted with them. The breach with Daudet hurt him more than the breach with Maurras, for Daudet was a man – indeed a musketeer – after his own heart. He had introduced him to the *Avant-Garde de Normandie*, and been a witness at his wedding. He had notably contributed to the success of *Sous le Soleil de Satan*. 'We have never doubted where his heart really lay, or that he would remember his own Journey to the end of Night with a man called Shakespeare' – for among the men of his generation in France, Daudet was one of the very few to have shown an understanding of Shakespeare. But the relentless classicism of Maurras, and the tyranny of his intelligence, had been too strong for that genial and combative epicure; and the great, the salutary, lesson that Bernanos drew from so bitter a parting of friends was the realisation of what Maurras really stood for – a cynical caricature of Catholicism and, implicitly, a betrayal of the Christian monarchy he claimed to serve.

When he was only about fifteen years old the future author of *Anthinéa* cherished the idea, almost monstrous in the head of a young Frenchman, of a kind of universal theocracy. Walking with a friend through Aix-en-Provence, only five weeks ago, we were thinking of that strange little boy, already conscious of defeat and very much alone among his own people, eaten up with the sense of injustice, inhabited by this dream. The world in the hands of the clergy, the world instructed, ruled and domin-ated by the priests. . . . Who could fail to see in this frantic, furious and almost ferocious attachment of a child to the notion of order, the fatal augury of a Christianity decomposing at the heart of a formal Catholicism still intact? M. Maurras has remained a churchman, a Dominican of the thirteenth century. Inflamed as he is with hatred, his natural reaction in front of any obstacle is only to excommunicate and to curse.[2]

[1] *Bulletin* 17–20, pp. 35–7
[2] Ibid, p. 54

Maurras had referred to the 'poison of the Gospel', while claiming every privilege for its ministers. The paradox secreted its own poison; and in freeing himself from the mind that had mixed it, Bernanos was at last in a position to speak, without compromise or equivocation, to a world that would soon be very ready to listen to him.

CHAPTER 7

NEW DIRECTIONS

I

EVEN before he had broken with Maurras, Bernanos kept his distance from certain Catholic writers with whom others might have supposed him to be in sympathy. Having placed so many of his characters in the sacristy – and the most memorable of them all was yet to come – he was anxious not to be placed there himself. The only other Catholic novelist to attract a similar degree of public interest was François Mauriac, and Mauriac had a much wider clientèle. He was now a member of the Académie Française, and a dominant figure on the literary stage. An early disciple of Marc Sangnier, he had been as frustrated by the suppression of the Sillon as Bernanos had been infuriated by the interdiction of the Action Française. Their origins were very different; Mauriac came from the higher, Bernanos from the lesser, bourgeoisie. And their temperaments were equally opposed. For Mauriac, the suppression of the Sillon had confined the Catholics of France to an intellectual ghetto. For Bernanos the interdiction of the Action Française had given the green light not only to democracy, but to modernism. Bernanos was never able to give Mauriac his due, either as a writer or as a man: Mauriac's appreciation of Bernanos was at once more charitable and more just.

There was a similar alienation from Claudel, whom the younger Bernanos had ardently admired. Claudel may not have swung his censer before the altar of democracy, but he was an important functionary of the Republic – ambassador, successively, in Tokyo, Washington, and Brussels – and a châtelain of considerable private means. He was visibly allied to the capitalism which Bernanos detested, and for which he held democracy responsible. Claudel's Catholicism was hardly less triumphalist than Maurras' opportunistic attachment to it, but his belief was deeply rooted – and he realised what it owed to Israel. Nor had he ever shown the slightest sympathy for the Action Française. In many respects – as he freely admitted – he was a product of the Revolution *embourgeoisée*.

Bernanos' irritation with both these considerable writers is shown in a letter to Vallery-Radot. Mauriac had criticised a novel of Vallery-Radot, and Bernanos had sprung to the defence of his friend in *Le Figaro*. This had caused some pain to Mauriac. Shortly afterwards Bernanos was shown a letter in which Mauriac had given his opinion on Péguy, describing his influence as 'illusory' – which was certainly not the case – and expressing both his admiration for the man and his surprise that he had been able to 'accept a situation, at the mere thought of which any Catholic would be horrified'. This was certainly putting it strongly. The unfortunate Péguy, having contracted a civil marriage with an unbeliever, was thereby excluded from the sacraments; and he was too honest a man either to force his wife to go through a religious ceremony, or to have their children baptised into the faith to which he had himself returned. Claudel's *L'Otage*, with its mixture of ultramontane piety and what Bernard Shaw would have described as 'Sardoodledum', where the heroine is persuaded to marry the revolutionary assassin of her family in order to save the Pope who has taken refuge in her château, was equally repellent to Bernanos. His view of this blasphemous procedure is echoed by the curé de Torcy in the *Journal d'un Curé de campagne;* and the curé de Torcy is the only character in the novels of Bernanos to bear a close resemblance to the author.

The collaboration with Coty had only slightly eased his financial straits; there were times when he had little more than 100 francs in the house. Except for visits to Paris – frequent but of short duration – and a tour of lectures in Algeria under the auspices of the Alliance Française, he remained at La Bayorre, slaving away at *Monsieur Ouine*. When he was not writing in a café, he used his son Michel's bedroom as a study. It looked on to the sea, and another spectacle – less inviting. For the owner of the villa, his wife, and his fat Bohemian gardener were all nudists, and they were occupied in building a wall underneath the window. Bernanos carried a number of other projects in his head, but few of them got down on to paper. Moreover an event was close at hand which would affect his future as decisively as the break with Maurras, though in a very different way. On the 31st of July 1933, he was riding on his motor-cycle through the town of Montbéliard, in the Doubs, when an elderly schoolmaster crashed into him with his car. The wing caused a deep wound in his left leg, and he was taken to the nearest hospital. Afterwards he was moved to Avallon, where Eugène Manificat and his wife – a sister-in-law of Vallery-Radot – took care of him. The Vallery-Radots also had a house at Avallon. Bernanos returned to La Bayorre in August where he was forced to submit to a diversity of medical treatment. He was unable to immobilise the leg at night for more than three-quarters of an hour without being woken up by intolerable pain, and the shattered limb seemed to be literally melting before his eyes.

A nursing sister was in attendance, and two surgeons examined him in the hospital at Toulon; but they were unable to agree upon the right treatment, merely advising him to be patient – and patience was not a Bernanosian virtue. In October a fresh abscess had formed; he was running a high temperature; and sleep was still almost impossible. After ten days the abscess was lanced, and this eased the neuritis from which he had been suffering. But all the skills of surgery could not restore the leg to its original length. The sciatic nerve had been so damaged that Bernanos would be lame 'until the resurrection of the Dead and the coming of the Kingdom of God'.[1]

In September he was prophesying the birth of 'a little boy' – his sixth child. The forecast was correct, although on this occasion Bernanos was unable to be at the bedside of his wife, and the new arrival had to be 'spanked and spanked and spanked again'[2] to confirm his foothold in a vale of tears. The addition of Jean-Loup Bernanos to the caravanserai did not lighten its budget; nor, save marginally, did articles for Le Jour, and Monsieur Ouine still hung fire, simmering at the back of dismal cafés in Aix-en-Provence. By the time he had corrected, erased, and recopied, Bernanos counted himself lucky if he completed one and a half pages a day.

In the train taking him the short distance from Aix to Marseilles the satchel containing three chapters of the manuscript was lost; and ten months later he was still at the beginning of the third chapter, dissatisfied with the previous version of it. In March (1934) he was describing the book as a 'lugubrious urinal', and confessed himself tired of 'relieving myself so miserably against the same wall'.[3] By

[1] To Dr Raymond Tournay, September 1933: *Correspondance* I, p. 489
[2] To Mme Manificat, October 1933: *Correspondance* I, p. 496
[3] To R. Vallery-Radot: *Correspondance* I, p. 513

September, however, he had added forty pages and could say that the book was virtually finished. But it was nearly ten years before he considered it fit for publication. Nothing he wrote was to cause him so much difficulty, and we shall examine later the reason why.

Not only the mischance, but the cost, of his accident had landed Bernanos in serious financial straits. He was legally entitled to an indemnity, but this had to be awarded by due process of law, and the law's delay lived up to its reputation. Hobbling about on his crutches, he felt that he had earned the right of entry to 'the Invalides of the blessed and Divine Providence, with a cap and uniform and twopenny worth of snuff'.[1] He now proposed, through the mediation of Vallery-Radot, that Plon should pay him so much per page of whatever work he had in hand, as the manuscript was delivered to Paris. His method was to revise each page with scrupulous care and not to touch them afterwards. This proposal was not accepted immediately, but it was finally agreed that he should receive sixty francs as advance royalty on every page of manuscript. The procedure was risky in the case of serial publication, and six months later Bernanos was warned by Plon that the monthly reviews envisaged for the publication of *Monsieur Ouine* would hesitate to serialise an unfinished manuscript. The *Revue des Deux Mondes* was hesitating between *Monsieur Ouine* and Montherlant's *Les Célibataires*, and since the latter was ready while Bernanos still had thirty pages of *Monsieur Ouine* to recopy, it was chosen instead.

On the 6th of February 1934, thirty to forty thousand malcontents of the extreme Right attempted to storm the Chambre des Députés and bring down the Daladier government. The *Camelots du roi*, members of Colonel de La Roque's *Croix de Feu*, and the *Union Nationale Des Combattants* were prominent among them. The ostensible cause of a bloody manifestation, in which a nephew of Bernanos was arrested, was the dismissal of Jean Chiappe, the Prefect of Police, but it reflected a fairly general *malaise*. Bernanos was not deceived by the appearances of a salutary, if abortive, *coup d'état*. He thought it an ineffective and hypocritical demonstration in the interests of the propertied *bourgeoisie*. Little as he sympathised with democracy as it was preached and practised, Bernanos knew his countrymen too well to suppose that Fascism would prove an acceptable alternative.

[1] To Marie Vallery-Radot: *Correspondance* I, p. 498

On the 3rd of May he was involved in a second car accident, less serious than the first, as he was driving through Toulon. This left him with an injured hand, and the shock, both moral and physical, was severe. In July, however, he was able to come up to Paris for a meeting with his publisher, and it was here that he conceived the idea of writing a 'whodunnit' under a pseudonym. The *genre* presented an attractive challenge. Georges Simenon, whom Bernanos greatly admired for his realism, ingenuity, and insights, had set a fashion which it might be profitable to follow, if not to imitate. The pattern of guilt, discovery, and judgment found an analogy in the spiritual sphere; there would be no need to labour it. Like any novelist who puts the whole of himself into his fiction, Bernanos faced the criticism that he was too subjective in his themes; and he could also be charged with an excess of rhetoric in his style. This was natural when he was speaking in his own person, but it is the business of the novelist to make other people speak. If he tried his hand at a 'whodunnit' he would be obliged not only to be true to himself and to other people as well, but to keep his readers alert and inquisitive as to what would happen next. This would be all the more important if the book were serialised. Here Simenon had a long start of him, for Bernanos had not a tithe of Simenon's narrative skill, although it might not be beyond his power to acquire it.

He returned to La Bayorre at the beginning of August, and with the help of Michel Dard, and another friend, Charles Singevin, elaborated the following plot. A woman assassinates an elderly châtelaine in a mountain village, and then, meeting in the middle of the night a young priest who has arrived to take possession of his new parish, albeit unknown to any of his parishioners, kills him, dresses up in his soutane, occupies the presbytery, and puts the police and the magistrate on a false scent. The real priest, stripped of anything that could reveal his identity, is found dying a few yards from the scene of the crime, and is assumed to be the assassin, killed by an accomplice. The false priest disappears, and only at the end of the book is the reader told who she is and why she has committed the crime. Bernanos told his publisher that the latter part of the novel particularly excited him, and for a reason easy to understand. It was here that he was able to use much of the material already sketched out for *Un Mauvais Rêve*, and to give to his story a dimension not usually found in a 'whodunnit' – even when Simenon is the author.

'I think that you will like the second part,' he wrote. 'It has allowed me to sketch the portrait of my criminal heroine in my own way . . . and this gives stature to the *roman policier*.'[1]

Pierre Belperron, writing on behalf of Plon, did not see the matter in the same light. He complained that the latter part of the book broke the interest of the reader just when it had been vividly awakened, and substituted for a curiosity looking backward to clues a curiosity preoccupied with the development of character. The *roman policier* had its own laws. The truth must be reconstructed from evidence available to those who were trying to discover it, and not from the point of view of an omniscient narrator. The reader must attempt to find his own solution while the enquiry was going on. This was as much as to say that Bernanos was writing two novels in one – which was, in fact, the case. He recognised the force of his publisher's arguments, but regretted the waste of time and effort over something he had thought worth doing. 'God,' he replied, 'has not put a pen into my hand for me to play the fool with. . . .'[2] Necessity is emptying my brain by the nose and ears, and after four or five years of this régime there will be nothing left of an organ which has only given me anxiety. Then I shall just have a pair of buttocks for a brain when I take a seat in the Académie.'[3]

Nevertheless he entirely rewrote the second part of the book, although, according to his contract, this would bring him no financial reward, the previous version having been already paid for. Belperron, however, agreed to pay him for it on the condition – proposed by Bernanos himself – that the second version should be entirely new, and that if he utilised the previous one for a long short story of a hundred pages or so, this should be published by Plon with other stories of similar or shorter length. In this way neither author nor publisher would be out of pocket.

The change of perspective imposed a fresh motivation for the crime. Instead of murdering the châtelaine in order to obtain a rich inheritance for her lover, the criminal acts in the interest of the châtelaine's niece with whom she – the pseudo-priest – is involved in a Lesbian love affair. She is herself the daughter of the châtelaine's housekeeper, who had carefully concealed the fact from her em-

---

[1] *Un Mauvais Rêve (édition Béguin)*, p. 118
[2] To R. Vallery-Radot, 6th January 1935: *Correspondance* II, p. 47
[3] 20th January 1935: *Correspondance* II, p. 53

ployer since she was a member of a religious order when her child was born. This explained how the pseudo-priest had managed to gain entrance to the château, just as the prospect of a rich inheritance had persuaded the niece to share her favours with an adventuress. Bernanos not only succeeded in abdicating an omniscience to which, in this instance, he had no right, but in giving a colourful ambiguity to his heroine. Her sexual tendencies presuppose a physique appropriate to the active partner in a Lesbian relationship, and explain – or at any rate excuse – the ease with which she is taken for a man. Here there are one or two faint clues for the attentive reader to pick up.

A hundred pages of the book were written before the end of August, and fifty more in September, but it was not finished until the spring of 1935, and it left Bernanos exhausted and discouraged. He had underestimated the challenge of a way of writing that was new to him, and felt that he should have thrown himself, heart and soul, into a great book. *Un Crime*, he told his publisher, had been a waste of time. It was certainly not a waste of time, but neither was it a great book. The great books were just round the corner. The soutanes had not, after all, been hung up in the cupboard, but they served a less sacerdotal purpose. Moreover Bernanos had shown an extraordinary realism in his characterisation of magistrates, *gendarmerie*, and peasantry. He had their vernacular at his fingers' ends; accompanied, as it is so often, by the wind blowing through the mountain passes above Grenoble. The pseudo-priest with her prototype haunting Bernanos all the time, is unlike any other character in his previous novels. She excites pity rather than repulsion, fascination as well as fear. The author, one may say, had stepped out of the sanctuary, even if he had not abandoned the soutane. Yet, for all that, the book, published under his own name, did not have the popular success he had hoped for. It was serialised in the review *1935*, which claimed to have lost a number of subscribers as a result. The claim could hardly be sustained, since the review ceased publication eight days after the last extract of the novel had appeared. The contributors were left unpaid, and Bernanos complained that the truncation of the final chapter had done the book a serious disservice. The complete text had come as a revelation to those who had only read it in serial form. *Un Crime* went some way to fulfil its promise of a Simenon *Bernanosié*, but it is less interesting for itself than for its close relationship to the much more important novel – *Un Mauvais*

Rêve – which was at the back of the author's mind all the time he was at work upon it.

But what had happened, one may ask, to *Monsieur Ouine* to which he had given so much of his thought and time, and which was already nearly complete? He had reached the point in Chapter XVI where the young curé of Fenouille is in conversation with the mayor. Why had he interrupted the story at this juncture? He was, it is true, hurt by certain of Plon's readers who had returned his manuscript with their criticisms – 'illegible and unintelligible' – pencilled in the margin; and he replied to them with some asperity that he was not the kind of writer on whom a publisher could rely for a regular sale by the exploitation of a familiar vein. There was nothing familiar about *Sous le Soleil de Satan;* yet the book was already off to a good start before Daudet's famous article appeared.

Maurice Bourdel, from Plon, wrote reassuringly, and Bernanos cleared up a number of points that the readers had raised. But it would seem that something far more significant had stopped him in his tracks. Behind the young curé of Fenouille had arisen the figure of another curé who was to be the *curé de campagne.* Thus from the corrupted heart of the *paroisse morte* was conceived the master-piece whose birth would not now be long delayed. It was easier, in these circumstances, to plunge into a *roman policier* than to pursue *Monsieur Ouine* to its conclusion. Bernanos had seen, already, some hope of salvation for the *paroisse morte* before the *paroisse* was really dead. It would die eventually, of course, but in its author's own good time.

All through this summer of physical pain, mental depression, and material anxiety a project, hardly less fantastic than the plot of *Un Crime*, was simmering in his head. The old dream of emigration to Paraguay returned to haunt him. The other two musketeers – Maxence de Colleville and Guy de Bouteiller – would join him. In 1914, only fifteen kilometres from Asunción, a cow could be bought for twenty-eight francs and a horse for thirty. Bananas, oranges, mangoes, and sugar cane were there in plenty for all who fancied them. Colleville had the money required for the expedition, and Bouteiller would exploit the capital of his parents. Bernanos would undertake a lecture tour in the Argentine or Brazil to cover the cost of the journey, and the establishment of his family in a new way of life. He would further promise his publisher, not only all his literary production until he was dead, or they were bankrupt, but one volume of his *Journal* every year to be sent in monthly instalments. It might even be amusing to report on the Gran Chaco war with Bolivia; and in Asunción there would be boarding-schools for the children, even though they were run by the Jesuits. He would leave before the winter, which was summer under the Southern Cross. He ought to have left twenty years before.

Bernanos had neither the will nor the capacity to lead the life, and earn the income, of a conventional *homme de lettres*. He could not write to order. 'I go about armed with a No. 12 revolver, which fires explosive bullets, and they want me to bring down a thrush on the grounds that this is still better than nothing.'[1] He was constantly in demand for lectures; but three lectures would demand 120 pages of text, and this would cost as much time and effort as 120 pages of a novel – with much less to show for it either in money or reputation. It would be too silly, he argued, to have waited forty years to write *Sous le Soleil de Satan*, and end up as a literary hireling, if not a literary hack. And so there appeared to him only two solutions – extreme poverty or flight.

These Utopian reveries were partially interrupted by the writing of *Un Crime*, and the emigration, when it came, was less spectacular. Abruptly, at the beginning of October, Bernanos, and all his family, took ship for Majorca without a word of notice to anyone. Since he owed the proprietor of his villa several months' rent, he left him his furniture and effects to be disposed of to the best advantage.

[1] To Marie Vallery-Radot, 26th June 1934: *Correspondance* I, p. 532

CHAPTER 8

GOOD DREAMS AND BAD

I

FOR three weeks Bernanos and the family found accommodation at Soller and then, from the beginning of November, at Terreno on the outskirts of Palma. Towards the middle of December they secured a house – 95 Calle de 14 Avril – with which Bernanos expressed himself delighted. Here they remained until March 1935, when the proprietor – an American nudist – turned them out into the street. At last they rented a comfortable house – 30 Calle de la Salud – a street which, in these circumstances, did something to justify its name. Living was forty per cent cheaper than in France, but it could not be too cheap for a writer whose ability to pay his monthly bills depended on his daily output. Bernanos' correspondence with his publishers is a litany of requests for payment – a first instalment by telegram, the remainder by post. Writing in the Café Borne he usually managed to complete five pages a day, but when he tried to bring *Monsieur Ouine* to its conclusion the going was a good deal slower. The French were not popular in Palma, and no allowance could be expected for rent unpaid and bills unsettled. Bernanos described the end of each month as a 'nightmare of anxiety', and an epidemic of scarlatina in the family added to it. Even the consolations of religion were not easily come by. There were only two priests on the island who could understand French; one of them was a Jesuit and the other was deaf. 'All I can do with my sins is to drop them in the compassionate lap of the tramway conductor at Terreno.'[1]

Madame Manificat and her daughter came to stay, but otherwise Bernanos was cut off from all those to whom he could open his mind. Friendship, he wrote to Michel Dard, had its 'divine rights', and he imperatively claimed them. He had come to Majorca for material security, not for spiritual detachment. Where others were

[1] To Madame Manificat, 30th October 1935: *Correspondance* II, p. 106

mistaking Mussolini's Ethiopian adventure for a civilising mission, he could translate it in terms of hilarious irony, imagining General de Bono raised to the purple, and the Pope himself turning the first sod of a tunnel leading from the Palazzo Venezia to Addis Ababa. As for the Maurrasian *pays réel*, Bernanos believed in it less and less. As Maurras himself had written, the feudal monarchy was religious in origin, and the administrative monarchy was legal in origin. From the administrative monarchy to the totalitarian state and the pagan society there was a logical progression. Democracy would long ago have secured the latter, if it had not flinched before the revival of slavery, at least in its legal form. It was to a living prince, not to a dead system, that Bernanos burned to give his allegiance: a prince who would 'reign boldly, strongly, and gaily ... as one eats, drinks, and makes love when one is twenty years old.'[1] Why, he argued, should French history revolve around the *grand siècle*, like the moon? For a young Frenchman the *grand siècle* should be in front, not behind.

Bernanos had seen his legitimist dreams smothered in rhetoric when he was young, and now he feared to see them crushed by an implacable dialectic under which a monarch – even suppose he were restored – would have no freedom of manoeuvre. He had little freedom of manoeuvre himself, his motor-cycle languished at the Customs Office for want of the money to pay for its importation. As recreation he saw a great number of foreigners, devoured the Spanish newspapers, and enjoyed the *corridas*. Belmonte, Lalande, and Mino de la Palma were at the top of their form, although Belmonte – whom Bernanos described as 'a glory' – was seriously injured by his first bull.

In the height of summer Bernanos took to writing at home; he found the cafés intolerable with their stertorous ventilators and elderly, malodorous Englishwomen. Resilience and melancholy alternate in his correspondence, as he sends Marie Vallery-Radot an illustration for his tomb, with a prayer to the angel of the Last Judgment to blow his trumpet very loudly, since the deceased is hard of hearing. In 1928 Léon Daudet had assured Bernanos that the normal rhythm of his production should be three books a year, and Bernanos agreed with him. He now had four in his head; *Un Crime*, which we have already discussed; *Monsieur Ouine*, which was to

[1] To Louis Salleron, 20th August 1935: *Correspondance* II, p. 92

defeat all his attempts to finish it, at least for the time being, although he regarded the part already written as his best work to date; *Un Mauvais Rêve*, for which he proposed to utilise the discarded second portion of *Un Crime;* and the *Journal d'un Curé de campagne*, which was beginning to stir in his creative consciousness. Although *Un Mauvais Rêve* was only published after his death, it will be convenient to discuss it here. Once he had *Un Crime* off his hands, he proceeded to remodel, and very considerably to amplify, the section which his publisher had rejected. The principal character, Simone Alfieri, is an enlarged and deepened portrait of the pseudo-priest. Widowed after two years of marriage to a rich Italian, she has become the secretary to an eminent novelist, Ganse, in whom there are certain features of Bernanos himself, and of what he feared that any novelist might become – a machine for turning out so many pages a day; pumping the world around him for a regular fodder of fiction; long since emptied of that interior life which alone could nourish the imagination; substituting bad dreams for good ones. Having long dispensed with the counsels of a priest, he cannot live without those of a psychiatrist to whom he confesses his faith – and his futility.

I only believe in literature – period! In nothing else. Literature does not exist for the sake of successive generations, but the generations exist for the sake of literature, because it is finally literature that eats them up. They are all eaten up, and then disgorged under the species of printed matter.[1]

Holding these beliefs, Ganse is naturally not a great writer. He had fancied himself a Balzac whom, indeed, he can quote to his purpose – 'nothing brings a man more shame or suffering than the abdication of his will' – and there is a kind of frenzy in the determination to maintain his output. But of course he is not a Balzac; still less is he a Bernanos, although he can remember writing his early novels 'at the end of a dairy in the rue Dante, borrowing the wobbly table, the ink, and the paper ruled in squares!' Ganse is not even a Zola, and his invocations to the god of literature are only the echo of an irremediable despair.

Equally hollow is the refined *bonhomie* of his favourite psychiatrist – a type upon whom Bernanos once again expends his irony.

---

[1] Editions de la Pléiade, p. 937

Dr Lipotte joined his long and nervous hands together under his nose, and sniffed his nails, polished every morning by the manicurist. Like so many of his kind he was proud of his reputation as a connoisseur, claimed to be ruining himself in his collections, patronised the young painters, and yawned at important concerts several times a month. He was in fact the victim of his own deceptions, for his contempt for the vices and misfortunes of mankind grew more venomous with age, and the bragging of the medical students who had been his assistants for so long was not enough to reassure him. An abject fear of death gnawed at him, like a hidden worm.[1]

It gnaws at each of the characters in this inferno, which may be read as a 'myth of the modern world'.[2] Ganse has an assistant secretary, Olivier Mainville, a young drug addict who has been initiated by his mistress, Simone Alfieri; and a nephew, Philippe, who is flirting with Communism, and kills himself in front of Olivier. Towards the end of the book *Un Mauvais Rêve* recalls many features of *Un Crime*. The landscape is the same; the housekeeper at the presbytery has the same name; in each book the châtelaine's housekeeper had also belonged to a religious order; and as Simone is approaching the château where she will presently assassinate Olivier's aged aunt, so that her death may relieve his poverty, she meets the young priest on the way to his new parish. When she is in flight from the scene of the crime, she meets him again, and the novel ends on a note of suspense.

Even before his silhouette had emerged from the shadow, she had recognised his voice – that unforgettable voice which, only a few hours before, had seized her with a sinister premonition – and it was not without fear that she looked into his eyes through the darkness. No lie sprang to her lips, for she knew that any lie would have been useless. This phantasmal figure of a priest, coming now for the second time out of the night, knew everything. She had only one chance left to her; to recognise his funereal power, and acknowledge herself vanquished . . .[3]

Long after losing the last vestiges of her faith, Simone Alfieri felt the urge to confession, for at the root of all her criminal designs and desperate drug addiction was the hatred of herself: 'Known, experienced, and drained to the last dregs.' This she has in common with the other lost – or apparently lost – souls that Bernanos

[1] Ibid, p. 934   [2] *Bernanos*. Max Milner   [3] Editions de la Pléiade, p. 1027

summoned up from the metaphysical depths of his invention; their destructive egotism is only a mask for self-contempt, and Bernanos goes so far as to suggest that no human being is totally exempt from it. Simone Alfieri's defence was the frequentation of sophisticated priests – naïve in their sophistication – who found in her an easy prey. Bernanos describes them 'wandering here, there, and everywhere, from one dinner table to another, in search of problematical miracles, stuffing themselves with *petits fours* and curaçao. They were much edified by her docility, her deference, her perfect acquaintance with the fashionable mystics, whom so many pretty lips boasted to have read, without ever having opened a book that they had written.'[1] Later, we are told, she did not hide her preference for priests who were in some way under suspicion. From mystery to magic, from the Eucharist to cocaine or heroin, the descent was easy. It was the descent from the truth half-remembered from her childhood to the total, the enveloping, lie.

Simone Alfieri and her crime occupy the entire last section of a book which is too short to realise all its possibilities. In their descriptive detail and analytical precision these pages are among the most powerful and persuasive that Bernanos was ever to write. The obsession, not only of a crime to be committed, but of a fate to be encountered, of a doom to be faced, brings us again very close to Dostoevsky. For this murder of a helpless old woman in a lonely château, for whom Simone bears no hatred and from whom she only collects a bundle of banknotes, is really a species of suicide. A comparison with *Crime and Punishment* leaps to the reader's eye, except that we are left in doubt as to how Simone will be punished, and whether she will be redeemed.

Bernanos had crowded too much into too small a compass to make *Un Mauvais Rêve* into the masterpiece to which his imagination, allied to his technique, was now moving forward. The generation gap, illustrated by the long conversation between Olivier and Philippe, is slightly reminiscent of a *roman à thèse* – or, if one prefers, a *roman à la Jules Romains*. 'I was born in little pieces, like specks of dust,' says Olivier. 'You need an eye that looks in all directions, like a fly, if you want to see me. All my generation are the same.' And when Simone takes the part of bewildered youth in her last conversation with Ganse, she borrows the accent of Bernanos:

[1] Editions de la Pléiade, p. 1011

As a schoolboy at Bourges

With his father

The dandy

No two generations ever looked at each other with a more covert hatred, from either side of the black hole where the stench of a million corpses still rises after so many years – the fearful crime for which you dare not openly admit your responsibility. Poor young things, if they came into the world with the grimace of disgust that so displeases you, it was because they didn't like the smell of it.[1]

Elsewhere, however, the author's commentary is too penetrating and, in its context, too appropriate, to be dismissed as irrelevant. 'Egotism is doubtless a sin of the flesh, and a secret triumph for the world of the flesh'; or when Lipotte compares Olivier to the Treaty of Versailles – 'too weak for the harshness of its content.' One is only left wondering why Bernanos left a work, on which he had expended such pains, lying for so long unpublished. Was he perhaps dissatisfied with the abrupt ending? Was he so depressed by the relative failure of *Un Crime* that he was afraid to publish a novel which had so much in common with it? Did the book appear to him, as it has seemed to some of his critics, an inconclusive sketch for *Monsieur Ouine*, of which he had already written a considerable part? The psychological ambience of the two books is very similar; nowhere else is the spiritual vacancy so unrelieved. In 1938 he showed it to a friend who expressed himself as disappointed, and Bernanos deferred to his opinion. It was not until after his death that the novel was published, most usefully annotated by Albert Béguin.

Yet the character of Simone Alfieri stands among his major achievements. Too strong for submission to any master but the one for whom she searched through so many deviations, and of whose reflection she perhaps caught a glimpse in the eyes of the young priest so unexpectedly encountered, she thought she had found him in Ganse only to discover that he had simply used her as material for the best of his books. Hers, too, was the fate of those 'successive generations' whom literature had 'eaten up'. For a few months she had enjoyed 'a kind of repose and almost voluptuous annihilation which the abuse of morphia had prolonged for a little while. This was followed by the crisis of mystical madness in which her reason nearly gave way, as she dashed hither and thither across a secret Paris of false priests and bogus magicians, black masses or grey – hell, in fact; until, all of a sudden, there was Olivier with his angel face.'[2] But Olivier was no more angelic than she was; and although

[1] Ibid, pp. 928   [2] Ibid, p. 985

G.B.–K

she was his mistress, he was certainly not her master. Having been destroyed by literature, and disappointed of love, she sought reality in a crime that was almost gratuitous – an escape from one bad dream into another. What happened to Olivier or to Ganse we are not told and cannot guess. Their fate, like hers, hangs suspended on the three dots that bring the novel to a halt which is hardly a conclusion.

2

On the 6th of January 1935 Bernanos was writing to a friend of his intention to write the diary of a country priest, who 'will have served God in exact proportion to his belief that he has served Him badly. His naïveté will win out in the end, and he will die peacefully of a cancer.' The *Journal d'un Curé de campagne* is the most famous, the most popular, and the most highly considered of Bernanos' novels. After a slow start, and a dishonest serialisation in the *Revue Hebdomadaire* – too solicitous for the feelings of its *bienpensant* public – it was awarded the Grand Prix du Roman of the Académie Française, translated into several languages, and turned into a film by Robert Bresson. No one else could have written it, and yet it is as different from *Sous le Soleil de Satan* as it is from *Monsieur Ouine* or *Un Mauvais Rêve*. The soutane is there, on every page, but the features of those who wear it have radically changed. The themes are familiar, but the variations are new. *Sous le Soleil de Satan* is a sad book, and *Monsieur Ouine* leads one to a precipice of despair. The *Journal* is a happy book, for all its burden of sin and suffering, because Bernanos found happiness in writing it. The face of the young priest, he told a correspondent, came up at him by day and by night, and he was straining every nerve to portray it.

No doubt the change of scene, and easier cost of living, were partly responsible for a balance which is absent from all his subsequent work, with the exception of the *Nouvelle Histoire de Mouchette* and *Dialogues des Carmélites*. Yet the *Journal* had its genesis in *Monsieur Ouine*, of which – we shall recall – Bernanos had already composed sixteen chapters at La Bayorre. For the reasons indicated above, or others, he switched his imagination from a parish that was 'dead' – *La Paroisse Morte* was still the provisional title for *Monsieur Ouine* – to one that was merely dying, and not quite beyond hope of redemption. It has been observed that the curé of the dead parish makes his appearance in the story just at the point where Bernanos laid it aside. Other characters were calling him, and even before the end of 1934 he was writing the *Journal* at the rate of three or four pages a day. For each one of these he received sixty francs, and more than ten years later, on his bed of mortal sickness, the supplications of his wife and children – 'Georges, your pages . . . papa, your pages' – still echoed in his memory.

Having given the curé no chance whatever of rescuing his parish from perdition, he was resolved, it would appear, to give him another chance in a different context – for, as we shall see later, the resemblances between the two priests are too striking to be fortuitous. There is no character in the *Journal* from whom Bernanos withholds his sympathy, and this alone was a victory over temptation. He wanted the typical village of Ambricourt to be a microcosm of the countryside he had known as a boy. The figures, grotesque but never implausible in their mediocrity, which had formerly provoked his satire – a Ganse, a de Clergerie, a Saint-Marin – have disappeared. The curé de Torcy, who is the nearest the author came to a portrait of himself, suggests a more charitable view of mediocrity:

Mediocrity [he tells his younger colleague] is a snare of the Devil. It is God's affair . . . too complicated for us. I told him [the local doctor] one day: supposing Jesus Christ was waiting for you in the likeness of one of these fellows you despise, for, except for our sins, He assumes and sanctifies all our miseries? This man you take for a coward is only an unhappy creature crushed by the huge social machine, like a rat caught under a girder. This man you take for a miser is only worried by his fear of not making the grade. This fellow who appears so pitiless in his aversion to the poor – for there are such people – is merely the victim of the same inexplicable terror which others feel for mice and spiders. Do you look for Our Lord in people like these? And if you don't, what are you complaining about? It's you who haven't made the grade.[1]

Bernanos told a friend that when he started to write the *Journal*, one winter evening, he had no idea where it would lead him. He had often begun a book in this way, and then abandoned it after twenty pages because it was leading him nowhere. Whenever he took up his pen, his childhood rose up before him 'a very ordinary childhood, like anybody else's'; and it was the faces and landscape

[1] Editions de la Pléiade, p. 1123

of his childhood, mixed up together in his unconscious memory, that were the matrix of his fiction. In the *Journal d'un Curé de campagne* they led him far from the Balearic shores to the chalk plateaux and sombre presbyteries of Artois, and the carefree playground of Fressin. Indeed certain readers accused him of modelling his châtelain on a respected figure in the neighbourhood, whom he had known as a boy. He was quick to deny any intentional resemblance, and wrote in desperate apology to the châtelain's daughter. Where other books had been a burden to Bernanos, he was always impatient to get back to this one. Never before, he believed, had he achieved such strength and tenderness. He wanted the *Journal d'un Curé de campagne* to 'radiate'. It radiated far and wide, and beyond his most optimistic dreams.

To reach the truth of objectivity without the chill of detachment is never easy. Bernanos was helped towards this by giving his novel the form of a diary, in which the writer should not be too obviously himself. The young curé of Ambricourt does, it is true, express many of the author's ideas, but there is no physical or temperamental resemblance. For these we must turn to the curé de Torcy. Yet is is interesting to note that Bernanos had begun to write his own private journal at the same time, devoting an hour a day to it, and practising – though for personal, not professional reasons – the technique he was employing in the novel. A comparison between the two diaries, if and when the private one is made available, would provide fascinating material for a thesis.

The first difference that strikes the reader in comparing the *Journal d'un Curé de campagne* with the other novels of Bernanos is the absence of sensation or melodrama. There is no Mouchette to be rescued, unsuccessfully, from the jaws of suicide; no miracle *manqué;* no murder and no apostasy; no spectacular demonstration of saintliness. To be sure, the young curé – we are never told his name – is no ordinary priest; for one thing, he has the Bernanosian gift of expression. But his parish is a very ordinary parish, and he exercises his ministry as any other of his cloth might be expected to exercise it. He baptises the infants, teaches the children, absolves the dying, and buries the dead. He lives alone in the poverty to which he has long been inured, and such food as an unsuspected cancer allows him to digest he cooks for himself. In his relations with the château he is correct without servility, and he leaves the peasantry

alone unless they ask for him. He watches, without surprise, the
habits of adolescence develop into the vices of maturity; and he sees
the little world for which he must answer before God devoured by a
mortal *ennui*. To keep a diary of his thoughts, and such encounters
as relieve the monotony of his daily routine, is one way of not being
devoured by it himself. He celebrates his Mass and says his prayers,
but prayer is not easy and it brings him little consolation. No one
thinks him remarkable, although his superiors think him odd. The
most that anyone would say of him is that he is slightly unusual –
by which they mean that he makes them uncomfortable if they
happen to have a bad conscience. He does not read their souls
like the curé of Lumbres, but he sees that there is something
written there. In the crucial passages of the book they tell him what
it is.

The curé de Torcy is a very different character. A native of
Flanders where the curé of Ambricourt is a native of Artois, he likes
to quote his Ruysbroeck: 'If a sick person asks you for a cup of soup,
come down from the seventh heaven when God has caught you up
there.' The sublimities of certain Catholic writers get on his nerves.
There is nothing sublime, he declares, about sanctity, and if Sygne
de Coufontaine, the heroine of Claudel's *L'Otage*, came to him in
confession, he would tell her to keep faith with her fiancé and acquire
a proper Christian name. The security of the Pope was not worth a
broken promise; and he would be more suitably housed in prison
than in a Renaissance palace, decorated by painters who took their
mistresses for models of the Blessed Virgin. Bernanos puts into the
mouth of the curé de Torcy his own thoughts about the Mother of
Christ:

The Blessed Virgin knew no triumph and worked no miracles. Her son
did not allow her to be touched by human glory, not even to be grazed
by its huge and savage wing. No one has lived, suffered, and died in
greater simplicity than she, more utterly unaware of her own dignity
which, for all that, places her above the angels. . . . Naturally she holds
sin in abhorrence, but she has no experience of it – and the greatest saints
have had experience of sin, even the seraphic saint of Assisi. Only the
Virgin looks at us with the eyes of a child; hers is the only truly childlike
gaze which has ever rested upon our misfortune and our shame. If you
want to pray well, you must feel it resting upon yourself. It's not an
indulgent look – because indulgence has some bitter experience behind

it – but it's a look of tender compassion, of sorrowful surprise, of some inconceivable, indefinable feeling which makes her younger than sin, younger than the race to which she belongs, and although Mother by the grace of God, Mother of the graces that flow from Him; the youngest daughter of mankind.[1]

The curé de Torcy emphasises to his *confrère* the importance of little things. 'They don't seem to matter, but they give one peace – like wild flowers. You think they have no scent, but taken all together they're balmy.' True to his character, he is orderly in his habits and appearance, decisive in his judgments, frank and fraternal in his manner. His robust common sense is not, in fact, common at all, for it reflects an accurate and experienced spirituality. He is the virile counterpart to the young curé's diffident sensitivity; each represents an essential facet of Bernanos himself, with this difference that in the curé de Torcy we recognise the Bernanosian features and catch, unmistakably, the Bernanosian tone of voice. In their conversations it is as if one part of Bernanos were coming to the rescue of the other.

A writer wishing to give the impression of the diurnal round, varying little from one day to another, will find the diary a con-venient – perhaps a too convenient – form. Bernanos does not fall into such traps as are here laid out for him. In conveying monotony he does not weary the reader, and he registers all the time a gradual progress towards the climax of the book. There is the progress, hardly suspected, towards death; and there is a corresponding growth in spiritual wisdom as the lessons of experience are digested. The curé's old friend from the seminary, in whose arms he dies, is introduced to us at an early point; it is already made clear that he has left the active ministry and is living with a mistress. Moreover, in eschewing melodrama, Bernanos does not dispense with dramatic confrontations. These revolve, principally, around the persons living in the château – the count, the countess, their daughter Chantal, and her governess.

Bernanos was not insensitive to the values of aristocracy; he knew that it was sustained from below. Imposed from above, it became something else. Olivier, the count's nephew, now engaged in the Foreign Legion, does not reject it; he merely finds it loveless. And the curé, as a poor man, knows what poverty expects from riches:

[1] Editions de la Pléiade, pp. 1193–4

You are always talking of their envy [he tells the countess] but you don't understand that what the poor are longing for is not so much your riches, but something they hardly know how to describe, which lends an enchantment to their solitude – a dream of magnificence and grandeur. It's a poor dream – a poor man's dream – but God gives it His blessing.[1]

The count himself realises just how poor a dream it is:

There is no longer a nobility [he reminds the curé]. Get that into your head. I knew two or three noblemen when I was a young man – ridiculous, but remarkably striking, characters. They reminded me of the oak trees, twenty centimetres high, that the Japanese cultivate in little pots. The little pots are our conventions and our morals. No family can resist the slow erosion of avarice when there are equal laws for everyone, and public opinion is the legislator. The nobles of today are simply bourgeois who are ashamed of themselves.[2]

The shame is concealed by a decorous façade which crumbles before the curé's clumsy simplicity. The count and the countess go to Mass, although the count is never seen to approach the altar. His casual and chronic infidelities forbid it. But it is the countess, scrupulous in her observance, who presents the curé with his challenge. She has never forgiven God for the loss of her little son, and this persisting rancour turns all her observance to sacrilege. She despises her husband, and hates her daughter, who returns the sentiment at compound interest. 'We talk about the Family,' reflects the curé 'as we talk about the Fatherland. We ought to pray very hard for the Family – the Family frightens me. May God take it to His mercy!' This reminds one of André Gide's 'O familles, comme je vous hais!'; but the curé's mission is to persuade the countess that the incapacity to love is the only accurate definition of Hell, and his argument wins the day. Just in time, however, for within a few hours of her surrender the countess is dead.

The *Journal*, despite its form, does not float on a stream of consciousness. It is built up on a massive rhythm of alternating duologue and soliloquy. Here is no catalogue of sacerdotal victories, no dissipation of the seeping *ennui*, no forcing of the barricades. Pride and scepticism maintain their foothold. Chantal, possessed by some demon of defiance, overhears the curé's last interview with her mother and duly circulates her slanderous and misleading account of

[1] Ibid, p. 1155   [2] Ibid, p. 1174-5

it. The doctor who tells the curé that he is dying of an inoperable cancer is discovered injecting himself with morphia. The ex-seminarian, himself incurably ill with tuberculosis, on whom the curé calls after hearing his sentence, and who absolves him as he lies in his last coma, reports his death to the curé de Torcy in a letter where the vanity of a priest, turned into a pretentious and provincial *homme de lettres*, still puts up its feeble defences. The *curé de campagne* will die in the odour of failure rather than sanctity; but the reader will not contest the rough compliment of the curé de Torcy: 'You're a famous little priest, all the same.'[1]

Much of Bernanos' writing is a passionate monologue; the *Journal* is a dialogue with himself, which he objectifies into a dialogue with other people. At no single moment does the Fury of satire get the better of him. When the curé observes that 'even a justified indignation is an impulse of the soul too suspect for a priest to give way to it', Bernanos may well have been thinking of his own temptation. The pessimism, of course, remains; but the window is left ajar to joy. When the curé de Torcy has the stage – and the *curé de campagne* never disputes it with him – the fresh air blows in. Nevertheless, these occasions are rare. The morning breaks, image of the first Paradisal dawn, and then the mists of the aboriginal calamity close in:

I am more and more convinced that what we call sadness, anguish and despair – to describe certain movements of the soul – are in fact the soul itself; that since the Fall the human condition is such that a man can see nothing inside or outside himself except in the shape of anguish. Even when he is most indifferent to the supernatural, and even in the throes of sensual delight, he still feels obscurely that the radiation of a single joy is a frightening miracle. For here is someone capable of imagining his own annihilation, and forced to justify by precarious arguments the furious revolt of his flesh against this hideous and absurd hypothesis. If it were not for the vigilant pity of God, I think that man would relapse into dust from the first moment that he realises what he is.[2]

How then is he to defend himself? Only the disarmament of the saints will serve him: poverty, simplicity, and the spirit of child-hood.

They keep on saying to me: 'Be simple.' I do my best. It's so hard to be

[1] Editions de la Pléiade, p. 1191   [2] Ibid, p. 1185

simple. But men of the world talk about 'the simple' as they talk about 'the humble', with the same indulgent smile. They should really be talking about 'the kings'.[1]

The curé, and Bernanos with him, is in the difficult position of extolling the blessings of poverty and condemning the riches that produce them. Here he stands in higher company than Bernanos. It was easy enough for Christian social democrats to speak of poverty as a kind of shameful illness, unworthy of a civilised nation, but they would not dare to speak like that about the poverty of Jesus Christ. The problem was insoluble – how to re-establish the poor in justice without establishing them in power, for the beggar did not realise that he was himself radiating with a grandeur beside which the wealth of the millionaire was penury. However severely he judged himself, the *curé de campagne* never doubted that he had the spirit of poverty. It was akin to the spirit of childhood; indeed the two were identical.

Where *ennui* reigns triumphant, as it does at Ambricourt, lust silently proliferates – for lust is 'a dumb devil', and the curé is afraid to look at it too closely. He remembered the *estaminet* in the village of his childhood, and the besotted stare of the customers fixed in poignant vacancy on the girl who was serving them:

Of course I don't deny that thousands of people live disordered lives, and extend the unsatisfied curiosities of adolescence right up to the threshold of old age – and sometimes beyond it. What can one learn from these frivolous creatures? Perhaps they are the playthings of the Devil; they are not his true prey. It would seem that God, in His mysterious designs, has not allowed their souls to be really engaged in their appetites. They are more probably the victims and the inoffensive caricatures of a wretched heredity; retarded children, little brats soiled but not corrupted; and they have the benefit of certain immunities which are the privilege of childhood.[2]

The carnal sinner imagines he is in revolt; but the world for which Christ refused to pray 'is not revolt, but acceptance, and above all things, acceptance of the lie'. For the lie is everywhere; 'voluntary humiliation is royal', but it should not be confused with 'a vanity which has lost its usual composure'.

So, in this greatest of his novels, one by one the central Bernanosian

[1] Ibid, p. 1245   [2] Ibid, p. 1128

themes are picked up and interwoven in the fabric of a single human destiny. The *légionnaire*, on leave from Morocco, speaks for a *chevalerie* which the mechanics of modern war have rendered superfluous – 'protectors, but not servants, of the City; not all of them either just or pure, but representing a kind of justice which for centuries had haunted the unhappiness of men, and occasionally fulfilled their dreams.'[1] But the soldier had been degraded into the conscript; and the wars of mutual extermination which 'appeared to be the signs of a prodigious activity' were only 'the evidence of an increasing apathy, leading vast herds of sheep, resignedly, to the slaughter.' The *légionnaire* had carried the curé for a ride on his motor-cycle, and the memory of the straight road flying past comes back to him, like a figure of man's journey through time to a destination which he now knows to be round the corner, or beyond the rim of the near horizon:

These roads of ours, the highways of the world, mysterious and changing and echoing with the footsteps of mankind – have I really loved them so much? Where is the child born to poverty, and raised amid their dust, who has not shared with them his dreams? Great rivers of light and shadows, bearing along the dreams of the poor, slowly and majestically, towards uncharted seas.[2]

In a book, whose character of a testament Bernanos admitted to be more explicit than elsewhere in his fiction, this episode had a very personal resonance. He wanted the curé to have loved and understood, for a single instant of his life, what he had himself loved so dearly. 'I needed some grand triumphal morning, and a soldier speaking.'[3]

Four years later Bernanos was writing to a friend that the 'artist's work is never the sum of his doubts and disappointments and sufferings, of what is good and bad in his life, but his life itself, transfigured, illuminated and reconciled.'[4] This is eminently true of the *Journal d'un Curé de campagne;* and when Bernanos had finished it he declared: 'Yes, I love this book. I love it as if someone else had written it. I don't love the others. *Le Soleil de Satan* is a display of fireworks shot up into the sky of a stormy evening, amid the wind and the rain. *La Joie* is no more than a murmur; you wait for the

---

[1] Editions de la Pléiade, p. 1217   [2] Ibid, pp. 1241–2
[3] To Pierre Belperron, 6th January 1936: *Correspondance* II, p. 120
[4] *Cahiers du Rhône*, p. 50

Magnificat, but you never hear it. *L'Imposture* is a face of stone.'[1]
And if the face of the *curé de campagne* was to remain so vividly and
affectionately in the reader's mind, one reason may have been that,
in the nature of the case, Bernanos had been unable to describe it.
But we should easily recognise it if we met it along the road – or
even, maybe, at times, in the mirror.

[1] *Bernanos par lui-même*, pp. 173–5

CHAPTER 9

THE CEMETERIES UNDER
THE MOON

I

FROM his position of complete detachment from any party align-ment, Bernanos agreed, in the same spring of 1935, to contribute three articles to *Marianne*, a weekly newspaper of the Left, founded by Emmanuel Berl. It was shortly to become a firm supporter of the Popular Front. Bernanos made perfectly clear the colours under which he was sailing. He refused to march either with the mon-archists or the revolutionaries, because he maintained that each was contaminated with the spirit of the bourgeoisie. What was the point of rallying to the salvation of a society that one did not wish to save? Let it, first of all, have the grace to disappear. Neither then, nor later, did Bernanos feel called upon to suggest what should be put in its place.

Such then were his political dispositions as events were moving towards the outbreak of the Spanish Civil War; his attitude may, in fact, be described as *disponible*. There were still distractions, with the matadors carried shoulder high in triumph from the Plaza to the Alhambra Hotel; and he had now recovered his motor-cycle, so grey with dust and abandoned in the depths of a hangar that he felt afraid of hurting its feelings. Moreover, the Grand Prix du Roman, awarded him by the Académie Française for the *Journal d'un Curé de campagne*, had earned him a certain local celebrity, and the obligation of addressing both the Castilian and Catalan literary societies in Palma – a mild foretaste of what it would be like to be caught between two fires. As the summer warmed up, the crisis of a Government incapable of protecting life and property was moving to a head; and in May 1936, a general strike was declared. For a single day Palma was in the hands of the Popular Front. The strikers, not unnaturally, stayed at home, and Bernanos limped, almost alone, along the deserted streets. Only a handful of militants, he was to record later, 'pretended to set fire to the churches, and prayed to God that they would not catch alight'. What had happened to make these reluctant and sheepish incendiaries disinter and desecrate the bones of Carmelite nuns, and turn them into the fanatical partisans of civil strife? This was the question that Bernanos was to ask himself in the most famous of his polemical works.

For the moment he was far from anticipating the dimensions, the duration, or the ferocity of the Spanish Civil War. What interested him was a certain analogy between the political situations in Spain and in his own country. He wrote accordingly to Père Boisselot, OP, the editor of *Sept*, offering him an article. He stipulated that it should be published unabridged; otherwise he would send it elsewhere. *Sept* was a weekly review of liberal tendency run by the French Dominicans. It had vigorously opposed the Abyssinian war, and later – at the instance of General de Castelnau, who was the Chevalier Bayard of the *bienpensant* public – it was suppressed by the Master-General of the Order. To edit a Dominican review is among the more risky of occupational hazards. Boisselot welcomed the article; he had read a report by Daniel-Rops, the well-known journalist and historian, of a conversation in which Bernanos had given his opinion on Gil Robles, the leader of the CEDA[1] and not long since Prime Minister of Spain. These views were not at all necessarily those of *Sept:* never, probably, since the far off days of the *Avant-Garde de Normandie* were the views of Georges Bernanos identical with those of the paper for which he happened to be writing.

By and large the Catholics of Spain had taken the abdication of King Alfonso fairly quietly, but the anti-clerical policy of the Republican Government had provoked a vigorous reaction, and in 1934 Gil Robles, with his allies standing further to the Right, came to power. He was not himself a monarchist, and this was enough to prejudice Bernanos against him. The Accion Popular, which he had founded, was a variant of Christian democracy, accepting the republic and the need for certain social reforms, but affirming the rights of Catholicism to respect as the religion to which the majority of Spaniards at least nominally belonged. Robles' bite, however, was sharper than his bark, if indeed so smooth a lawyer could be said to have a bark at all. When the Asturian miners rose in revolt against what they regarded as the betrayal of the Revolution, they were

[1] *Confederacion Española de Derechas Autonomas*

ruthlessly suppressed. Robles chose as his agent for this operation a certain General Lopez Ochoa, who had been cashiered from the army under the monarchy for a particularly repellent form of immorality – *immoralité crapuleuse*, as Bernanos put it. The choice was hardly reassuring. No doubt the Asturians needed to be pacified; but the notion of pacification includes the notion of reassurance – and they were anything but reassured. 'Christian democracy' continued to proclaim its principles, but it had already moved some way from the Mount of Beatitudes; and in 1936 Robles fell from power to be replaced by a Popular Front. The CEDA remained, however, a formidable opposition; and when Calvo Sotelo, an outstandingly able deputy on the extreme Right, was murdered on the 12th of July, no one could foretell to what lengths opposition would go in retaliation. Bernanos concluded his article as follows:

M. Daniel-Rops is perfectly right to blame the selfishness of the ruling classes in Spain. But M. Largo Caballero[1] has reason to reply that the conscience of these classes has been formed, from one generation to another, by the Religious Orders. My old master Drumont used to observe, in days gone by, that the Communards had been educated by the Christian Brothers, and the officers at Versailles by the Jesuits.[2]

Bernanos despatched his second article on the 16th of July, but it did not appear until the 31st. He warned Boisselot that if he did not wish to publish it, he would pass it on to *Humanité*. He noted that the avant-garde of the Catholic party – by which he meant, no doubt, the Falange – was frankly anti-capitalist, but he wondered what confidence these eleventh-hour militants would inspire among the workers when they were 'not even capable of defending their churches, and were content to move from one street to another to avoid the sight of a handful of fanatics beating up an aged priest.' As for neutrality, 'it was all very well to hold oneself above one's party, or above one's country. But one ought to make sure whether one was above or beneath them.'[3]

When the war broke out Bernanos was in wholehearted sympathy with the Nationalist insurrection. He felt no tenderness for a republic founded by neo-Encyclopaedists, and when his attitude had changed he reproached General Franco not for reneging on his oath to the republic in 1936, but on his oath to the King in 1931. Majorca

---

[1] The Socialist trades union leader.   [2] *Bulletin* 28–9, p. 4   [3] Ibid, p. 7

looked to be safe in the hands of the Nationalists, and Bernanos noted with scorn the ignoble flight of the foreigners, particularly the French. It was extraordinary how many of them had suddenly discovered that they were suffering from weak hearts. Nothing would induce him to desert his friends who might soon be in danger if the Catalan Marxists succeeded in crossing to the island, for the Spanish fleet had remained generally loyal to the republic. He was glad not to have taken his holidays in France. Moreover his eldest son, Yves, aged only sixteen and a half, had enlisted with the Falange, parading in uniform with an enormous Mauser rifle, and riding a BSA motorcycle of the latest model. He was soon promoted lieutenant by the Marquis de Zayas, governor of the island. The temperature in Palma was very high, from every point of view. 'Thirty-six degrees in the shade, and a *coup d'état* – just what suits me.'[1] To any suggestion that he should return to France Bernanos replied that he could not breathe freely in France while his son was risking his life in Spain.

On the 15th of August the Catalan militia disembarked at Porto Cristo, and there was heavy fighting; but the Nationalists had effective aerial support from Mussolini, and after two days the invaders were thrown back into the sea. Later in the month Bernanos went up to the scene of the fighting. He found his son shattered by the death of his lieutenant – a young cavalry officer from Madrid, killed at his side. Already, it would seem, the shadow of a doubt is beginning to take shape in his mind. Whatever the rights or wrongs of a civil war, to see it close at hand is a 'bitter experience',[2] and he hopes to formulate in writing what he thinks about it. For the moment he concludes that

this great people is acting today in accord with its deepest instinct and its immemorial tradition – which is above all to assure its moral and religious unity, if necessary by fire and sword. Fratricidal strife is a thing one is bound to deplore, but it is better to fight and die for one's altars and one's gods than for one's national commerce and economic outlets. I must add that Communism can destroy a great deal, but it can construct nothing lasting. In spite of appearances, the '*Requetès*'[3] of Navarre and the Asturian anarchists are equally remote from a conception of social

[1] *Bulletin* 28–9, p. 7
[2] To Marie Vallery-Radot, August 1936: *Correspondance* II, p. 149
[3] The Carlists from Navarre, so called for their red berets.

life which would sacrifice the human person to the State. These are men of the Middle Ages. If the new Middle Age that Berdiaeff writes about is to be born one day, it will be here, in this old land, inhabited by the only race in Europe which has kept the virtues and the faults of childhood, its disinterested heroism, and also – alas! – its cruelty. These events were expected for months, but they were retarded by tortuous politics which turned a simple police operation into a veritable civil war. I hope to write one day about the heads on whom the blood should fall.[1]

Whatever sympathy Bernanos still professed for the Nationalist cause, warmed by his son's active adherence to it, he had none for its supporters in France, where the nationalist press, cheering from the sidelines, filled him with disgust. All they could do was to send unarmed demonstrators into the Place de la Concorde.

Throughout September the traces of progressive disillusion are plain to read. The ferocity of the civil war was as implacable on one side as the other, and Bernanos took comfort from the conduct of his son, who maintained the traditions of military honour, with its respect for the defeated – not without causing some annoyance to those under whose orders he served. Bernanos was beginning to annoy them himself; but whatever he said – and he was to say a good deal – 'the cemeteries would speak in the end'.

2

Bernanos sent five further articles to *Sept* between October 1936 and February 1937. The last of them was never published, but the manuscript was found many years later among the papers of Vallery-Radot. Each was intended to form part of *Les Grands Cimetières sous la lune*, but Bernanos had to be careful what he wrote. He could say what he liked about the French, but the Spanish authorities in Majorca, no longer quite certain of his support, would be suspicious. Censorship of one kind or another appeared to them so much a matter of course that General Queipo de Llano could not believe that a denunciation of the Nationalists by the *Echo de Paris* had been published without the permission of the French Government. So far was the average Spaniard from understanding the French that he imagined that the French agreed with one another! It was upon

[1] *Le Jour*, 16th August 1936: *Bulletin* 28–9, p. 8

With his future wife, 1917

With his family at La Bayorre, 1932

these national differences, rather than upon the specific issues of the civil war, that Bernanos now concentrated his attention.

The Spaniard is a creature of faith. The Asturian miners believed firmly in the arrival of 100,000 comrades from the Popular Front in France, and the Catalans are still on the look-out, from the heights of Montjuich, for the army of Tarascon – in the name of Mistralian solidarity. The Nationalists believed in General Pétain – not a week goes by but they announce his *coup d'état* – in Colonel de la Rocque, and even in M. Charles Maurras.[1]

But all these beliefs were illusory; and if the Spaniards were putting their trust in those who could talk of nothing but the 'French order', Bernanos asked where that 'order' was to be found:

in their books? But people don't care a damn for their books, even supposing they have read them. If there is a French 'order', let someone create it! The situation of a Frenchman abroad would be considerably improved, I can assure you. For, after all, when we have been told a hundred times over that the *pays réel* is not the *pays légal*, and when they ask us, 'Where is it, your *pays réel*? Show it to us', it's annoying to have to refer them to a Bibliography.[2]

The Spanish Nationalists readily spoke of their war as a crusade, and their claim was as readily admitted by those conservative elements in France to which Bernanos particularly addressed himself. What exactly, he asked – now speaking from some personal observation – was the quality of the Spaniard's religious faith?

You will not make me believe that unfortunate people who go slyly trotting from one chapel to another, and place their hand on the dusty pedestal of statues, fortunately out of their reach – who then put it convulsively to their lips, repeating the gesture as often as they think necessary, and then again to make sure that the number is right – you will not make me believe that such people are not obeying some obscure instinct which impels them, not so much to pray to God and the Saints as to appease them, *if they exist*. . . . A superstitious person of this sort may be quite incapable of passing under a ladder, and yet he does not – in the exact sense of the word – believe in the virtues of the ladder. His belief is founded on fear. It is so true that more importance has always been attached to bad omens than to good. I am well aware that doubt has always played its part in what men believe; and that this gives to faith its moral colouring. But if doubt, like the spectrum of light, has its divisions of infra-red and ultra-violet, the part familiar to people over here is the part shading from disquiet to anxiety. The anxious character of the Spanish faith seems to me fully to justify the views of Lenin on this extraordinary people. We Frenchmen – you may think it deplorable or not, no matter – are not afraid of God.[1]

Bernanos could not, of course, avoid a more specific discussion of the issues and personalities of the war. He had joined in public homage to Calvo Sotelo and Ramiro de Maetzu – an erudite and respected publicist of the Counter-Revolution. Bernanos ardently admired his *Defensa de la Hispanidad*, and the following tribute appeared in *Le Figaro* of the 12th of September 1936:

The death of M. de Maetzu does honour to every thinking man – to every man, that is to say, who prizes his thought a thousand times more dearly than his life. But in so far as this death sets the last seal – the seal of the supreme sacrifice – on a work devoted entirely to the glory of Spain and Hispanidad, we can write that it honours also those misguided Spaniards under whose bullets the illustrious master has fallen. Today I offer to his memory the tribute of a French royalist. The writer who raised so high the standard of his country will not be surprised if I salute his tomb with the colours of my own flag. . . . Yes, Maetzu, Europe has need of Spain, and of the greatness which should be hers.

For a number of the generals – Varela, Yagüe, and Franco himself – Bernanos expressed a warm admiration. They had temporised for as long as necessary, and then they had struck. When the situation was compromised – or apparently lost – they had redressed it with a mastery that proved their mettle. No man with a drop of military blood in his veins would not be proud to serve under Yagüe or Varela. For Queipo de Llano and his 'radio' war from Seville Bernanos had less regard; these jokes were wearing rather thin and Spain was not laughing any longer.

I am writing these lines on the evening of All Saints day. Tomorrow is the feast of All Souls. Spain is living under the reign of death, and the abstract symbol of mortality is no longer enough. Death roams around the vast cemeteries like a famished lioness, digging up the corpses, crouching on top of them, haunted by the secret which it is trying to make them reveal. Spain is living one of these moments today. Oh yes, the thing began very simply with a military *coup d'état*. I lived through

[1] 11th September 1936: *Bulletin* 28–9, p. 18

those weeks of waiting, and I know what I am talking about. For a Frenchman like myself the atmosphere was already intolerable. But the people over here paid no attention to it. 'It will be over in a day or two,' they said. The less optimistic gave it a week. And now months have passed, and Spain is filling its lungs with a mist of blood.[1]

Queipo de Llano had declared that the civil war was a 'war to the death – to the total extermination of the enemy' and that 'whoever did not realise this was no good servant of Spain, and the sacred cause.' Bernanos described these words as 'terrible', and admitted that the sentiment they expressed was now generally shared. The interior life of the Spaniard was not easy to read; he could only suspect its fearful aridity. 'With him asceticism is not a vocation but an instinct, and the most powerful instinct of all. He can only conquer it – he can only enjoy his life – at the price of a tension so painful that it gives to his face, one of the most beautiful faces on earth, an expression that one can hardly bear to look at.'[2] Bernanos had caught it on the face of a gipsy in the last ecstatic throes of a *flamenco* – for one was born with a sense of sin as one was born with an ear for music; and it was the sense of sin which made the vengeance of the Spaniard so implacable.

He knows the value of intention and that is, primarily, what he punishes. He recognises no legal protection, and the theory of *habeas corpus* makes him laugh. Respect for the life and liberty of another man is no more than an obligation of gentlemanly behaviour, or of common politeness, only valid for as long as circumstances allow him to keep the rules of the game. After which, he politely kills his adversary, very much as one declines to raise one's hat if one meets a man in doubtful company.[3]

On the 25th of July, the military cadets of every garrison in Spain had been drinking merrily under the tricolour and the portrait of the Señor Presidente. It was not quite the same as drinking under the portrait of the King – presidential portraits tend to drabness – but still it implied a recognition of constitutional authority. Five days later the cadets were killing each other, as if they were obeying a regimental order. Chance, no doubt, had played a part in deciding on which side they found themselves; but they had engaged their lives in the business, and they were not like other people – Frenchmen for example – who insisted that their actions should accord

<hr>

[1] *Bulletin* 28–9, pp. 16–17   [2] Ibid, p. 19   [3] Ibid, p. 20

with their beliefs. They were not afraid of contradiction. They believed because they had decided to believe; and like the furious gamblers that they were, they understood only too well the wager of Pascal. 'I should add that the sincerity of an opponent can inspire respect for his character without inspiring the least desire to spare his life. Obviously, for the true believer, a convinced heretic is more dangerous than any other.'[1]

The keynote of these articles for *Sept* was a growing detachment and a compassionate irony; Bernanos reserved his indignation for the book that was boiling in his head, and of which they were intended to be a part.

Certain passages in his letters let drop a hint of the bomb that was presently to explode. 'We are soldiers and what they are doing here is not our sort of work' – and he admits that what he confides to his daily journal is, for the time being, unpublishable – if only because his son was in the firing line with the insurgent forces, and smoking a cigar in gay defiance of the enemy. He had made several attempts to join the Nationalist armies on the mainland; but the Italians, who viewed him with particular disfavour – probably aware of what his father thought of their fellow-countrymen – and who had forty-three aeroplanes on Majorca, succeeded for a time in preventing him. Bernanos wrote of trigger-happy desperadoes, with the mentality of colonial adventurers, playing dominoes in the cafés, when they were not driving their opponents to summary execution. The Counter-Revolution bore no resemblance to what its partisans in France, and elsewhere, imagined it to be on the word of a press manifestly sold to Mussolini. He described how entire villages had been purged of anyone suspected of republican sympathies, for no better reason than a casual denunciation by the servant or mistress of a parish priest. They were shot in front of the cemetery at Manacor, and the bodies, soaked in petrol, were burnt before the eyes of the next batch of victims. And the Bishop of Majorca had allowed this to happen without a murmur of protest. The Dominicans of *Sept*, for all their liberal pretensions, were afraid to let the articles of Bernanos appear without a caveat of editorial neutrality, and he resolved to write no more for them. In his last article, never published, he spoke his mind without ambiguity – and with prophetic insight.

[1] *Bulletin*, 28–9, p. 20

The few readers curious to know what I think about affairs in Spain must wait for my forthcoming book. This civil war appears to me, more and more clearly, as the first in a long sequel of events, each leading to the next, until the final catastrophe which would give us the clue to the enigma, if we could predict or merely conceive it. Certain crimes in the lives of men are no more than a simple and tragic event, irreparable but without significance. I am not speaking only of violent acts which justice can absolve, but of deliberate crimes – or at least of crimes perpetrated in a sort of cold blood and with a due calculation of risk. Even then the disproportion between the act and the evil thought which inspired it, like a monster risen from the motionless waters of the deep, often overwhelms the author so that he loses conscience, and becomes a stranger to his dreadful misfortune. But some crimes are essential, and stamped with the mark of fatality. The war in Spain is one of them.[1]

Life in Palma was becoming increasingly difficult, and the popular success of the *Journal d'un Curé de campagne* had not made it easier. Postal communication was uncertain, and the surest way for Bernanos to receive the money-orders or banknotes on which he and his family depended for their daily bread was to send them care of the French Consulate. Occasionally a French warship would take his private mail, but money or letters often became lost in transit. Except for a fortnight's complete rest in the Spring of 1935, he had never stopped working; his nerves were raw with the strain; and now the health of his wife was giving cause for serious concern. This was the sixth house or apartment the family had occupied within a space of two years, and its minimal furnishing reminded Bernanos of the booking-hall at a railway station. He remembered such places from his days as an insurance agent, and he now seriously thought of asking the same company for a job in the south of France. This would enable him to live, although it would disable him from writing; to such desperate measures was the famous author of the *Journal d'un Curé de campagne* now reduced. Eugène Manificat had made two offers to defray the cost of an operation on his foot, but Bernanos knew himself too well not to realise that, once in bed, he would only be impatient to get up again, and that the promised convalescence would be anything but a rest. François Mauriac had published a *Vie de Jésus*, and both Gabriel Marcel and Jacques Maritain were encouraging Bernanos to do the same. Plon were enthusiastic, and Bernanos allowed the idea to take root in his mind,

[1] Ibid, p. 27

where it never ceased to obsess him. He wrote a few pages while he was still on Majorca, and it is a loss to literature that he never added to them. Driven by these preoccupations, his horror at the turn the Nationalist crusade had taken, and the knowledge that Yves was now fighting on the peninsula, he decided to return to France. He left with his family on the 27th of March 1937, but he had already despatched to Plon the preface and the first thirty-six pages of *Les Grands Cimetières sous la lune*.

3

These pages were mysteriously lost in transit – if the authorities in Majorca had known what they contained, they would happily have consigned them to the fire – and Bernanos rewrote the book from the beginning, making no direct use of the material which had already appeared, or been destined to appear, in *Sept*. He was now settled at Nogent-sur-Marne, a small town he must have visited on his rounds as an insurance agent. It was characteristic of the author, and indicative of his universal approach to a particular problem that not until page 72 does he mention the Spanish Civil War. He was not concerned to debate the rights and wrongs of the *coup d'état*, or to establish a balance sheet of atrocities. He did not discuss, or deny, the facts asserted by Gil Robles in the Cortes on the 16th of June 1936. In the four months since the advent of the Popular Front to power, 160 churches had been burned to the ground; there had been 269 murders, mainly political; 1,287 assaults of varying severity and significance had been committed; 69 political centres had been wrecked; 113 general strikes and 228 partial strikes had been declared; and 10 newspaper offices had been sacked. 'We are today present,' Gil Robles declared, 'at the funeral service of democracy.' Professor Hugh Thomas, an impartial historian, does not refute these figures, nor deny that the situation was as grave as Robles had depicted it.[1]

At the same time it was ridiculous to suppose, argued Bernanos, that the military revolt had been organised, over night, after the murder of Calvo Sotelo; that General Franco had telegraphed his accomplices: 'I am rebelling tomorrow. What have you decided to do?' or telephoned his own decision to Mussolini from the

[1] *The Spanish Civil War* (1961)

Canaries. Three months would hardly have been long enough to prepare so concerted a conspiracy. Bernanos did not fail to point out that General Sanjurgo, who was to have led the revolt but whose aeroplane crashed on its way from Portugal, had forced the abdication of King Alfonso – for it was he who assured the defection of the Palace guard. Evidently the Spanish generals rode loosely to their oaths, whether to the constitution or the throne. For the moment they were saying nothing about the altar, having shrewdly kept the Spanish episcopate in ignorance of their plans; for these shepherds, anxious only to preserve their flocks from mortal sin, were naturally the declared enemies of violence. Yet Bernanos noticed how quickly their croziers acquired a cutting edge. On that bright Sunday morning in July, when he found the road into Palma unexpectedly barred by armed pickets, a young Falangist – only seventeen years old – had been killed, almost under his eyes. The Bishop of Majorca held the Falange in such reprobation that he only reluctantly allowed the young man a Christian burial, and forbade his clergy to attend the obsequies in a surplice. Six weeks later Bernanos discovered the brother of the victim dead on the road to Porto Cristo. He received a public funeral; a street was named after the two brothers; and a plaque registering this decision was solemnly blessed by the same Bishop. When the false news arrived that Madrid had fallen, his Lordship was prominent in applauding them from the balcony of the City Hall. On the 17th of July there were 500 Falangists in Majorca; a few weeks later there were 22,000. The reasons for this remarkable recruitment were clear to Bernanos; if they were equally clear to the Bishop, he remembered the long-standing tradition of the Church to make the best terms it could with established authority. Majorca had its concordat, as well as its cemeteries – and the moon shone with a tranquil indifference on both.

The clergy were less compliant. When a lady of title ventured to ask a canon of the cathedral, reputed for his eloquence in the pulpit, whether he approved the systematic extermination of all judged lukewarm in their sympathy for the *movimiento*, he replied as follows:

I neither approve nor disapprove. Your Grace has unfortunately no idea of how difficult is our ministry in this island. At the last general meeting of priests, which his Lordship presided over, we had the proof that last year only fourteen per cent of Majorcans made their Easter duties. So grave a situation justifies exceptional measures.[1]

They were certainly exceptional. In 1937, every citizen was obliged to fill in a form stating if, and where, they had been to confession and received Holy Communion during the prescribed period. Needless to say, the altars and confessionals were besieged, but the guilt of sacrilege was upon the heads of those who had provoked it.

God knows [wrote Bernanos] the names of those few irreconcilables, who, doubtless believing themselves to be His enemies, had enough Christian blood in their veins – though they were not aware of it – to resent the injury to their conscience, and to say no to these insolent demands. May they one day sit in judgment on their judges![2]

Bernanos knew personally the Capuchin friar whose task it was to absolve the Communists before their execution. Whatever comfort he may have drawn from the fact that they nearly all asked for his ministrations, the time came when he begged to be relieved of them. While the rest of the world regarded the war as a duel between Democracy and Fascism, or between Christianity and Communism, Bernanos was concerned to denounce a reign of terror masquerading as a crusade. Why did these *preux chevaliers*, who liked to present themselves as the descendants of El Cid, follow so dutifully in the footsteps of Fouquier-Tinville? When the Catalan militia landed at Porto Cristo in August 1936, they occupied a school run by a religious order. The children were of course on holiday, and the sisters were put to work turning the place into a hospital, under the direction of a South American who declared himself to be a Catholic and a Communist and threatened to blow out the brains of anyone who treated them with disrespect. He brought food to the nurses, helped them to dress the wounded, and spent his rare moments of leisure in good-humoured controversy with the Superior. The Catalans were not able to make good their landing, and on the third day – as the Superior herself reported to a local newspaper:

We heard a lively burst of rifle fire; the wounded men were anxious; the militiamen took to their heels; and we threw ourselves on our knees, beseeching Heaven to aid our rescuers. Then we began to hear cries of

[1] *Les Grands Cimetières sous la lune*, p. 141   [2] Ibid, p. 143

Arriba España! and the doors gave way. What can I tell you more? The brave soldiers came in from every direction, and settled their accounts with the wounded. *Our South American was the last to be killed.*[1]

Bernanos had many friends among the Falange and their sympathisers; the idea of a military insurrection against a Government incapable of defending life and liberty, and notoriously hostile to religion, did not shock him in the least. He could now explain why he had stayed in Majorca for so long:

We stood our ground, my wife and I, not out of bravado, nor even in the hope that we could be of much use – there was, in fact, very little we could do – but rather from a feeling of deep solidarity with the good people – and their number grew from day to day – who had known our hopes and shared our illusions, had defended them, inch by inch, in face of the evidence, and at last came to share our anguish. We were free, and they were not. I am thinking of the young Falangists or *Requetès*, and the old priests. One of them was forced, at the point of the revolver, to drink a litre of castor oil, as punishment for an imprudent word. ... You woke up in the morning, pretty worried; you went out, and there – in the street, or in the café, or in the porch of the church – you met someone you believed to be on the side of the butchers. With tears in his eyes, he said to you all of a sudden: 'This is too much! I can't stand it any more. Look what they have just done.'[2]

It might have been the mayor of a small village, who was dragged out of his hiding-place in the cistern one December morning, shivering with cold and crouching in several inches of water. He was taken to the cemetery and left there with a bullet in his stomach. Since he showed a certain hesitation in dying, his assassins, by now slightly drunk, returned with a bottle of *eau-de-vie*, stuffed the neck of the bottle in his mouth, and, when it was empty, broke it over his head. It might have been yet another knock upon the door in the early morning; the crisp command to 'follow'; the reassuring words to the frantic wife, and the reassurance of the officer in command that of course they were only taking him to prison; the jolt of the lorry; the order to get out – not too far from the cemetery; the holy medal to kiss, if the fancy took him; and the *Pan*! *Pan*! of the revolver. No difficulty about a death certificate: 'So-and-so, and so-and-so, and so-and-so, died of cerebral congestion'; and the gravedigger would find the corpses in the morning. Bernanos had seen what

[1] Ibid, p. 139   [2] Ibid, p. 133

they looked like, twisted into attitudes almost obscene, when all the Catalan prisoners were executed in a single night – with the clergy in attendance. It was not the first time that Bernanos had looked on violent death; but in war the enemy's life was very much like one's own, and it was difficult to hate him.

The daily gift of oneself does not excite any of the feelings – hate, envy, and avarice – which throw a man back upon himself, and give him the idea that his life has no purpose beyond himself alone. One gets very easily used to the sight and stench of the dead. But a charnel-house is a charnel-house. . . . As long as there are soldiers in the world, you will not prevent them from honouring the risk they run, and whoever honours his own risk honours his enemy. Such is the law of sport and of war.[1]

But the terrorists of Majorca were neither athletes nor warriors, and they ran no risk whatever. The civil war was what many had believed it to be in the beginning – a police operation. But it was anything but simple, and it certainly was not short.

Bernanos was alive to the objection that his view of the war was a partial one; he had only seen what happened on Majorca, and Majorca was a small island. Nor was it representative of Spain as a whole. Its inhabitants were peaceful; they lacked the ferocity and fanaticism of Castile. Bernanos' son, now fighting in the trenches outside Madrid, could no doubt have told him a story of courage and idealism; and of cruelty on the other side – for the Republicans tortured their victims as well as killing them. He protested when *Humanité* added his signature to a letter denouncing the Nationalist atrocities in Malaga. 'I would willingly protest against the massacres in Malaga,' he wrote to Christiane Manificat. 'They seem, alas! more than probable. But the people on the Left don't appear to me any better qualified than the people on the Right to defend the unfortunate. It is all hideous.'[2] Bernanos admitted that if he had frequented Left-wing circles in Palma, certain reflexes of a temperament inflexibly Royalist, even if it could no longer be called a *tempérament de droite*, might have been aroused. For the founder of the Falange – José Antonio Primo de Rivera – he had unqualified admiration. If he had studied the Falangist programme, with its anti-clerical and anti-capitalist overtones, he might well have

---

[1] *Les Grands Cimetières sous la lune*, p. 194
[2] 27th February 1937: *Correspondance* II, p. 178

approved of it. But Bernanos did not believe in programmes, any more than he believed in principles; he believed that a society was created, or recreated, by men and women. If you had talked to him about 'Christian principles' he would have laughed in your face. The makers of medieval Christendom had not believed in Christian principles; they had believed in Christ.

But if his attitude to the war was partial in the sense that he recorded only what he himself had seen in a particular place, or what he knew to be true from common knowledge and irrefutable evidence, it had a general application. Almost alone among Catholic publicists of the day, he hammered home what no somersault of casuistry could conceal – that crimes committed in the name of religion were more reprehensible than those committed against it. This conspiracy of silence on the part of those who should have been the first to denounce, not necessarily the Nationalist uprising – here there was certainly room for two opinions – but the terror it unloosed, was the supreme scandal of the Spanish Civil War, and the Church was to pay a heavy price for it. Why had the Bishop of Vitoria refused to sign the manifesto of the Spanish episcopate? Because the percentage of the Basque population who made their Easter duties would have caused the Bishop of Majorca, not to think again – for he was clearly incapable of thought – but at least to rub the eyes which he had so carefully kept shut. The connection between the maintenance of Christian principles and the destruction of Basque autonomy was no more apparent to an impartial observer than to the defenceless victims of Guernica. Bernanos admitted, again, that when the first Italian aeroplanes landed on Majorca he had welcomed them; but a subsequent arrival from Italy, General Count Rossi, carried his *fasces* with a difference.

The newcomer was naturally neither a general, nor a count, nor Rossi, but an Italian functionary and a member of the Blackshirts. We saw him, one fine morning, getting out of his scarlet trimotor. . . . A few days later he took effective command of the Falange. Dressed in a black boiler-suit, with an enormous white cross on his chest, he dashed through the villages, driving his own racing-car, while other vehicles, packed with men armed to the teeth, did their best to keep up with him in a cloud of dust. Each morning the papers recorded these oratorial excursions, where he preached the crusade in a strange dialect of Spanish, Italian, and Majorcan, flanked by the mayor and the parish priest.

Certainly the Italian Government had at its disposal in Palma collaborators less showily conspicuous than this brute of a giant, who declared one day at the table of a great lady of the town – as he wiped his fingers on the tablecloth – that he required 'at least one woman a day'. But he was perfectly suited for the mission entrusted to him – which was to organise the Terror.[1]

The activities of this sinister *farceur* only underlined the international character the war had now assumed, and reinforced the warnings that Bernanos gave to his own countrymen. For he was looking beyond the cemeteries of Majorca to the greater holocaust which he saw looming, ineluctably, ahead. At least half of this tremendous polemic was addressed to those who, despairing of democracy and terrified of Communism, saw salvation in the nostrums of Fascism. Douglas Jerrold, who had played his own part in getting Franco flown from the Canaries, himself admitted that the chief argument against Fascism was its tendency to produce Fascists. Bernanos had closer experience of them than Jerrold – or Charles Maurras and the demagogues with whom he was now allied. Bernanos had long since despaired of the Republic, but he had not quite despaired of France. For that reason he was eager to get back to it.

[1] *Bulletin* 28–9, pp. 127–8

CHAPTER 10

A WORLD ELSEWHERE

I

We must retrace our steps a little. Some months before he sat writing *Les Grands Cimetières* in a café at Nogent-sur-Marne, Bernanos had sat at the table of another café in Palma, writing the *Nouvelle Histoire de Mouchette*. The genesis of the book tells a great deal about the ways of his inspiration.

I began to write it as I watched the lorries go past, and there, under armed guard, were the unfortunate fellows, their hands resting on their knees and their faces covered with dust, but very upright, head erect, with the dignity of Spaniards even in the extremity of misfortune. They were going to be shot the next morning. That was the only thing they knew. For the rest, they understood nothing. And if one had questioned them, they would have had nothing to say in their defence. Against what? That is what you would have had to tell them. I realised how impossible it is for the poor to understand the frightful game to which their lives are committed. I was struck by the horrible injustice of those in power who, in condemning these miserable people, speak a language completely foreign to them. This is an odious imposture. And I cannot say how much I admired the courage and the dignity with which they died. Naturally, I did not deliberately decide to make a novel out of it. I didn't say to myself: 'I shall transpose what I have seen into the story of a young girl pursued by misfortune and injustice.' But it is true that if I had not seen these things, I should not have written *Nouvelle Histoire de Mouchette*.[1]

It would seem, nevertheless, that Bernanos was speaking here with a certain degree of hindsight. On the 3rd of June 1936, six weeks before the civil war broke out, he was telling his publisher of his intention to write a story which would 'show the desperate awakening of the feeling of purity in a miserable child – an entirely carnal purity, you understand, for she would be incapable of discussing this virtue with a theologian. It's an immense subject.'[2]

[1] Interview with André Rousseaux: *Candide*, 17th June 1937: Milner, pp. 251–2
[2] To Pierre Belperron: *Correspondance* II, p. 136

An immense subject for what is little more than a long short story. Bernanos was still uncertain, three weeks later, what name he should give to his heroine. 'Mouchette' attracted him for obvious reasons; he remembered, with some affection, his first Mouchette in *Sous le Soleil de Satan*, and the history of the second would be equally, though differently, tragic. And even if the story had begun to take shape in his mind before he saw the lorries of the Terror clatter past, they undoubtedly influenced its development. The book, though it never transgresses beyond the limits of fiction – and indeed observes them more strictly than any other of the author's novels – is none the less a protest as compassionate as *Les Grands Cimetières sous la lune*. Its violence – murder, rape and suicide in the compass of 200 pages – is a microcosm of the violence which was the order of the day when Bernanos was at work upon it.

His claim to be regarded as a born novelist, as distinct from a born writer pouring out certain obsessive feelings and beliefs indifferently into fiction and polemic, is substantiated by *Nouvelle Histoire de Mouchette*. Perhaps this was why Paul Bourget liked to tell his friends that he would gladly have sacrificed all his own novels to have written this one. The form and character of Bernanos' fiction had hitherto allowed him to say pretty well what he wanted. But where he had stated, he was now forced to imply – often by a symbolism not too obviously contrived. A lesser novelist will rummage in his mind or personal experience for the themes that suit him; they came to Bernanos unbidden, and after giving them a short run for their money he was always ready to dismiss them. The second Mouchette, like the first, came to him from the grey skies and dismal *estaminets* of Artois; and it mattered nothing that he wrote her story in the shade of the scorching Majorcan sun. Death was at his elbow, as it was at hers.

The technique of narration is skilfully varied. Sometimes a scene is described with its direct impact upon Mouchette; sometimes with the impact on the author looking, so to speak, over her shoulder.

Bernanos keeps the advantages of the narration in the third person, but he tries to incorporate in this method certain advantages of narration in the first person; we are allowed to hear simultaneously the voice of Mouchette and the voice of the man who is telling her story; and the complete, if not omniscient, awareness of the narrator, with his ability to draw conclusions and propose interpretations, is varied with the limited knowledge of the world which is all that Mouchette possesses.[1]

This extremely subtle alteration of perspective enabled Bernanos to register a paternal sympathy with his heroine, and to turn what might have been a sordid melodrama into a sombre idyll of compassion.

The story is divided into four parts, and can be briefly told. Mouchette escapes from school to avoid the singing lesson, and running across the fields she meets a poacher, Arsène, who leads her into his hut to shelter from the rain. Then he takes her into a second hut; confesses to a fear that he has killed the gamekeeper, Mathieu; and falls into an epileptic fit. Mouchette is seized with a sympathy hardly distinguishable from love, and when Arsène returns to consciousness he rapes her in a moment of passion, and under the influence of drink. She returns home, trembling with shame and humiliation, to learn that her mother has died in the night. Later she discovers Mathieu, alive, when he comes to ask her if she can confirm Arsène's alibi – for he is threatened with prosecution for poaching. Thus she finds herself enmeshed in troubles which she cannot understand – like the victims of the Majorcan Terror – and the notion of death is brought closer to her by the woman of the village whose mission it is to prepare, and watch over, the dead.

Death is something I understand; and the dead, I understand them, too, very well. When I was your age they frightened me. Now I talk to them, as you might say, and they answer me. They answer me in their own fashion. It's a sort of murmur, a little breath which seems to come out of the depths of the ground. I explained it one day to the curé, but he scolded me. For him, the dead are in heaven. I don't want to contradict him, but I have my own idea all the same. In the old days, it seems that they worshipped the dead; the dead were a kind of gods. That's the true religion, my girl. Everything that lives is filthy and corrupt. You'll tell me that the dead don't smell very nice. Quite true – they don't. When the cider is fermenting, it's as beastly as a cow's piss. Death is like the cider; it must first of all get rid of its froth.[2]

This sibylline character had seen Mouchette as she came back in the chill of the early morning:

[1] P. Fitting, *Etudes Bernanosiennes*, p. 9
[2] Editions de la Pléiade, pp. 1331–2

When you came by the first time – you remember? – you stopped a
moment in the middle of the road. All your poor little face was asleep,
except your eyes. When I saw you again, your eyes were asleep too.
What was the good of waking you up, I said to myself? Isn't she unhappy
enough, as it is?[1]

Here we see the misery of Mouchette through the eyes of a third
person; but when the idea of death as an escape, and also as a
discovery and a compensation, is firmly implanted in her mind,
Bernanos takes over:

And today she was dreaming of her own death, her heart contracted not
with anguish, but with the disturbance of a prodigious discovery, the
imminent revelation of a secret – the secret which love had refused her.
To be sure, she had a childish notion of this mysterious event, but the
image of death, which left her insensitive the evening before, now
intoxicated her with a piercing tenderness. In the same way a familiar
face will appear different to us when we see it in the light of desire, and
we realise all of a sudden that it is dearer to us than life itself.[2]

It was only a short step now to the pond where Mouchette
drowned herself like Ophelia but, unlike Ophelia, in her right
mind:

Mouchette let herself slip over the side until she felt the gentle bite of the
cold water on her leg and thigh. An immense silence suddenly filled her
being – like the silence of the crowd holding its breath when the acrobat
reaches the last rung of the giddy ladder – and into this silence her failing
will power managed to lose itself. Obediently, she crept down a little
further, one of her hands resting on the bank. The mere pressure of her
palm was enough to keep her body on the surface of the water, which
was not, however, very deep. For a moment, as if she were playing some
sinister game, she threw back her head and fixed her eyes on the highest
point of the sky. The water insidiously lapped about her neck, and filled
her ears with a gay murmur – like the music at a fête. And pivoting
gently on her loins, she felt the life stealing away from underneath her,
while the odour of the tomb mounted to her nostrils.[3]

It has been debated how far, in fact, Mouchette was in her right
mind, and whether she found salvation. No priest is at hand to
rescue her with his prayers, as Donissan had rescued her elder sister.
But it has also been observed that in a story packed with violence

[1] Editions de la Pléiade, p. 1332   [2] Ibid, p. 1339   [3] Ibid, p. 1345

the scene of her suicide is among the rare passages of calm, and that the waters in which she drowns herself are an opening towards the love which she had not found on earth. Her last deliberate look at the open sky would seem to bear out this interpretation. Even more persuasive is the tenderness with which Bernanos envelops a character he could not have intended to condemn, and Mouchette's total ignorance of the moral law which might have dissuaded her. Like the victims of the Falangist terror, she could not have answered to an accusation couched in language she did not understand. In contrast to the nocturnal landscape of the novel – the adhesive mud, the pouring rain, the clammy peat bog, and the squalid interiors, physical counterparts of a world which had lost the secret of innocence – the placid waters of Mouchette's deliverance are an image of rescue rather than despair. They only thinly disguise, with a discretion that did credit to the author's integrity, his own commendation of a suffering humanity to the *douce pitié de Dieu*. As Albert Béguin pointed out, *Un Mauvais Rêve* and *Nouvelle Histoire de Mouchette* are both 'novels of a negative theology, where the world of the deepest night becomes a world of grace'. 'Hell is the hollowed out inverse of Heaven,' said Barbey d'Aurevilly; and Bernanos, 'All the breaches open on to the sky'.[1]

Apart from his revisions and completion of *Monsieur Ouine*, Bernanos never again put his hand to fiction. The loss to literature was incalculable, for he had attained in *Nouvelle Histoire de Mouchette* a mastery which would have served him well in novels of larger scope. The book has a clarity, a concentration, and a structure which are quite absent from *Monsieur Ouine;* and whatever the partisans of that hermetic work may pretend, it might have been as well for the reputation of Bernanos if it had been allowed to rest on a work minor in scale, but major in substance. *Les Grands Cimetières sous la lune* is a transcription of actuality; the *Nouvelle Histoire de Mouchette* is a transposition of it, and by that much the more considerable achievement.

2

After disembarking at Marseilles on the 31st of March, the Bernanos family went straight to Paris where they spent several weeks with

[1] *Bulletin* 5, p. 16

the Manificats in their apartment. There was no lack of cafés to write in, but Bernanos was missing the Borne at Palma, and the *camereros* who were so sympathetic, and the policemen who collected the pages he had torn up, whenever he disappeared to the lavatory. Later he moved to Nogent-sur-Marne; and then, shortly afterwards, to Toulon. Yves had been repatriated from Spain, and had now joined the French Merchant Marine, cruising happily off the coast of North Africa. On the 10th of May Bernanos was lecturing in Zürich, but a slight motor accident in September prevented him from attending the Book Fair in London, organised by the *Sunday Times*. The sales of the *Journal d'un Curé de campagne* had risen to 74,800, and translations of the book had appeared in German, Czech, Polish, English, and Dutch. A Simca was among the visible signs of his success. At the end of October he moved closer in to Toulon at 'Hermitage', Avenue Louis-Sorel, Petit-Bois. This was home ground, in so far as any ground was home to Georges Bernanos.

He was hard at work on *Les Grands Cimetières sous la lune* – telling Maritain that he had 'greased my big boots' and was committed up to the hilt, 'according to the good traditions of the French cavalry.'[1] He had chosen the title after much deliberation, and somewhat to the surprise of his publishers. It conveyed, he thought, an 'image of peace and mournful reconciliation'. The book was finished in April 1938, when he wrote to Maritain again with the assurance that he had said all he wanted to say and had compromised no one. Comparing his opinions to the 'irregular cavalry' of Vercingetorix, he hoped that he had 'got them through'.

The hope was an understatement. In France the Spanish Civil War divided the Catholics more seriously than elsewhere; in Britain or America to be 'sound on Spain and birth control' was a passport to clerical approval. But François Mauriac had too many friends among the Basques, and too keen a sense of justice, not to take their part; and when Bernanos read certain passages of the book to the Dominicans at Marseilles, they warmly approved of them. Maritain pleaded for appeasement and neutrality in a struggle where there was right and wrong on either side. He hoped that 'after the terrible purifications now being undergone, certain historical values will appear complementary which today, mixed up as they are with so many faults, are setting unfortunate and exasperated men at each

[1] 19th December 1937: *Correspondance* II, p. 189

other's throats'.[1] This calm and charitable reasoning was enough to make those who had previously sat at his feet denounce him from the pulpit. It was a long time since Bernanos had sat at his feet, and he had never felt at home in the neo-Thomist cenacle at Meudon. He was even less at home with the democratic sentiments that now reigned there, for these had replaced the conservative influence of Clérissac and Garrigou-Lagrange. Yet for all his diatribes against Christian democracy, Bernanos was capable of the *amende honorable*. Something he had written to the detriment of Marc Sangnier had wounded Henri Guillemin, then Professor of French literature in Cairo. He assured Guillemin that he would ask his publisher to suppress the passage in any future edition of the book. Whether he liked it or not, the Christian democrats were in future to be Bernanos' surest allies, and we now find him at Meudon, with Maritain and Mauriac, testifying to what he had seen. His witness was irrefutable; and all the *Action Française* could say in reply to it was that he was now 'writing with his feet'. He would have preferred the reputation of writing with the soles of his feet to that of writing with the tips of his fingers.

In July Marcel Arland, in *La Nouvelle Revue Française*, hailed the achievement of *Mouchette*, shrewdly pointing out how the author had identified himself with his heroine.

Is it Bernanos speaking, or is it Mouchette? Rough and tender, often hasty, and sometimes confused, loud all of a sudden and yet concise, the voice that we hear – the voice of Bernanos and of Mouchette – is not quite an explanation or a commentary. It participates in the drama; it is an action in itself. And if it throws a light on the heroine which she could not have furnished for herself, I find the same astonishing lucidity in the heroines of Racine. It derives, no doubt, from the author, and no less deeply from the character.

The book sold more than 20,000 copies, and its success was eclipsed by *Les Grands Cimetières sous la lune* which detonated with predictable effect. When bishops and heads of religious orders demanded that the book be put on the Index, the Pope had no ears for them. Mgr. Fontenelle, the Rome correspondent of *La Croix* had written to Bernanos: 'Your book is the work of an *enfant terrible*, but I will confess that I am not frightened of *enfants terribles*,

and I am even rather fond of them.' The Monsignor had been asked
to take the book to the Secretariat of State. 'What will they think
of it? A bombshell, certainly, and its splinters will have caused some
pain, but the explosion is still beautiful.' 'It scorches, but it clears the
air' was the comment of Cardinal Pacelli. Bernanos was particularly
proud of the Monsignor's letter, and carried it about in his wallet to
Brazil and elsewhere. André Malraux, who had fought for the
Republicans, invited him to dinner and congratulated him on the
'inflexible sincerity' of the book. When Bernanos rejoined that
Malraux would have spoken with an equal sincerity, Malraux's
reply was disconcerting in its candour.

That is not the same thing. You are a Christian, and you act like a
Christian. I am a Communist, and I shall never write a word that might
cause the slightest injury to the party.[1]

'That is your affair,' said Bernanos, 'but in that case, what value
can I place on your congratulations?' Bernanos was to remember
this exchange when Malraux was no longer considered a Communist, and others were conducting the inquisitions of the party.

But the most remarkable tribute to *Les Grands Cimetières sous la
lune* came from Simone Weil. She did not know Bernanos, but she
had admired his books; and although she was not, and was never to
become, a Catholic, she wrote that 'nothing Catholic and nothing
Christian has ever seemed foreign to me.' Her instinctive sympathy
went out to the poor and dispossessed, but it was not until she
joined the anarchists in Spain that she found a grouping to which
she could happily belong.

They were an astonishing mixture, and admitted anyone into their ranks.
In consequence you saw immorality, cynicism, fanaticism, and cruelty
side by side; but there was also love, and the spirit of brotherhood, and
above all the sense of honour and its rights which is so fine a thing on the
part of men who have been humiliated. It seemed to me that those
inspired by an ideal came in greater numbers than those who were moved
by a taste for violence and disorder.

Simone Weil spent two months with the Republican forces in
Barcelona and on the Ebro, and returned completely disillusioned.

---

[1] Bernanos recorded this episode more than once, but Malraux states in his *Anti-
mémoires* that he had never been a member of the Communist party, although he
had fought beside the Communists in Spain.

I no longer felt any inner necessity to take part in a war which was no longer what it had seemed to me at the beginning, a war of famished peasants against landed proprietors and their clerical accomplices, but a war between Russia, Germany and Italy.[1]

She told Bernanos of the atrocities she had seen; she recognised in his book the odour of blood and terror mounting up from the soil of the country she had loved and thought to save; she described how her comrades took the death of the innocent in their stride; she gave examples of the priests shot without mercy; of the boys massacred. She had begun by believing in the Republicans, as Bernanos had once believed in the Nationalists; and like him, all she could see, as the conflict moved to its finale, were the vast cemeteries under the moon.

Of course the book was widely criticised, as well as voraciously read. When *Combat* – the successor to *Réaction* – published certain reservations, Bernanos stormed into the Brasserie Lipp where some members of the editorial board were dining. Brandishing his stick and talking at the top of his voice, he delivered a violent indictment of his own generation, while manager and waiters stood aghast, and the crockery trembled on the tables. No one hearing him would have been surprised to learn that the material consolations of success had failed to exorcise the adolescent dream of Paraguay. Bernanos was not the man to go back on his dreams, however capricious. He knew little of the country, but he still imagined that he could set up as a farmer, sustain his family, and write his books. It was often said that the shame of Munich drove him into exile, but this cannot have been true since he embarked on the *Florida* from Marseilles on the 20th of July 1938. Certainly he felt the shame acutely, and he must have sensed the disunity and demoralisation of France as soon as he returned from Majorca. It would be more exact to say that he was literally asphyxiated by the attitude of the Church to the civil war in Spain, and by the scorching memories he brought back from it.

I am ashamed of them [he wrote in *Scandale de la Vérité*], I am ashamed of myself, I am ashamed that we are so powerless – that we Christians are so shamefully powerless in face of the peril that threatens the world. Are we really the Church of Christ? The charnel-houses open their doors

[1] *Correspondance* II, p. 201

and we can't say a Yes or a No. The charnel-houses open their doors, and we think we have done our duty when we warn the junior curate to hurry along and jabber the absolutions in the afternoon, as he does for the funerals of the poor.[1]

If Bernanos wrote *Les Grands Cimetières sous la lune* to get the cemeteries out of his system, he had certainly failed to do so. He also felt that the only way he could preserve intact the image of the France he cherished was to absent himself from what she seemed to be in the way of becoming. This could be fairly criticised as escapism, but hardly as disengagement. It was the effect of an experience that few of his countrymen had shared; his friends had reason to regret his departure, but not to misjudge it. He was not to be sparing of his own judgments, as he sat writing under the Southern Cross.

He embarked with his wife, six children, and a friend – Dr Jean Benier – who was also accompanied by his family. Only a handful of friends were on the pier to see them off, and the journalists were fully occupied with the departure of Cécile Sorel. As the ship drew out into the channel, the silhouette of a friar in the white habit of the Dominican Order was seen with his arms raised wide in benediction. It was Raymond Brückberger speeding Bernanos on the first, and last, of his missionary journeys.

As if in answer to Père Brückberger's blessing, the boat anchored at Rio de Janeiro on the Feast of St Dominic, a fact of which Bernanos took grateful note. The crossing had been calm, except for two days of a tiring swell. Cécile Sorel had done her best to get herself introduced to Bernanos, but he had managed to avoid her. At Rio she disappeared in a haze of publicity. The journalists were also interested in Bernanos, and he treated them to various incendiary declarations. The poet Auguste Frédéric Schmidt and Amoroso Lima, a philosopher and influential member of Catholic Action, came aboard to welcome him and invite him to luncheon at Copacabana. He was heartened by the warmth of their greeting.

Proceeding to Buenos Aires he lectured for Victoria Ocampo, the editor of *Sūr*, and then, on the 16th of August, sailed up the Parana River in a paddle steamer, with the crocodiles drowsy on either bank. Dr Benier was waiting for him in Asunción, where their dreams were quickly dispelled. The country was exhausted by the Chaco war with Bolivia; the climate was atrocious; and an abortive

[1] *Scandale de la Vérité* (1939), pp. 69-70

expedition held out no prospects of subsistence farming. Bernanos had set out for the Promised Land only to discover one of the most unpromising countries on earth.

He remained in Paraguay for only ten days, and then decided to return to Rio, encouraged by the welcome he had been given there. He arrived on the 1st of September, putting up for a few days at the Botafogo Hotel overlooking the bay, and then moving to a smaller house at Itaipara high above the city. It belonged to a French aviator. The beauty of Rio was overwhelming; it surpassed any idea he had conceived of it; and he was woken each morning by strange birds, mewing like cats. Only twenty minutes ride beyond the city, the tramway crossed the impassable forest with its smell of rotting leaves and stagnant pools, reminiscent of the countryside in France at the fag-end of the year.

The news of the Munich agreement came to sear Bernanos as bitterly as the cemeteries under the Majorcan moon. Even the most Francophil newspapers were crushing to read. In these hours of humiliation he was sustained by the friendship of Amoroso Lima, who introduced him to Virgilio de Mello Franco, brother of the Brazilian ambassador in Paris. Virgilio had the impression of a 'biblical exodus', as various plans for the family were discussed. All Bernanos wanted was a *fazenda*, which would benefit from his literary earnings and where two of his sons could learn a little about agriculture. They had not, it seems, shown much aptitude for learning about anything else. Bernanos' nephew, Guy Hattu, joined the party in December, and they all set out for Juiz de Fora in the state of Minas Gerais. Here, with five horses to feed and look after, as well as to ride, and the rain, wind and mud to contend with, Bernanos felt very close to the soil. The word 'home' was beginning to mean something.

The euphoria was short-lived. Although the place had been lent to them, servants had to be paid for and food to be bought. There was running water, but it ran according to its own sweet will, and the bathroom was a quagmire. It would have been much cheaper to rent a more habitable house, and in February 1939 – after declining the Légion d'Honneur for the third time – Bernanos moved to a little farm, further to the south, at Vassouras. Here there was land that could be made productive. three cows, six pigs, seven horses, and the rudimentary necessities of life. But within doors the picture was less encouraging. The house was virtually unfurnished, with nothing on the walls and no carpets on the floors. For twelve large rooms there were only two cupboards, three chests of drawers, a few tables and chairs, six beds and five mattresses. Even the two cases of *eau-de-vie*, which supported one of them, were empty. Bernanos was forced to do his writing from a ruined shanty where he was visited by enormous lizards. The place was so small that it was difficult to enter it without hitting one's head against the lintel, and once the table and chair were in position there was scarcely an inch of space. It was in this primitive *cabinet de travail*, and in the midst of a 'hard, inhuman, silence', that Bernanos completed *Nous autres Français*.

There was a Salesian mission at Vassouras, and Yves Bernanos, armed with a repeater carbine and a Colt revolver, left with one of the Fathers and five converts for a six months stay on the Rio das Mortes, utterly remote from civilisation. The Indians in the country around Vassouras made themselves very scarce – only visible, now and then, when they came to barter their gifts.

In July of the same year the caravan moved again to Pirapora – 1,200 kilometres to the north on the banks of the São Francisco River, and at the mouth of the *sertão*. Mello Franco had large properties in the state, and he advised Bernanos to rent some pasture, buy some lean cattle, and fatten them for market. A bullock could be bought for 200 francs and sold at double the price. Mello Franco was on the point of buying 6,000 of them, and a small number of these he would sell to Bernanos for what they had cost him. He also owned the company which navigated the São Francisco – which would greatly facilitate their transport. Such money as Bernanos had brought with him was inadequate to buy a *fazenda;* so he leased instead what he required at San Antonio – eighteen kilometres from Pirapora – and bought 200 head of cattle, with a few saddle-horses. While he was waiting for the *fazenda* to be made habitable, he stayed at the Hotel Internaçional in Pirapora, and it was here that he wrote *Scandale de la Vérité*.

This was intended as the preface to a collection of extracts from Drumont, but his publisher – Gallimard – judged the moment hardly propitious to recall the author of *La France Juive* to the memory of a public outraged by the Nazi persecution of the Jews. The pamphlet, as it stands, is little more than a postscript to *Les Grands*

Cimetières sous la lune. Bernanos wrote it in two months, working eight hours a day in a rented house 'grated by the sun, without water or furniture, where we were sleeping more or less one on top of another and virtually eating off our knees.'[1] It repeats a great deal of what he had said before, and would say again. It was also the first public explanation of his exile.

To those who ask why I have left my own country for Brazil, I can say that I came here to cover my shame. Some people are overcome by shame; others it reduces to despair; and I am one of them. I want to go on writing, and to witness on behalf of what I love. And I know very well that shame and disgust would have reduced me to impotence, or to the hatred which is impotence in its pure and demoniacal form. . . . From this distance, among the sincere friends of my country, the *diktat* of Munich appears to me in its true colours – a macabre farce, but still a farce, one of those events that can have no root in our history – a kind of miscarriage, where France was raped in her sleep by blackguards in the corner of a wood.[2]

The first of his *bêtes noires* is Maurras, whose recent election to the Académie had enraged him. How could a man who for fifty years had declared war on the Establishment now solicit its accolade? And by what right did he speak in the name of the French tradition

when he remains willingly a stranger to what is for us the most precious part of our national heritage, the Christian tradition of France, the Christianity the French have made? We readily express our gratitude for the respect with which he speaks of France and of the Church, but when he claims to serve them, let him serve them from his own rank, which is not ours. He can no more claim to absorb the cult of the Fatherland in his brand of nationalism than his master Auguste Comte to absorb the cult of the Blessed Virgin in his religion of positivism. For us the France of Maurras is as empty and hollow as his Catholicism without Christ, his Catholic 'order' without grace. This is not the country that we honour; this is not the France of Chartres.[3]

Bernanos' second *bête noire* was Mussolini, whose demands upon 'Corsica, Tunisia, and Nice' had not deterred Maurras from a slavish support of his policies.

When M. Mussolini owes so much of his credit with the population of

---

[1] To Christiane Manificat, November 1939: *Correspondance* II, p. 273
[2] *Scandale de la Vérité*, pp. 73–4   [3] Ibid, p. 17

Norman bastards, Lombards, and Levantines that he rules, by an appeal to its fabulous Roman origins and the majesty of the Roman Empire, why should we renounce the Christian vocation of France?[1]

It was his very attachment to the monarchy that made Bernanos so anxious to save it from Maurras. When the theorists of the Action Française quoted Louis XIV's '*L'Etat, c'est moi*', Bernanos reminded them that he also spoke about '*mon peuple*' – and not one of these cynical realists would have the effrontery to speak of the French people as being 'theirs' in any sense whatever. The *Roi Soleil* had spoken of 'my people' as he might have spoken about 'my conscience' – for they were in fact his conscience, and just as he answered for the State before the people, he answered for the people before God.

There are several long quotations from Péguy in *Scandale de la Vérité* – all of them from *Notre Jeunesse*. Bernanos did not realise, or at least he could never admit, a certain contradiction in his dual attachment to Péguy and to Drumont – for the *Dreyfusisme* of the one was at mortal odds with the anti-Semitism of the other. What mattered to him was that both were men of flesh and blood, where Maurras was a man of brains. When Péguy spoke of the 'intellectual party', he was referring to the anti-clericals of the Chambre des Députés and the Sorbonne – to the transformation of the Dreyfusard *mystique* into the *politique* of those who had turned it to their own advantage. Bernanos drew an analogy between Maurras and Jaures; both were professors who mistook themselves for politicians. He was to write to a Brazilian friend[2] of the need 'to liberate the Intelligence from the exploitation of the Intellectuals'. Men like Péguy and Drumont had nothing in common with those in France who now claimed to represent the Right, and who clung to the intellectual coat-tails of Maurras, as Maurras clung with an abject submission to the opportunism of Mussolini. Péguy and Drumont were heirs to the men of 1798, and to the Communards of 1870; Maurras stood in the posterity of Robespierre, little as he would have cared to admit it. So did Mussolini; Bernanos had not forgotten the accomplished terrorist who was 'neither general, nor count, nor Rossi'. He did not allow his readers to forget him either.

By what right does M. Maurras appropriate Proudhon? By what right

---

[1] *Scandale de la Vérité*, p. 18   [2] Alvaro Lins

does the heir to the centralising legists of former times – who only a few months ago was presenting his respects to the executioner of Catalonia and the Basques – claim as his reference the liberties which monarchy bestows? There is nothing more foreign to our traditions than dictatorship, and M. Maurras has done more than anyone else to create a Mussolinian *mystique* among our people on the Right.[1]

Meanwhile the *Action Française* was busily informing its readers that Bernanos had bought a magnificent house in Rio, and was earning enormous sums of money by lecturing on the folk-songs of his native country. The inventive genius, which no one had ever denied to the *Action Française*, must have curiously deserted it.

Both in Spain and in Italy the Church was the spiritual buttress of Fascism, and it was a little late for Pius XI to speak to Hitler *mit brennender Sorge* when he had publicly expressed his satisfaction with the Abyssinian conquest. Bernanos spared the Pope, but not his curia:

In a few months from now, and in face of the immense ordeal which awaits the world, any one of these astute little Monsignori diplomats, for example, with his fat fingers and cunning smile, may well seem as incongruous a figure in the Church as he would have appeared in the time of St Peter. You may persuade me to tolerate the existence of these intermediaries for the sake of the Church's temporal needs, but you would not dare forbid me to look forward to the day when they will have become useless parasites, easy to dispense with. 'But these Monsignori are officials of the Church.' No doubt they are: and we poor devils, believers or unbelievers, are precisely the world with which the eternal Church employs them to negotiate. That is why we have a perfect right to express our opinion about negotiators who exist for our convenience. We do not find them in the least attractive, and we find them even less convincing. What purpose do they serve? None whatever.[2]

If Bernanos had ever set eyes on Angelo Roncalli he would hardly have guessed how far this 'Monsignore diplomat with his fat fingers' would go in restoring a more apostolic image to the Papacy. People were not always quite so bad as Bernanos painted them. In an article otherwise friendly, appearing in *Temps Présent*, Pierre-Henri Simon accused him of generalising too freely in his attacks on the clergy, although Simon did not dispute the evidence he had brought back

[1] *Scandale de la Vérité*, p. 43   [2] Ibid, p. 61

from Majorca. Bernanos replied that three professors of theology had examined and approved his manuscript.

The Comtesse de Paris and her children had come to Brazil, and Bernanos met them in Petropolis. He wrote to her, discreetly, of the opportunities that future events might offer to her husband. Not even the restoration of the House of France would have seemed more improbable than the catastrophe now in preparation; and Bernanos confided some of his more intimate feelings to one whom he relied upon to serve, if not to rule. In doing so he was paying homage to an *idée de la France* which few, perhaps, even of his warmest admirers may have shared. *Scandale de la Vérité* was his last word to them. He described it as a *grand cri*. On the 3rd of September he was still living at Pirapora, having moved to a house where the most elementary conveniences were lacking. Dr Benier was at his side, listening to the news in a café. Suddenly the *Marseillaise* came over the radio, and all the customers stood up, moved by a spontaneous impulse of sympathy. They were looking at the two Frenchmen for as long as the anthem lasted, but Bernanos was looking at the thoughts in his own mind.

CHAPTER 11

HOPE AND HUMILIATION

I

B Y November 1939 Bernanos was in occupation of the *fazenda* of San Antonio. His nephew, Guy Hattu, had received his mobilisation papers and left for North Africa on the 15th of January 1940. Dr Benier also returned to Europe, leaving his wife and family behind. Yves had come back from the Matto Grosso with a severe attack of fever. He and Michel, his younger brother, were responsible for pastures spread over 5,000 acres – clearings in the forest – with cows giving birth to their calves in disconcerting secrecy. The calves were attacked by the wild cats, almost as large as leopards, and the cows looked more like zebras, with a hump on their backs, galloping like horses and jumping over fences several feet high. Claude Bernanos, assisted by a pair of half-castes, cooked the meals for fifteen or twenty people; smoked meat, rice in place of bread, black beans, and tepid water from Rio. And Jean-Loup had a little horse which he had christened 'Fleur-de-Dieu'. Bernanos himself rarely went in to Pirapora, since the journey would cost him a day's work.

He was getting used to the house of chalk and clay, and the bats swarming in the roof; to the *va-et-vient* of settlers and cowherds, coming at all hours to sell a couple of chickens or buy a bottle of medicine; to the everlasting lowing of the cattle, and the Negroes, ubiquitous and obese. It was not, he concluded, such a bad life for anyone. But although Bernanos had never found the coming and going of other people a hindrance to his pen, these were not the faces to find their way, no matter how transposed, into a novel. Besides, he was not writing a novel, but a Journal. Its fate was dramatic. In January 1940, he gave his only copy to the poet, Henri Michaux, who was returning to France. The *Nouvelle Revue Française* published the first pages in its issue of the 1st of May, but after that the NRF, like a good many other things in France, changed hands. The manuscript, however, had been entrusted to Père

Brückberger, then serving on the Saar front; he in turn lent it to a
superior officer whose belongings disappeared during the retreat.
They were rediscovered only in 1948. Bernanos, already mortally
ill in Tunisia, re-read the text which he had forgotten, made a few
corrections, and gave it to his publisher. It appeared after his death.
He had not given it a title: *Les Enfants humiliés* was a phrase taken
from the Journal, and chosen by Gallimard. It expressed a theme
constant in the author's writing before, during, and after the Second
World War. He had never been so close to France, and never so far
away from it.

Every evening I shut this notebook, resolved not to open it again – at
least for a long time. And each morning I come back and seat myself in
the fast retreating shade of the wall, under a withered mango tree. The
fruit hangs from the end of a dead stem, and drops one by one, bouncing
on the hard soil. Opposite me is another wall, stained with bright patches,
scaled, peeled, and grated by the sun, stricken by that solar itch, which I
shall always take as the almost abstract sign of extreme poverty – a
poverty without hope or remedy. At the end of this little courtyard, only
sixty feet wide, the heat lies in successive, horizontal layers, like still
water, and of unequal temperature. The faint breeze pushes it slowly
towards the flaming canal of the road, and the road rolls back towards
the liquid stream another rivulet of burning air. The leaf fallen from the
tree already snaps in one's finger, breaks like glass, and by the end of the
day you can hardly distinguish it from the other refuse, for the sun makes
everything equal and its austere dung-heaps, without colour or smell, are
more dismal than the most disgusting products of rain, snow, and mud.
Out of a corner of sordid earth, a leprous little courtyard open to an
apparently inflexible sky which the approach of evening turns suddenly
to green, it creates a patch of solitude, as if the unchanging heat and light
concentrated all life at a fixed point, in a strange equilibrium which gives
one the illusion – or perhaps the reality – of silence, while behind my
back – as usual, as always, my friends – cries, arguments, and insults
reverberate in three languages. The eccentric parrots gravely answer
them – great clowns they look like, painted in yellow, blue, scarlet, and
Veronese green, and they make the black vultures with their scaly heads
dance nervously from one foot to the other. . . . I draw the table closer
to me, I prop myself against the back of the chair and the back of the
chair against the wall, because I know that I shall not have this spot of the
shade for long, and that I shall have to change it presently for another
spot even more unhealthy, under a tree riddled with holes like a sieve. I
did not choose this place, and it was not forced upon me either. I drag

myself along easily on my two sticks – that's all. The time is past for me to go any further – and where should I go? All that matters at my age is not to go back any more . . . and now, caught as I am between the table and the wall, I am certain not to retreat an inch. So I stretch out my hand towards my notebook, because there is nothing else I can do, nothing else I can take hold of; otherwise it would close upon the void. Anywhere else but in this country, which is absolutely foreign to my soul, I should be tempted to put off writing until tomorrow. But I am too recent an exile, and I have not yet succeeded in making for myself a new tomorrow – could I, one day, make myself a tomorrow in Brazil? Is it possible? My tomorrow is still a French tomorrow; it has the colour and the smell of the mornings I knew as a child, and it can be of no use to me here. My time, here, is as limited as the shade.[1]

Yes, it was quite possible. Many people believed that if Bernanos had lived, he would have returned to make his home in Brazil; but for the moment he was far from the friends in Rio who expected of France what he expected of her himself. The war had come to find him

in the middle of the Brazilian *sertão*, on the banks of an enormous river. I don't know where it comes from, and it probably goes nowhere. It flows for the sake of flowing, rolls along for the sake of rolling, for thousands of miles – league upon square league of earth – one can't tell whether the soil is rich or poor, or where a stake turns into a tree or a tree into a stake, according to the hour or the season. But why talk about times and seasons? Dryness and humidity divide the year between them. Now the wandering cattle grow fat, and now they grow lean and die, buried up to their bellies in the venomous grass which the chemical Furies of the Sun turn into a matter that no beast can feed upon, into a kind of mineral poison. I don't hate this country, and I can't say that I love it. I should love it if it could love me, if it was capable of the exchange to which our lands in the old world have accustomed us. But then we have given them everything, whereas this country has received nothing of anybody. For centuries it has done nothing but chew the cud of its hunger and thirst, waiting for the daily companionship of man, his smile and his caress. How we have caressed our own! . . . Each square inch of French soil has no doubt been paid for by the life of a man; but this huge, uncultivated land, where mere municipalities are as big as a State and provinces as large as a continent, has assuredly not drunk, in the course of centuries, much more blood than a single one of our rich, free, cities.

[1] *Les Enfants humiliés*, pp. 105–8

When it has made men suffer enough, and when men have suffered enough on its behalf and at its hands, they will understand its language, or give it their own; but, thank God, it does not speak as yet, and one does not even feel inclined to engage it in conversation. This perpetual silence adds to one's perpetual astonishment, but in the long run it weighs more heavily than you think. Before I felt it, I would never have believed that our French countryside was so talkative. Our smallest village, if you race through it on a motor-cycle at eighty kilometres an hour, fills your ears with a murmur which is partly tender and partly gay and partly mocking; it follows you for a long while; and in the evening, when your head is on the pillow, it's still humming in your head. Here there is nothing like that. After twenty leagues on horseback, if anything is humming in your head, it is useless to ask this unintelligible confidence for a meaning. You've narrowly escaped a sunstroke. Take an aspirin and sleep.[1]

The São Francisco River rises just to the north of the great lakes at the southern part of Minas Gerais. It flows directly north through fairly hilly country and is joined, a few miles beyond Pirapora, by the Velhas. It then flows north again for thousands of miles until it turns east and falls into the sea halfway between Salvador and Recife. It was upon this thread that hung suspended the dialogue of Georges Bernanos with a nature more monstrous than any landscape he had ever known. Forced by chance and necessity into a retreat more rigorous than any monastery could have offered him, he turned – antiphonally, so to speak – from the war in whose reality he did not believe – with reason, for it was still the *drôle de guerre* – to the implacable forest, more hostile to the little band of exiles than the armies, inactive behind the Maginot and Siegfried lines, then appeared to one another. It was

the dwarf forest, not its splendid equatorial rival with its tall trees; the dwarf, which infallibly recovers what it has lost, encircling the villages until it crushes them like glass. Even over there, to the west, it defeated the patience and skill of the Jesuit colonisers. I can imagine the expression on the face of a friend, suddenly transported here from the clearings in the forest of Fontainebleau, and having seen nothing on the way, if he woke up one morning in face of this horizon without a single landmark, this billowing infinity of peaceful green where there is no hint of a skeleton underneath, and where the smallest spur of rock stands out like the spire of a village church. 'Ah! look at the brushwood,' he would say.

[1] *Les Enfants humiliés*, pp. 109–11

But it is not the brushwood; it is the martyred and suffering forest, the waterless forest, dying of thirst for six months of the year to the distant grumbling of streams and cataracts. Any good fellow, at his table in the dear old Brasserie Lipp, who looks through the window at the darkened tarmac of the Place Saint-Germain des Près, bitterly sorry to have left his mackintosh behind, can have no idea of what it is like when the rain falls over here.... As I listened to it ringing on the roof, the familiar picture of a bursting cloud never once came into my mind. I thought, rather, of a river majestically flowing on its way, or again of a great liquid arch between earth and sky. It was peace and pardon and reconciliation and universal remission, a night within night, a sleep deeper and sweeter than the sleep we know. And yet I knew very well that it would bring no salvation to this country, that it would even less bring repose and sleep. It would not straighten in two months the twisted forest, or loosen its deformed and contracted limbs and its knotted joints. It would only turn these hardened cripples into monsters more powerful than any athlete from the forests of France. Their wood blunts the steel of the axe; fire blackens but does not kill them; they pump up their own cinders from the roots and transform them into sap which suddenly breaks out into green buds of an inexpressible purity and freshness.... Yes, I really think I know what I could say about this country to my friends, over a fire of cuttings from the vine, some clear winter evening in Provence.... I now feel I have the right to speak about it because our destinies, our effort, and our poverty are humbly linked together. I no longer regard it from without, I am now inside. I have left the railway behind me, and seen it disappear like a thin steel trap under the parasite vegetation. I have seen the last station and the last bridge. In front of me, to right or left, the squat trees creep and creep for thousands of leagues towards the Matto Grosso, Paraguay, the Amazon, and even beyond, to the shores of the Pacific.[1]

It is tempting to multiply quotations from *Les Enfants humiliés*, even in a translation that cannot hope to recover the extraordinary richness of the original. Nowhere else were the descriptive powers of Bernanos deployed to such accurate and emotional effect. The thing seen is made one with the man who sees it, without any blurring of shape or colour. Past and present, sensation, thought, and memory, are wonderfully fused. The controversial issues of the war into which Bernanos was later, and often recklessly, to plunge have little place in it. The opening sentence gives the key: 'We are going back into war, and it is like returning to the house we knew

[1] Ibid, pp. 65–7

G.B.–N

when we were young.' The book is a retrospect rather than a commentary; less a polemic than a meditation, conceived in the 'heart of darkness'. There are the old tilts against the modernism which would 'substitute for dogmas and ceremonies an elegant symbolism capable of rallying to traditional beliefs the most distinguished minds'.[1] There was a radio station at Bello Horizonte, 400 kilometres away, but Bernanos conceived a distaste for the 'sexless' voices – the only contact he had with the outside world – all speaking 'in the same tone of false cordiality, false emotion, false candour, feigned indignation and sharp impertinence, recalling irresistibly the face of a lady of a certain age in discussion with her son-in-law.'[2] He reminded the propagandists of 'order' that it was their business 'to settle problems, not to prevent one from stating them';[3] and he made a distinction between the State and the Fatherland, for 'naturally no man in his senses would treat the State as a comrade'. He took a long look back to the disillusionment of the *après-guerre* when 'justice had Briand for its advocate, and hatred went by the name of Maurras, the empty threat and the empty word.' Bernanos speaks of the 'mistakes and misdoings' of those men and women who, like himself, were possessed by the demon of the Absolute, and he prays that the 'hard sun may dry up in me all the springs of bitterness'. But it was not in the *sertão* of Brazil that his prayer was eventually to be answered.

2[4]

In February Yves was suffering from a severe attack of hæmotypsis, but Michel had succeeded in mastering the recalcitrant cattle. To relieve the monotony of writing Bernanos had taken to painting, although of this recreation only a single landscape of Pirapora survives. He had already abandoned the dream of writing his books without depending on his publisher for the necessities of life. If he had realised the difficulties he might not have come so far for so little, but since he was there he would stay. The resolution, however, was short-lived. The last three months of summer, after the departure of Guy Hattu, had placed an unbearable strain on Claude and Michel,

---

[1] *Les Enfants humiliés*, p. 126   [2] Ibid   [3] Ibid, p. 84
[4] For much of the information in this section I am indebted to the article by Geraldo Franco de Lima in *Bernanos no Brasil*.

and by the middle of April Bernanos was thinking of moving to Minas Gerais, among the great forests, on a plateau 3,000 feet above sea level.

In the meantime he completed, on the 10th of May, the last chapter of *Monsieur Ouine* – which had occupied him for the best part of four months. He placed little hope in the diplomatic activities of the Pope; they merely seemed to him quite natural, since Pius XII was a professional diplomat. He was not impressed by the report that the Pope slept on the floor; such reports got abroad, he thought, only by permission of the interested party. Without casting any aspersion on the personal holiness of Pius XII, Bernanos could never forget that he had been elected under the shadow of the Palazzo Venezia. Then, in May, came the news that Corap's ninth army had been broken on the Meuse. Bernanos, still at Pirapora, wrote in agony to Mello Franco: and also with some shred of hope that the nightmare would have an end. After all, one did not master a country like France with 'rope-dancing parachutists' and tanks roaming the Pas-de-Calais at thirty kilometres an hour.

That, however, was precisely what one did. Bernanos did not expect the millions of square kilometres of forest which surrounded him to show much concern for the fate of Chartres Cathedral, but he knew that among his friends in the cities of Brazil he would find something of the human sympathy he was missing. On the 21st of May Yves received his mobilisation orders, but he was in no state of health, as yet, to comply with them.

Bernanos was still at San Antonio when a nasal voice on the radio announced that the swastika was flying over Notre Dame, but it was only later, in a railway carriage, that the full horror of humiliation was brought home to him. The other passengers, seeing that he was French, spoke in lowered voices, and he seemed to read on their faces a conclusion that the war was lost. But then they turned to him and reiterated the only words that he wished to hear: 'England will hold out, England will hold out.' This meant that the war would not finally be lost for France, and for Bernanos the honour of his country and his flesh and blood rested for a moment in the custody of these sympathetic strangers who would presently return to their work and pleasures. They would never know what reassurance they had given him at a time when he had never needed it so much.

He now resigned himself to the loss of three years' rent, paid in advance, and of twenty head of cattle which disappeared at the last moment with the man who was looking after them. He learnt afterwards that the subsequent owner had discovered gold on the property, and he thanked the Providence which had preserved him from temptation. He left San Antonio in June; sold what remained of his herd; returned to Rio; stayed for a time at Bello Horizonte, where the passers-by wept openly in the streets at the news of the French capitulation; and then at a hotel in Barbacena. From here he sent regular articles to the Brazilian press, notably to *O Journal*, which was under the control of Assis Châteaubriand, Dario de Magalhaes, and Austregesilo de Athayde. One cold afternoon in July a young Brazilian writer, Geraldo Franco de Lima, was sitting on a bench in the public gardens, reading the *Mercure de France* and making the most of the thin sunshine. Presently a corpulent figure, leaning on two sticks, approached him and sat down at his side.

Seeing that I had stopped reading, he said: 'Forgive me, I'm disturbing you.' I shut the magazine and was about to say something when he exclaimed: 'Ah! my poor *Mercure*! Allow me.' He took it from me and stared at it as if it were a piece of French soil. I simply followed his gestures, and observed the contractions and workings of his face. Who could it be? 'Since they love France and speak French in Brazil, one feels at home. My poor, unhappy France!' Perceiving something grand and passionate in that masculine figure, I felt too shy to say anything. Yet I was about to open conversation with what French I could then muster, when the fabulous presence opened the floodgates of its eloquence and began to shout aloud. . . . He started to curse, and how well he cursed! With what precision, energy, and grace! It was magnificent. He was overwhelming, sublime: an angel, sword in hand, choking the conspiracy of evil. Then the storm abated, the waters became calm again, the smoke of the explosion dispersed and gave way to the murmur of a profound lament. 'France has been betrayed, but all that will pass.' Then he asked softly: 'Do you speak French, sir?' 'Yes, I speak it a little.' He held out his hand and introduced himself: 'Bernanos – Georges Bernanos. *Enchanté*.' Never, no matter how hard I try, shall I be able to express what I felt. Perhaps the emotion of that moment was so strong that it has destroyed my power to recapture the glory of it. 'But you're trembling, my friend.' 'Yes, sir, I was dying to make your acquaintance.'[1]

They were staying at the same hotel, and the next day they both

[1] Geraldo Franco de Lima, *Bernanos no Brasil*

lunched with Virgilio de Mello Franco, with whom they toured the locality 'to find a small refuge for a great bitterness'. Bernanos was difficult to please. He had practically no money; yet he demanded a wood and a little spring. At last they heard of a small villa for sale, with three acres, on the top of a hill overlooking the town, and close to one of Mello Franco's own farms. There was a stream which flowed into a pond and a patch of dense woodland. But none of this appealed to Bernanos until he was told the name of the place: *Cruz das Almas*. Then his face lit up and he decided to take it. The formalities of the sale were arranged through Mello Franco and Franco de Lima; and although Bernanos spent everything he earned, he insisted on a strict accounting of every *conto* paid out in his name. The refitting of the house both excited and irritated him a good deal.

Barbacena was little more than 200 kilometres to the north of Rio – an eight-hour journey by train – on the plateau between two tributaries of the River Mortes. It was still in Minas Gerais, and Bernanos was to admit later: 'In order to become a little bit of a Brazilian, I first of all became a *mineiro*. I tried to root myself somewhere – and one can't root oneself on a railway line.'[1] The house stood at the end of a side road, surrounded by lean and deserted pastures. With various out-buildings, joined by connecting walls, it took on the appearance of a French farm, and Jeanne Bernanos filled it with pleasant furniture. The open door disclosed a statue of the Blessed Virgin in a niche, and the tricolour with the Cross of Lorraine – for Bernanos was quick to declare his adherence to de Gaulle. The stables and barns were converted to family use, and a kind of turret served as quarters for Bernanos and his wife. He occupied the lower part of this, a square room which gave one the impression of a crypt or a catacomb, since you were obliged to descend two steps to enter it. Here he slept, wrote, and studied. A camp bed stood along one of the walls, and on the table was a half-broken crucifix from which he refused to be parted, and a couple of school notebooks. One of these he used for the first version of whatever he was at work on, and the second for the fair copy. This was made immediately, since his handwriting was difficult to decipher, even for himself, complicated as it was by the drastic revision to which his tumultuous feeling, allied to his care for

[1] To Virgilio de Mello Franco: *Cahiers de L'Herne*

language, compelled him. From the window one saw the line of hills stretching to the white fringe of Barbacena.

Bernanos was now within easier reach of his friends in Rio – intellectuals, for the most part, who shared his view of the war as it developed. There was also a Benedictine monastery on the outskirts of Rio, and one of the monks, Dom Paul Gordan, a native of Germany, became his confessor. Almost for the first time in his life, since he had married, Bernanos had what he could call a home. Only at Fressin and at Cruz das Almas is there now a plaque to tell us that he once lived there – and the house at Fressin has been demolished. He remained at Cruz das Almas for five years, longer than he had stayed anywhere before; and when he left it he was to become, once again, a wanderer.

He was not always easy to approach; Cruz das Almas acquired the reputation of a sanctuary or a lion's den, according to the way he looked at you. An Englishwoman, who had trekked up to Barbacena to protest against Bernanos' criticism of Allied war policy, found herself shown the door without ceremony. On the 7th of September 1940, a British diplomat sought him out, and found him smarting from the refusal of the British Government to accord immediate recognition to the French National Committee. To cap a pretty rough conversation Bernanos exclaimed: 'My dear diplomat, in a year from now you will see Germany invading Russia.' The diplomat laughed; such an idea was inconceivable. Bernanos shouted in reply: 'My dear friend, you are an imbecile' – and then, very slowly, repeated the word, syllable by syllable. 'Im-be-cile.' The visitor, faithful to the tenets of his profession, declined to be ruffled, merely answering: *Comme vous êtes aimable*! When Germany did invade Russia he sent Bernanos a telegram of congratulation.

On another occasion a fellow-exile, who had an immense fortune in France, was bold enough to stand up to Bernanos in defence of Pétain. He was missing his young wife, he said, who had remained in Paris instead of joining him in Rio. Bernanos, having listened quietly, now exploded: 'Your wife will not come, I am quite sure of that. She is betraying you with the *Boches*. Go and look for her. *A bientôt!*' – and he turned the man out of the house. Stefan Zweig, who descended unexpectedly at Cruz das Almas, had a very different reception. A sad and broken man, Bernanos received him with immense courtesy and kindliness, asking him to stay with him for a few days, and inviting him to join in a world-wide protest against Hitler's persecution of the Jews. He escorted him back to the town hall, and saw that he was made an official guest of the municipality. Not even the war distracted Bernanos from an interest in local affairs. He followed the fortunes of the football clubs, and the vendettas of municipal politics. To the German Fathers of the Divine Word, who had a chapel in the town, he allowed no quarter, regarding them one and all as agents of the Gestapo. Even the parish priest, a man of deep piety and a proclaimed Francophil, met the edge of his intransigence. Passing the presbytery one night, he observed a red lantern hanging from the eaves, and requested Franco de Lima, who was with him, to ask the priest either to remove the lantern or to change its colour. Knowing the priest to be a man of some obstinacy, Franco de Lima hesitated to undertake so delicate a mission. Bernanos grew exasperated; the little red light became an immediate obsession. At last he sent a message through one of his daughters – hardly a suitable emissary. To this there was no reply and none to the message that followed it. Only when Bernanos spelt out his objection in plain and peremptory French – that the red light suggested a brothel rather than a presbytery – was the lantern removed.

He had his own circle of friends in Barbacena; the Mineiro poet, Honorio Armand, whose verses in French he knew and could recite by heart; his doctor, Galdino Abranches, who was also an amateur of philosophy; M. Brut, a French radical who had a textile factory in the town; and Dr Paulo da Rocha Lagoa, for whose scientific erudition he expressed his gratitude on the fly-leaf of one of his own works. Bernanos would spend hours in a café helping students with a French syllabus, for he believed that if anyone could save the world it would be the young. On one occasion Franco de Lima found him weeping with emotion. He had been riding by on his horse when a coloured newspaper boy ran up beside him, signalling him to stop. Opening the *Correio da Manha* he pointed to the headline of an article by Alvaro Lins: 'Homage to Bernanos.' The subject of the article was more impressed by this interest on the part of a semi-literate youngster than by an offer of the Légion d'Honneur, which he had already three times refused and was to refuse again.

If he was sometimes referred to as the 'hermit of Cruz das Almas', it was because he resented intrusion as much as he enjoyed society. Two Brazilian writers, having announced their visit at an inconvenient time, perceived Jean-Loup acting the role of Cerberus and overheard him crying out, as he ran into the house: 'Papa, Papa, these idiots of yours have arrived.' Two years before, the same efficient watch-dog, seeing a Franciscan look inquisitively at the houses next door to where the family were then living – presumably at Toulon – asked him whom he was looking for. On learning that he was looking for Bernanos, Jean-Loup replied: 'But you know, sir, my father is not fond of the clergy.' Many of the clergy, in Brazil as in France, were no fonder of Bernanos; and in more than one diocese it was rash to mention his name. Dom Gordan, however, was not deterred from seeking an interview, and after an exchange of telegrams this was arranged.

He dismounted painfully from his high saddle, and came towards us in his top boots, dressed in a shirt and grey riding-breeches, carrying a broad-rimmed hat and supporting himself on two sticks. He embraced us, and, talking volubly all the time, he led us into the hall, gesticulating and asking us questions without ever waiting for a reply. Before I had properly understood why he broached the subject, he burst out into a vehement tirade against the Action Française . . . speaking with fire, but not at all unfairly. His eloquence was pathetic, roused as it was by his passion for justice, but without any trace of play acting. Everything about this man was spontaneous; and in his blue eyes with their heavy pockets, in his strong, sun-tanned face under the smooth and greying hair, you could read the most subtle reflection of his interior life. I fell at once under the sway of his whole personality and we had hardly exchanged more than a few words before contact was already established. . . .

When night fell and we wanted to be going, he came up to me and asked me, with an insistent simplicity, to stay with him. No doubt he had seen that I had been moved by what he said. Without a single word of a personal kind having passed between us, deep links had been forged and they were never to be relaxed. After the other guests had gone we spent half the night together. In the morning, which was a Sunday, I had the joy of celebrating Mass in his house, and he served it himself with a touching simplicity. A table had been turned into an altar, with the Cross of Lorraine above it. . . . I prolonged this first visit for a whole day before returning to Rio.

In a subsequent letter to a friend Dom Gordan summed up his impressions:

His instinct is so sure, his intuition so marvellous, and his conscience so prodigiously sensitive that one doesn't know how to speak about it. . . . He literally trembles with anger in every limb – and one trembles with him – when he speaks of corruption, mediocrity, or untruth. This 'anti-clerical' pamphleteer . . . loves the Church with a deep, unshakable, attachment, and the thunder of his voice becomes as sweet as music when he talks about the humanity of Our Lord, or of the saints who had the spirit of childhood, Jeanne d'Arc and Saint Thérèse of the Child Jesus. One unforgettable picture I took away with me. We had returned to his 'crypt', and he was lying on his bed. I was sitting in front of him on the only chair, and he was trying to define what, in his eyes, was the mission of France. This was difficult for him, because he was afraid that a German would not spontaneously understand him, and he was struggling to find the clearest and most acceptable formula. If I said that, for him, the mission of France was to proclaim the Humanity of God, the Incarnation of Christ, I should only be giving a crude outline of his thought. But in the vision that he gave of it, the words of incarnation and divine humanity took on an extraordinary intensity and a strangely complete significance. This excited his anger and contempt when the authenticity of human beings was under attack, whether by some philosophy, or by science enslaved to technique. This inspired his respect and his deep love for the poor. So I had no difficulty, when he had finished talking about France, in understanding him when he told me that he wished to write a Life of Jesus.[1]

It is important to realise that through the years of impassioned polemic, of alternating hope and disappointment, that lay ahead, this idea was never far from his mind.

3

England had not meant a great deal to Bernanos. For one thing, he had never been there. It was a long time since he had called himself a nationalist, but when he had done so British nationalism had always appeared in rivalry with French. The shades of Fashoda had only reluctantly retreated, and the Action Française looked upon the Entente with anything but cordiality. Now that he abhorred the idea of nationalism, there did not seem to be much difference to Bernanos between the British and the French varieties; each had become an instinct of self-preservation, leading France at the heels

[1] *Bulletin* 5, pp. 2–6

of Britain to surrender and betrayal. Moreover Britain had fathered the mystique of *laissez-faire*, and if there was one place on the map that roused the hackles of Bernanos more than Munich it was Manchester. When it came to religion, which mattered rather more than economics, England had first secured that Joan of Arc should be burnt as a heretic, and had then fallen into heresy herself. Bernanos knew very little of England apart from what he had gleaned from the novels of Sir Walter Scott, and the English poets could tell him nothing, because he was unable to read them. He only knew that 'every great drama of history is Shakespearian'. Nevertheless, throughout that smiling summer of 1940, England had astonished the world, and London was 'the most glorious city of the universe'.[1]

One day in November, when the spring rains had come to Cruz das Almas, Bernanos perceived a strange object, not immediately identifiable, lurching and spluttering up the road that led to his house. Splashing him with oil and mud, this revealed itself as the motor-car of a neighbouring farmer. It brought the news that a telegram from London was awaiting him in Rio. Attempts had been made to transmit the contents by telephone, but the storms had made communication impossible. 'Everyone knows,' Bernanos wrote, 'that in whatever country you happen to be, the telephone suffers from a chronic cold, but in the tropics it coughs and spits more than in all the other countries put together.' If he set off at once there was a chance that he might reach Barbacena before the road became impassable, for it looked as though the rain would last for three days. When he reached the Post Office, the Negro on duty was coughing and spitting as badly as the telephone, but he managed to inform Bernanos that the editor of the *Dublin Review* wished to know what he thought of 'St Louis and the honour of France'. The *Dublin Review* was then under the editorship of Christopher Dawson, and it was partly on account of Bernanos' reply to the telegram that he was afterwards, and unscrupulously, removed from it. Those who had helped to get General Franco flown from the Canaries had not forgotten that Bernanos had views on that subject which differed from their own.

Lettre aux Anglais was written in four parts between December 1940 and November 1941. It was published in Rio the following year, with a phenomenal number of *errata*, and very few of those to

[1] *Lettre aux Anglais*

whom it was addressed can have read it. The *Dublin Review* published a few pages, but the *Dublin Review* never had a large circula-
tion, although Dawson had quickened it into a semblance of life.
Nor, it must be confessed, had *Lettre aux Anglais* very much to do
with England, and it was quite as much concerned with the First
World War as with the Second. Bernanos naturally made his salute
to the Battle of Britain. If people observed – with a certain admiring
condescension – that this was something out of a child's story-book,
he replied that that was exactly what it was. The England of Adam
Smith and Neville Chamberlain had rediscovered its childhood; the
military and intellectual *élite* of France had forgotten theirs. That
was the difference and the tragedy.

When he allowed his thought to rest upon the cemeteries, not of
Majorca but of Artois, Bernanos realised that there were other
differences as well. France, it was freely said, had two million
prisoners of war; in reality she had four, and half of these would
never come back. The only English Bernanos knew, or might have
known, he had met 'between Loos and Vimy, or later still – much
later – in that windy and sunless March, along the roads so terribly
empty and gaping, of Albert and Montdidier'.[1] But they were
strangers to him, and to those who fought at his side.

With your smart uniforms, your shining straps, your curious sporting
knapsacks, and your lady-like cigars, they took you for sons of the house –
boys from the château – who had kindly come to lend a hand with the
harvest. And if you warmed their tarts, they were rather proud of it. I am
afraid you will think all that very vulgar, but you didn't hear, as I did,
the navvy from Aubervilliers on the road to Peronne. He was pale and
hollow-chested, black with powder and mud, and his shoulder was torn
by the tripod of his machine-gun. When he saw your handsome Scotsmen
stretched along the grass, he spat out a thick clot of blood and said in a
rough voice: 'It wouldn't be such a bad idea to send hefty fellows like
that to kingdom come.' And as I looked at him, he added at once, and
charmingly: 'Don't worry. This blood is only from the throat; the rest
of the carcass is sound.'[2]

Bernanos simplified the English into a race of seamen and shop-
keepers, the French into a race of soldiers and peasants. But it
remained true that the 1914–18 war belonged to the French in a
way that it could never quite belong to the English, if only for the

[1] Ibid, p. 19   [2] Ibid, pp. 50–1

reason that it had been fought on French soil. If the war had cost the French more dearly, the peace had more deeply demoralised them. The unholy Trinity of 'Work, Property, and Savings' had sapped the spirit of risk, and was now baptised as 'Work, Family, and Fatherland'.

The word 'conservation' flatters the blind resignation of the sheep, just as the word 'destroy' flatters the blind violence of the wolves. The wolves destroy what deserves to be kept, and the sheep preserve what ought to be destroyed. What is the point of distinguishing between them? To preserve at all costs prevents the birth of what might have come into being; to stifle the future in bud seems to me no less reprehensible than to overthrow the present, even though a crime of this sort exhibits no outward sign of disorder; and I have no doubt that many people will think, as I do, that it is better to kill a man than to castrate him.[1]

The *Dublin Review* had invited Bernanos to say what he thought about the 'honour of France', and he replied by saying a good deal about its dishonour. When he came to answer the question, he contrasted the indignation of Maurras at the attachment of so many young Frenchmen to the memory of their honourable defeats, with the message of *The Song of Roland*. This was the story of a defeat, and it was the only popular epic in the French language.

For a thousand years the hearts of our boys and girls have beaten for a vanquished child of their race, dying with his face towards the enemy, one hand raised towards the Angels, and the other humbly searching for the hand of his friend. For a Frenchman this is the infallible choice of honour.[2]

The shame of the Armistice, for Bernanos, was not the senile defeatism and political illusions of Marshal Pétain, but the support he received from the self-styled guardians of the nation:

Neither Marshal Pétain, nor anybody else, could have surrendered at a stroke the Fleet, the Empire, and Paris without the support of an important fraction of public opinion, and this fraction was perfectly aware of its responsibility. There was, and there still is, a party of the armistice, a party eager to renounce and to resign. You know as well as I do, I trust, that this party was not recruited from the ignorant masses of our people. If the word *élite* has any meaning, it was recruited from the *élite*. It is even an *élite* of the *élite*. You think that I exaggerate? Not in the least. You might have supposed, for example, that certain democratic measures having considerably augmented the number of officers risen from the ranks, who seemed to exercise their profession like needy little bureaucrats rather than as soldiers – you might have supposed that these would have been the first to support a policy so obviously void of prestige. On the contrary, it was the most distinguished and best instructed officers, the aristocratic and *bienpensant* corps of the Marine, who spontaneously, passionately, and angrily declared in favour of Peace at any price.[1]

Bernanos was to repeat this accusation throughout the war, and after it, wherever a platform or a newspaper gave him the opportunity. It was easy to reply that he was judging from a distance, but the evidence has not given him the lie. His diagnosis was confirmed by a far more sober, if less inspired, commentator – a Frenchman, like himself, and an ardent Christian democrat – writing from the United States.[2] If the word 'nationalist' had come to stink in the nostrils of Bernanos – easily inflamed as they were – it was because the nationalists had betrayed the nation. They had systematically attacked the League of Nations, and in so doing had made it weaker still. The campaign against the repayment of American debts had alienated a country upon whom they were quick to call in the trouble they had brought upon themselves, and whose sympathy Hitler was only too keen to win. The support for Japan against a China not yet enslaved to Communism; the hatred for Czechoslovakia because Dr Beneš was a Freemason; the campaign against the Russian military alliance, and for Italian rather than British collaboration, which the abject performance of the Italian army revealed in its true absurdity; the campaign against sanctions which had jeopardised the situation of the British fleet in the Mediterranean; and the campaign in favour of Finland which would have thrown Stalin, irremediably, into the arms of Hitler – these were the cherished themes of Right-wing propaganda, and not in France alone. In mounting his indictment, however, Bernanos fell into the trap of condoning the unrealistic realism which he condemned. No doubt the collaborationist *salons*, for cynical reasons of their own, were more anxious for the French to fight the Russians on behalf of the Finns than the Germans on behalf of the Poles. But this did not alter the fact that the defensive war of the Finns against the Russians

[1] Ibid, pp. 99–100
[2] Yves Simon, *La Grande Crise de la République Française*

was a just war, if ever there was one. It was a *locus classicus* of defeat with honour. Again, it was the imposition of sanctions, not the campaign against them, which had thrown Mussolini into the arms of Hitler. The case against sanctions was not that they had been imposed, but that they were ineffective. They had endangered the Royal Navy without saving Abyssinia. And even if one had hoped for a Republican victory in Spain – here Bernanos called 'a plague on both your houses' – it was plain as daylight that Spanish neutrality, however malevolent towards the Allies, had in practice served their cause. With a revolutionary government in power, nothing would have kept Hitler from Gibraltar; the North African landings would have been impossible; and even the collaborationists might have sprung to arms.

The letter of Bernanos to the English was written before America had entered the war, but Russia now stood suspiciously at their side. It no longer made sense to describe the war as a struggle between democracy and dictatorship. Bernanos had never seen it in terms which were so often interchangeable, and as the Allied victory drew nearer, he wavered between hope and foreboding. For Bernanos the point of the Battle of Britain was that it was fought, not that it was won. Even if the 'knights of the air' had gone down to defeat, they would have joined hands with Roland at Roncesvalles; and for this Frenchman who knew so little about the English, and so little understood them, the last siren would have carried across the Atlantic an echo of Roland's horn.

CHAPTER 12

THE DEAD PARISH

I

At Barbacena the routine varied little from day to day. Before the sun was high Bernanos mounted his horse, Oswaldo – so called from the stables of Oswaldo Aranha, the highly intelligent Minister of Foreign Affairs and later Ambassador in Washington, from whom he had bought it. A magnificent animal, it fulfilled his exacting requirements; handsome, inexpensive, long in the neck and oblique in the shoulders, with sound withers and a wide girth. He rode it at a walking pace, and baptised it with wine from Rio Grande do Sul. When he was obliged to walk with his two sticks, he felt his age; but on horseback he felt thirty years younger. To those who saw him in the saddle he appeared magnificent. Dismounting before the principal church, whose ostentatious baroque decoration he did not find conducive to prayer, Bernanos would painfully drag himself up the stone steps of the porch, and hear Mass. Afterwards he tethered Oswaldo outside the café where he read his mail and such newspapers in the French language as reached him. Then he would settle down at a table to write, remaining there for the greater part of the day – unless one found him thundering against Vichy in the vestibule of the Grand Hotel. In the evening he would read aloud to the family – Racine, Corneille, Homer, *Les Châtiments* of Victor Hugo, and *Cyrano de Bergerac*. As the boys grew up he had taught them to swim, box, fence, and to ride.

On the 19th of July he sent his first message to the French for transmission by the European Services of the BBC; the communication of the text to London was facilitated by the British embassy in Rio, where he was quick to establish friendly relations with the ambassador, Sir Geoffrey Knox. He requested that nothing in it be changed: 'I know my public,' he assured Virgilio de Mello Franco, who was acting as his intermediary. He asked that each message, which he composed at fortnightly intervals, should be prefaced by the following statement: 'French listeners will not be surprised that

Georges Bernanos should denounce a treason which he had foreseen, and whose authors and abettors he had denounced beforehand.' Every week a similar message was broadcast from Brazzaville, for Equatorial Africa, under Félix Eboué, had rallied to de Gaulle. On the feast of Jeanne d'Arc, in 1941, Bernanos reminded his listeners – and indeed the saint herself – that

The enemy is at Orléans, but he is also in the city of the Coronation. Notre-Dame d'Amiens, Notre-Dame de Reims, Notre-Dame de Rouen, Notre-Dame de Chartres, are in his hands. His horses are drinking in the Seine, the Meuse and the Loire. He is also in your own little native village, and when autumn comes it is he who will be gathering the *mirabelle* plums of Domrémy.

Whatever conditions Bernanos may have laid down, such messages were naturally subject to censorship. He could say what he liked from Brazzaville, but from London he was not allowed to insult the Marshal. The British government was anxious to keep the door to Vichy ajar, and the American government was eager to keep it open. The French section of the BBC's European service were resolutely hostile to Vichy, but they were not unanimously favourable to de Gaulle. Nevertheless Bernanos was the only French writer of the first rank who was free, and willing, to speak his mind openly against the Vichy government. Malraux joined the *maquis* as soon as it was organised. Valéry was silent, and Gide equivocal. Mauriac was condemned to clandestinity, and Claudel composed a sycophantic ode to Pétain – although he later gave sympathetic asylum to more than one diplomat who was on his way to join the Fighting French. Alexis Léger – *alias* St Jean-Perse – remained in Washington but said nothing against the new masters of the Quai d'Orsay, of which he had formerly been the permanent head. André Maurois, who had made his name as a professional Anglophil, escaped to America, thanks to the Ministry of Information and the Royal Air Force, occupied as they were in 1940 with more important matters. Maurois' *The Tragedy of France* was described by a cynical observer as a 'tragedy written in the style of Marivaux'. It was not quite that; but many of his English readers echoed the comment of Winston Churchill that 'we thought we had a friend, and found that we had a client.' Maritain, whom the outbreak of war had surprised in the United States, analysed the causes of the catastrophe, exposing the hypocrisy of a régime which pretended to restore the morale of a nation under the jackboot of the enemy. But even Maritain was careful not to impugn the personal integrity of Pétain, and he requested the BBC not to broadcast such passages from his book as might alienate the uncommitted listener. Nor did he give an unqualified adherence to de Gaulle. Where Maritain wrote with a philosopher's definition of his terms – and these included a definition of Christian democracy – Bernanos wrote with a prophetic insight into the nature of totalitarian evil, inherent, as he believed, in dictatorship and capitalist democracy alike; with no respect for the opportunism of political warfare, but alert to all its opportunities, he was merciless towards his enemies and candid towards his friends.

It is interesting to note that the Preface to *Lettre aux Anglais* was addressed to those who had welcomed him in Brazil. 'After Munich I wrote that I had come to Brazil "to let my shame cool down". It has not cooled down, but I have recovered my pride, and the people of Brazil have given it back to me.'[1] As always, he came back to Munich – for it was neither at Bordeaux nor at Rethondes, but at Munich that the victory of 1918 had been annulled. The impoverished peasantry among whom Bernanos lived had renewed his hope that 'the gentle and laborious patience of men' would eventually triumph over the power of money and the forces of material destruction; and as for the intellectuals among whom he had found so warm a sympathy: 'they make use of our culture because it seems to them the most appropriate instrument for our common defence; but it is from the people that they derive an almost physical sense of the danger which faces them, and the will to overcome it.'[2] He did not forget the old Brazilian abbé who had asked with his dying breath what was happening to '*our* France'. The men who gave Bernanos his audience in Brazil were no sycophants. Not all of them shared his political options or his religious faith. But they realised, in the words of Charles Morgan, that France was 'an idea necessary to civilisation', and that when Bernanos dragged his burly frame on to the platform the idea stood up and spoke.

The Brazil that Bernanos knew was the *Estado Novo*, founded by Getulio Vargas in 1937. Popular with the workers to whom it had given the first measures of social security – no employee could be dismissed after ten years' service – the régime was detested by the

---

[1] *Lettre aux Anglais*, p. II   [2] Ibid, p. VII

intellectuals, who naturally resented the censorship of their articles, though not of their books. Bernanos was careful not to involve himself in domestic politics, but the Vargas dictatorship was too like its European counterparts for him to smile upon it. Most of his friends felt as he did. Mello Franco, having supported the revolution which brought Vargas to power in 1930, and his election to the Presidency in 1934, parted company with him over the *coup d'état* which inaugurated the *Estado Novo*. When Brazil entered the war, however, he immediately offered his services. Among the others, Amoroso Lima, the convert president of Catholic Action, had drunk too deeply of Maritain's integral humanism to lend an ear to the corporative doctrines by which so many of the clergy were seduced. Editor of *A Ordem*, he was a leader of critical expressionism, and also director of a factory. Then, as later, he raised his persuasive voice against authoritarian government in any form. He did not always agree with the idealised anarchism of Bernanos, but after a hesitant start the two men became devoted friends. The Catholic leader and jurist, J. Hargreaves, whom Bernanos had known at Juiz de Fora; Alvaro Lins, the critic and journalist, later ambassador in Lisbon, whose style had a 'Pascalian tremor, nervous and supple, recalling some of the finest pages in our language';[1] Helio Pellegrino, the poet, causeur and psychiatrist, from Bello Horizonte; Fernando Carneiro, president of the Dom Vital Centre for Catholic intellectuals in Rio; Murillo Mendes, the poet and professor of literature at Bello Horizonte – were all of the same political shade of thought. Edgar Mata-Machado from the Academia Mineira de Lettres at Bello Horizonte, who translated a number of his articles, was almost alone in combining a friendship for Bernanos with support for the Vargas régime.

The *Estado Novo* was neither brutal nor vainglorious; nor, of course, was it remotely racist. Vargas had concluded that responsible democracy was impossible in a country where so many people could neither read nor write, and where the vast distances made free elections very difficult to enforce. The régime was from the first favourable to the Allied cause, and the single pro-Nazi newspaper, *Meia-Dia*, controlled by the German Embassy, was suppressed after an angry crowd had stoned its windows. Of the highly cultivated *élite*, among whom Bernanos moved in so far as he moved from

[1] *Le Chemin de la Croix des Ames* (Gallimard 1948), p. 132

Barbacena at all, some were more interested in literature than in politics. Jorge de Lima had been converted to Catholicism in 1935, turning from the primitive syncretism of his earlier books with the aim, as he put it, of 'restoring Poetry in Christ'. His great lyrical epic, *Invencao de Orfeu*, had as its central theme 'a poetical reconstruction of childhood'. This was written after the death of Bernanos, but the theme had an obvious Bernanosian resonance. Augusto Schmidt, the other outstanding poet of Brazil, also stood outside immediate political engagement. Like Jorge de Lima he represented a modernist and anti-Parnassian movement in literature, with romantic and pessimistic overtones. *Mar Desconhecido*, which appeared in 1942, with its mute rhymes, conveyed his sense of the transitory in a time of almost universal apocalypse.

Bernanos was at Barbacena when Brazil entered the war against Germany in August 1942. Returning on horseback to Cruz das Almas, and listening to the festivities of the town grow faint in the distance, he felt attached to the soil of Minas Gerais for all eternity 'like a dead man to the soil which covers him and where, like the dead, I await the resurrection.'[1] The movement of opinion which had led Brazil into war seemed to him more interesting than the volatilities of interventionism and isolationism in the United States, since it was much less influenced by propaganda. His daily contact with a laborious and largely illiterate peasantry, whom the communications media could reach only by radio when it reached them at all, was inclined to shrug its shoulders in face of issues far too complicated for their understanding. In so far as events came within their knowledge, they judged them as human beings, unconditioned by manufactured *partis pris*. Brazil – concluded Bernanos – had 'entered the war with clean hands and a pure heart'.[2]

This was not a certificate of immunity from the infection of Fascist doctrine. In Brazil, as elsewhere in Latin America, a powerful fifth column was at work, and if the war had developed differently the whole sub-continent would have been at its mercy, not to mention a United States well and truly insulated in its isolationism. Apart from the accredited and clandestine agents of Germany, important sections of the clergy were, consciously or unconsciously, sapping morale – with a nostalgic glance to the Portugal of Salazar, which Bernanos described as 'an elegant necropolis'. These elements

[1] Ibid, p. 229   [2] Ibid, p. 232

were all the more dangerous when they professed to speak *au dessus de la mêlée:*

It is intolerable when people who never hesitated, in Italy, Spain, France, or elsewhere, to show their sympathy for a realism which itself admits no scruple in the choice of the methods it employs, should claim to impose upon other Christians, in temporal affairs, a supernatural detachment of which they are very far from setting an example themselves. When their friends shoot, imprison, or sterilise, they never accuse these madmen of compromising the Church; but if, on our side, we merely express the wish that their activities should be controlled ... they accuse us of mixing up religion and politics, and of stamping on their privileges and prestige. In short, they claim for the Fascists the right to employ such methods as are normal in human affairs, but they are scandalised when we claim an equal right to defend ourselves otherwise than by fasting, prayer, and abstinence.[1]

It did not escape the attention of Bernanos that the French episcopate, which had judged the Action Française so severely in 1926, were now prodigal of their benedictions on a régime which owed so much to it. Marshal Pétain reminded him of the heroine in Claudel's *L'Otage* who had given herself to Turelure as an 'expiatory victim'. He had not been content 'to sign the marriage contract with a failing hand, but had appeared at the wedding in the uniform of a Head of State, and presented M. Turelure[2] to the nation'[3] – even daring to affirm, in *La Revue des Deux Mondes*, that the spirit of Nazi Germany was 'the legitimate heir to French classicism'. For those who exalted, or excused, the Marshal as 'the victor of Verdun' Bernanos compared the signature of the Armistice to the 'spittle of the men who had died there'.[4] Nor was he disposed to accept the invitation of Père Gillet, Master-General of the Dominican Order, to extend the notion of infallibility to a Head of State 'with a head like a sergeant-major',[5] and whose speeches reminded him of 'a sermon preached by Bishop Cauchon at the funeral of Jeanne d'Arc'. He never concealed the immensity, both moral and material, of the French disaster. He could admit, what the adherents of de Gaulle could never admit, that the vast majority of the country had not only suffered defeat but positively espoused it at the hands of a 'vain

---

[1] *Le Chemin de la Croix des Ames*, p. 259   [2] Character in Paul Claudel's *L'Otage*
[3] *Le Chemin de la Croix des Ames*, p. 145   [4] Ibid, p. 258
[5] Ibid, p. 295

and sententious old man, in whom a fierce ambition had become an unmentionable vice with advancing years, kindling a sort of lubricious spark in his speeches where the unction of a shady solicitor was strangely combined with that of a priest no better than he should be'.[1] Such language did scant justice to the honest intentions of the Marshal, however misguided, and Bernanos did not employ it until events had demonstrated the truth of his thesis – that the people of France had been bemused and betrayed by their élite.

Even in the summer of 1940 his intransigence was an embarrassment to the French embassy in Rio. He had more than one interview, and some correspondence, with the ambassador, Jules Henry, who urged him to suspend his judgment. On the other hand many people were surprised that in his articles he made so little mention of de Gaulle. He replied that naturally de Gaulle had his support, but that he wished to say nothing that might compromise his loyalty to the Royal House of France – 'the only legitimate authority to which I really feel myself bound – not because I have more or less freely chosen it as a matter of taste, but because the history of my country has given it to me; because it has its birth and derives its principle, not from the will of this or that generation of Frenchmen, but from the fidelity of countless generations through the centuries; because it springs, so to speak, from the bowels of the nation.'[2] In the general catastrophe of 1940 the death of the Duc de Guise had passed almost unnoticed, except by those attached to his person and his cause. 'Like most of the Princes of his House,' wrote Bernanos, 'he was of a liberal humour and formation, moderate by inclination but also by a sense of duty and royal vocation'; of a temper similar to the Comte de Chambord – who for Bernanos was 'Henry V' – when he called upon the workers of Paris: 'Together, and whenever you like, we will take up once again the great movement of 1789.' Rumour – later proved to be untrue – had it that his son, the Comte de Paris, had given his support to Vichy; Bernanos replied that there was every reason to affirm his own royalism when there was so little comfort in doing so. The dauphin that Jeanne d'Arc dragged reluctantly to Rheims had been notably improved by his coronation.

Bernanos showed no mercy to the attempts of Washington or Whitehall to spare the feelings of Vichy in the hope of rallying its resistance when the moment was ripe. The scuttling of the fleet in

[1] Ibid, p. 294   [2] Ibid, p. 172

the harbour of Toulon showed how vain were such illusions. This abject catastrophe was presented as an epic of heroism by German and Allied propaganda, and for directly opposite reasons. Bernanos thought that Admiral Laborde would have done better to go down with his ships, even if he had one foot on the gangway. Nor was the presentation of Giraud as an alternative to de Gaulle any more reassuring. His physical resemblance to Pétain lent a sinister plausibility to a candidature so evidently favoured by the State Department. But Bernanos pleaded that the French should be allowed to choose their own heroes, and not have them imposed 'by the same trusts which formerly eulogised Franco, affirmed the peaceful intentions of Hitler, imposed Lindbergh on the admiration of the world, and predicted the defeat of Japan within a matter of six weeks.'[1]

Bernanos could not help seeing the American landings in North Africa as a further humiliation; if bolder counsels had prevailed in 1940, a French army would have been there to welcome them. But the prospect of victory was now clear, though distant. He saw the New Year in with a 'Salute to Brazil'.

From the height of our little hill of Cruz das Almas we have seen, for many weeks, our bad roads melt little by little like butter on a hot plate. The gracious white town, half a league away, seems quite near, but no car would dare to risk the journey up here, and even the horses distrust the road which has collapsed and slips gradually under the weight of its own incline.[2]

As for the future, he placed all his hopes 'in the hands of the children of France, of the France of the day after tomorrow, whose hatred is innocent today, and whose vengeance will also be free from guilt.'[3] The épuration, when it came, was not, however, to be quite so pure as he predicted.

2

In 1943 *Monsieur Ouine* was published by the Atlantica Press in Rio. It will be useful to recapitulate the strange story of its composition. The book was begun early in 1931, and by the end of the year a manuscript of about 150 pages appears to have been completed.

---

[1] *Le Chemin de la Croix des Ames*, p. 312   [2] Ibid, p. 297   [3] Ibid

This was revised two months later, and Bernanos worked on, not without difficulty, until, three years later, there were still nearly 100 pages to write. At this point, as we have seen, he was distracted by *Un Crime*, having been already distracted by *Un Mauvais Rêve*, to which he returned when *Un Crime* was finished. A further forty pages were completed in Majorca until the person of the *curé de campagne* intervened to relieve him from what he had at one point described as a 'dismal urinal', and elsewhere as the really 'great novel' which he had it in him to write. He took it up again in March 1936, but without success; and it was not until 1940 that he completed the final chapter in Brazil. The loss of six weeks' work in the briefcase that vanished between Aix and Marseilles was a further discouragement; and the temporary disappearance of a *cahier* containing the whole of one important chapter towards the end of the book handicapped the reader and embarrassed the author when it was published in Rio.

It might have been anticipated that a novel so frequently interrupted and laid aside would show signs of its difficult composition, more especially since this was a book quite unlike anything that Bernanos – or anyone else for the matter of that – had written before. When it appeared in Paris in 1946, and subsequently in an English translation – free from a number of textual errors, though not yet in the definitive version which a study of the recovered *cahier* made possible – many critics and readers were disconcerted. *Monsieur Ouine* was not only mysterious; it was mystifying. Yet for Albert Béguin it was the key to the whole of the author's work; and Claude-Edmonde Magny, in an article[1] which won his enthusiastic approval, justified her description of the book as a masterpiece. For others it looked back to Dostoevsky, sideways to Sartre, and forward to the *nouveau roman* of Robbe-Grillet and Nathalie Sarraut. These voices could not be disregarded, and they have not become less persuasive with the years.

Bernanos, as we have seen, was incessantly preoccupied with the mystery of evil, and in *Monsieur Ouine* he attempted to plumb its depths – or, more exactly, to get to the bottom of something which had no base, to circumscribe something which had no contours, and to seize something which had no substance. It was, of its nature, a paradoxical experiment. The previous novels had been stories of

[1] *Poésie 46*

conflict – Donissan and the horse-dealer, Cénabre and Chevance, Chantal and Fiodor, the *curé de campagne* and the châtelaine; they were chronicles of desperate activity. But the characters in *Monsieur Ouine* are like fishes in a stagnant pond, and the world they inhabit – the world of the *paroisse morte* – is without feature or relief. Even the 'road', which for Bernanos was the surviving symbol of hope, had become the symbol of despair, since the very idea of destination had disappeared from the minds of those who travelled upon it.

The title of the book has a deliberate ambiguity. *Ouine* is a composite of *oui* and *non*, and Bernanos certainly had André Gide in mind when he conceived a character remarkable for the absence of what the French call *caractère*, whose ability to say *oui* and *non* at the same time masqueraded as sincerity. But there the resemblance stops. Ouine has nothing of Gide's distinction, and even less of his charm. He is both abject and absurd. If the essence of evil is negation, as the theologians maintain, Ouine fits the definition – for with him, and with other characters in the *paroisse morte*, negation has the sense of absence rather than refusal. He does not even swim in his stagnant pond; he floats upon it. We do not know where he has come from; we only know that he is a professor of languages; and he does not himself know where he is going, except to a death which, for him, is without significance. If *Monsieur Ouine* has meant little to a good number of readers, it is because nothing means anything at all to Monsieur Ouine.

Bernanos was faced with the difficulty of giving some degree of concrete reality to a world which is morally concave. His *paroisse morte* is clearly situated in Artois, familiar to us from *Sous le Soleil de Satan;* the *campagne* is the same as that in which the *curé* penned his *Journal;* and Artois is not a no man's land, although it sometimes looks like it. The physical presence of Ouine is at once vacant and oppressive. Day and night, we are told, he is at his window 'observing everything' – and doing nothing. He sits on his bed, dangling his short legs and caressing his felt hat. Even his voice has the softness and imprecision of felt. His person is at once fat and fragile, with its 'thick, pro-consular neck and massive chest, like the body of a mature woman'. The absence of muscle in his body reflects the absence of muscle in his mind. He is a dreamer – and his dream is a *mauvais rêve*. The claret-coloured scarf around his head, 'like a thin pink crescent', reminds the adolescent Steeny – whom he morally, and perhaps physically, seduces – of a 'delicate mouth'. He compares himself to a 'jelly-fish at the bottom of the sea. I float and I absorb.' With his smooth cheeks, and eyes half-closed, 'his sleepy look which seems to float on the surface of grey water', he might be almost anyone – 'a road-surveyor, or a renegade priest'. But Steeny will follow him to the end of the world – to which he significantly replies: 'There is no end of the world, my dear boy.' If the character of Monsieur Ouine has much in common with André Gide, his physical presence is reminiscent of George Moore. Supposing that he ever 'told', one might reasonably doubt that he had ever 'kissed'.

When Jorge de Lima published the first critique of *Monsieur Ouine*, Bernanos thanked him for not describing the novel as 'surrealist'; it was better defined as '*onirique*' – for there was 'nothing more real or objective than a dream'. For Bernanos the dream was a structure of the shaping imagination, not a vague apparition risen from the subconscious self. Yet *Monsieur Ouine* cannot be judged by those canons of realistic fiction before which the *Journal d'un Curé de campagne* and *Nouvelle Histoire de Mouchette* stand up so triumphantly. As in those two masterpieces the element of satire, rather too self-indulgently intrusive elsewhere, is wholly absent; and the author's own voice is rarely heard, although his presence is pervasive. The reader is made to feel that he has entered a room full of people to none of whom he has been properly introduced. He has to pick up from hints dropped casually in the course of their conversation who they are, what they are talking about, and what is their relationship to one another. Where the classical novelist is like a polite host who effects the introductions all round, and puts the newly-arrived guest at his ease, Bernanos deliberately leaves him stranded – for it is not his intention that he shall be at ease. He is meant to ask many more questions than answers will be given him, because Bernanos does not know the answers. The point of the novel is the disquieting depth of the questions which it poses. It represents the abdication of the omniscient narrator. There were more things in this hell upon earth 'than are dreamt of in your philosophy', and Bernanos does not trust in philosophy to find them out.

We may suggest the quality of *Monsieur Ouine* by categorising the questions it leaves unanswered. We never know who killed the young cowherd, or why. What looked like the *début* of a 'who-dunnit' turns into an inconclusive 'dunno'. We can only guess at the

sexual relationship between the young adolescent Steeny and
Monsieur Ouine. We do not know what happens to the mayor
after he has gone mad. We do not know whether the old wood-
cutter, de Vandomme, has a right to his prefix; what matters is the
reality of his genealogical dreams. We are not sure whether Steeny's
mother and his governess have illicit relations. We do not know
how or why Monsieur Ouine came to be lodging with Madame de
Néréis, the crazy châtelaine, or what exactly they had been to one
another. Yet we ask these questions as we should ask them in real
life, and to that extent the novel is far more realistic than one in
which the author has everything up his sleeve – and produces it.
Nor is there a direct sequence of cause and effect between the
presence of Monsieur Ouine in the village and the poison he distils –
murder, madness, and lust. Steeny and the curé are the only characters with whom we see him in direct contact, and it is only to
Steeny that he reveals himself. Monsieur Ouine is dying, and this is
the nearest he comes to a death-bed confession:

I had no wish to make them my prey. I watched them in their pleasures
and their sufferings, just as He who created them might have watched
them Himself; I wasn't responsible for what they suffered or enjoyed. I
only flattered myself that I gave them an imperceptible push, as you push
a picture towards the shade or the light. I felt that I was their providence,
almost as inviolable in its designs, and almost as unsuspected, as the other.
I thanked my stars that I was an ugly and grumpy old man. I expanded at
the sound of my own voice, I was careful to exaggerate its timbre of a
nasal bassoon, made to amuse the nursery. The security of these souls was
in my hands, and they didn't know it. I let them see it, or concealed it
from them, turn and turn about. I played with this crass security of theirs
like a delicate instrument, and drew from it a particular harmony of a
superhuman sweetness. This is the way God passes His time, these are His
amusements, and this is how He employs His long leisure – and it was the
same with me . . . Such were the souls with whom I played. I was
careful not to change them, I simply discovered them to themselves, with
all the precaution of an entomologist unfolding the wings of a nymph.[1]

And what was his motive?

I am eaten up with curiosity. At this very moment it gnaws and hollows
out what little remains of me. Heaven knows how curious I was, but I
was only hungry for souls.[2]

[1] Editions de la Pléiade, pp. 1558–9   [2] Ibid, pp. 1557–8

Naturally his hunger is unsatisfied, for all he can do is to communicate his own sterility. It is not that he disbelieves in the soul, but he has lost all feeling of his own:

whereas only an hour ago, I felt it like an empty space, an expectation, an inward longing. I suppose it has swallowed me up. I have fallen into it . . . as the elect fall into the hands of God. No one troubles to ask me to account for it; and it can't ask me itself, since it ignores me and no longer even knows my name. From any other prison I could escape, if only in desire. I have fallen just where no judgment can touch me. For ever and ever, my child, I go back into myself.[1]

Bernanos has travelled a long way from Donissan's nocturnal march with the horse-coper at his side. In the earlier novel Satan was personified as an almost irresistible force; in *Monsieur Ouine* he is an impalpable and quite irresistible influence. In the one case he was a formidable substance; in the other a fascinating vacancy.

What links the two novels, and integrates the whole work of Bernanos in a single theme with multiple variations, is the loss of childhood. Maturity is disillusion; experience is disappointment; all the children of Bernanos are *enfants humiliés*. They all go forward to adventure, but sanctity is the only adventure that succeeds – and sanctity is sacrifice. Joan of Arc is burnt at the stake; Chantal de Clergerie is murdered by the Russian chauffeur. The first Mouchette has looked for love, and is humiliated by the aristocrat and the doctor who have ravished her. The second Mouchette is humiliated by the poacher to whom she had given herself with a pity equal to desire. Olivier and Philippe in *Un Mauvais Rêve* are the lost generation of the *après-guerre*, humiliated by the society which has betrayed them. The one turns to drugs, the other to Communism – and suicide. In *Monsieur Ouine* the central character himself has been humiliated by the coarse Norman schoolmaster who corrupted him all those years ago – for Monsieur Ouine had also been a child, hard as it is to believe it. Steeny's English governess had lost her innocence in the cotton towns of Lancashire before she sealed the loss with Steeny; and Steeny had already been betrayed by his mother's lie which told him that his father was still alive. Only in the poor young cripple, Guillaume, whose crutches convey a reminiscence of his author's infirmity, does a kind of innocence survive.

[1] Ibid, p. 1560

Guillaume is the grandchild of de Vandomme; and his parents are both dead. It is Guillaume whom Steeny meets on the road after the interview with Monsieur Ouine, with which the book begins. Guillaume has often seen the professor pottering around the village, and wonders if he 'can ever love him', for innocence and infirmity have preserved for him, intact, the primary obligation of love. And he has seen Steeny, in a dream, 'nailed to a dry rock . . . and before I could even say a word, you cried out to me: "No, no, stay where you are, don't move, leave me alone", just as if you were already damned.'[1] This is the true portrait of Steeny, but it is not the portrait he paints of himself. Fixed in his obsession with Monsieur Ouine, he imagines himself heroically on the move.

I always drive straight ahead of me. If life is nothing but an obstacle to overcome, I overcome it, and I shall come out on the other side, all foaming and bloody. And you follow me, but a long way off, and we shall see you come out as well, carrying the burden of my sins. In fact, you are my soul, so leave me in peace – our salvation is your affair.[2]

– and perhaps it is. But of course Steeny realises none of his fine ambitions. We take leave of him half-drunk beside the death-bed of Monsieur Ouine, with an empty bottle of Madeira on the table. The empty bottle is a symbol no less significant than Guillaume's crutches. It stands for the emptiness of Monsieur Ouine, and for the emptiness of Steeny also. Guillaume's crutches are far ahead of him on the road which he thought to tread so triumphantly, and his only hope will be to lean on them – if one can speak of hope in a book so redolent of despair.

Monsieur Ouine himself makes only spasmodic appearances in the novel that bears his name. As often as not, we see him through the eyes of others. Madame de Néréis, the flamboyant châtelaine of Wambescourt, commonly known as Jambe-de-Laine, careering down the road behind a mare as mad as herself, is a tremendous – and ultimately a pathetic – figure of misdirected energy. She has Steeny's eyes, and there is a narcissistic reverie in the way she looks at him. She remembers the sad and soggy evening in September when Monsieur Ouine confessed to her: 'I have just been looking at myself again, like a dead man looking into the past. I saw the little boy that I used to be, I could have touched him and heard his

[1] Editions de la Pléiade, p. 1580   [2] Ibid, p. 1581

voice.'[1] And since that day no one had seen him smile. 'We hate him, like death,' she goes on, 'but alas! he so needs protection. One has to be at his beck and call. His naiveté is extraordinary, it's quite incalculable. One has to serve him – and service is the word. He does nothing for himself, he's as helpless as a child. You have to honour him and serve him blindly, as you would a god. And don't talk about his will – he has no more will-power than a child.'[2] And yet – asks Steeny – does she not also love him, after her fashion?

'Love him! He's large and fat and sticky, and his hands are slippery. Pouf! Don't you know that he's ill? His ageing voice vibrates as if he were speaking inside a drum. Good God! love him! But whoever goes near him, my angel, has no more need of love. Oh, the peace of it, the silence! Love him? I'll tell you what, my heart; where another person radiates warmth, our friend absorbs every scrap of warmth and every spark of radiation. The genius of Monsieur Ouine, don't you see, is cold; and the soul is at rest in the cold.'[3]

But if Jambe-de-Laine is at rest in the cold, where does she find the strength to hate him? Hatred, for Steeny, is an impulsive force.

'If you were a man,' she replies, 'and not an argumentative youngster, you would know that the one thing hatred doesn't do is to move. A clear, frozen water – that's what hatred is. At least, that's how it seems to me. But you see it as an enraged beast...'

'Don't let us play with words. In your language, to love and to hate mean the same thing.'[4] For Jambe-de-Laine, like Steeny himself, has been infected with the *oui* and *non* of Monsieur Ouine.

The parishioners of the *paroisse morte* are brought together for the funeral of the little cowherd – a scene of macabre and grotesque horror, which leaves one thinking of a picture by Hieronymus Bosch.

The church had lost its sweet odour of resin and moss and withered leaves. It was as dark and warm as a stable. The light from the candles in the apse trailed along the flag-stones of the nave, crept up the stone pillars which were always sweating with an icy water – a dead water that left the hands greasy – and then was lost in the vaulting. The choir was full of men standing immobile, or braying in unison, now and then, like a herd of cattle. Alone, absolutely alone, among the shadows, more isolated by the double row of candles than by an abyss, stood the tiny coffin draped in white.[1]

What mattered now was not who had killed the cowherd; all that mattered was the fact that he had died, drawing after him under the earth all those who, day and night, for a week past, had been so busily spinning their theories above it. The victim now had the upper hand; for 'one does not exhaust so easily the patience and the cunning of the dead.'[2] Here the author's commentary is unmistakable; but elsewhere it is left to the villagers themselves to describe their own *Walpurgisnacht*. 'The air had become thick and warm, like the air of our bakehouse when I kill my pig.'[3]

The young curé de Fénouille is preaching. Certain traits of the *curé de campagne* are clearly visible. He is a man to whom prayer had once come easily, and who now finds it difficult. He, too, lives alone and cooks for himself his *maigre*, vegetable meals. Once a week the bellringer calls for the laundry. But no matter – he is bred to poverty. Here, though, the resemblance ends. Contact with his parishioners is not merely difficult; it is non-existent – and now he tells them so.

'What are you? Why have you come here this morning? What do you want from your priest? Prayers for this dead person? But I can do nothing without you, I can do nothing without my parish, and I have no parish. There is no longer any parish, my brethren; a commune and a curé – if you can call it that – is not a parish . . . What am I doing here among you? Have you ever seen a heart that beats outside its body? Well that is what I am, my friends. A heart, remember, is like a pump that sets the blood going. I beat for all I am worth, but the blood doesn't respond any more. The heart inhales and compresses nothing but wind. And you . . . and you . . .'[4]

But he cannot proceed, and as the astonished murmur of the congregation grows, Monsieur Ouine, who is standing near him, begs him to recover his control. He continues:

'It takes a long time to kill a parish, and this one has stood for a good time. Now it is dead. . . . There are sinners among you – great sinners – but that is of no consequence. Every parish has its sinners. As long as the parish is standing firm, the sinners and the rest make up a single, great body, where the pity, if not the grace, of God circulates like the sap of a

[1] Editions de la Pléiade, p. 1482   [2] Ibid   [3] Ibid, p. 1484   [4] Ibid

tree. You may well say, my friends, that man is not made to live alone, or in couples, like the tigers and the snakes. Alas! the smallest community of men carries its burden of impurity; but what of the great cities? When night falls, the city awakes and inhales through every pore the filth of the day which is just over; mixes it up in its ditches and gutters, until it is no more than lime, rolling little by little towards the sea in vast, subterranean streams.'[1]

If *Monsieur Ouine* is the key to Bernanos' work, the curé's sermon is not less a key to his biography; for the 'dead parish' is a microcosm of the inorganic society, of a Europe in decomposition, as Bernanos had come to see it, and as Georges Sorel had once described it to him: 'a nest of vipers'. The curé goes on to remind his people of the double suicide of the poacher, suspected of having murdered the cowherd, and his young wife. She, too, had dreamt of escape – 'to a great forest with very tall trees, nothing but trunks, straight as columns, all black, and between them, very far away, the blue fringe of the sea.'[2] Her suicide, with that of her husband, has much in common with the suicide of the two Mouchettes. Like theirs, it is a supreme gesture of disappointment. It has the innocence of a justified rebuke, and of a love which, of all the sexual attachments in the novel, is alone free from guilt. And it is just when the curé refers to it that old de Vandomme pushes back his chair, and turning his face to the serried faces in the nave, quietly observes: 'The boy was not guilty.' The truth – if truth it were – should not be allowed to sully that fabulous escutcheon.

The curé – and Bernanos with him – plunges deeper into his analysis of evil.

'The devil himself has withdrawn from you. My brothers, we are alone in evil. From one century to another, the unfortunate race of men have dreamt of breaking that solitude – but their labour was lost. The devil, who can do so many things, will never succeed in founding his church – a church that will put in common store the merits of hell, that will create a common store of sin. From now until the end of the world sin must sin alone, always alone – we sin alone, as we die alone. For the devil, you see, is a friend who never stays with us to the end.'[3]

The scene in the church is brought to a close, upon a note of stupendous irony. After remonstrating with the curé about the scandal and severity of his address, Monsieur Ouine remarks:

[1] Ibid, pp. 1486–7 [2] Ibid, p. 1477 [3] Ibid, p. 1490

'I have always held childhood in honour ... loved it and honoured it. Childhood is the salt of the earth. If it loses its savour, the world will soon be nothing but gangrene and corruption. Gangrene and corruption,' he repeated in a voice loud and strong. He remained still for a long time, one of his hands, swollen no doubt with the same serous liquid that flowed, inexhaustibly, from his eyelids, hanging open on a level with his face. Then he turned his back and moved off without a word, walking very rapidly, among the tombs.[1]

By the time the curé has reached the newly-dug grave his surplice is black with mud, and there is a low, hostile murmur among the crowd which now includes the whole village. The inspector of education proffers his anodyne platitudes in the name of the Republic, and then it is the turn of the mayor. As he speaks from a sheet of paper, on which his wife has inscribed a few words in capital letters, it is plain to all around that he has lost his reason. He spews forth the catalogue of his carnal obsessions, and rediscovers his innocence in insanity, as the dead couple had rediscovered theirs in suicide.

The expectation of salvation and the certainty of winning it caused his knees to tremble and his bones to shake, while the words flowed in an unending stream. ... In the noise, now become appalling, he explained that he had finished for good with the fetid, filthy, and faded object which stuck to his soul, like something sticking to the skin. He stamped on the ground, pinched and pulled at his nose, suddenly looked around with astonishment, his hand wet with tears, and at last fell on his knees in the midst of the booing and the laughter.[2]

At this moment of hysterical panic Jambe-de-Laine appears like a horsewoman of the Apocalypse, and jumps out of her carriage, leaving the impetuous mare foaming on the other side of the hedge which borders the cemetery. She walks to the graveside, the perspiration mingled with the rouge running down her cheeks, 'pale as a Pierrot in the heat of the day'. By the time she has reached the edge of the grave 'there was so deep a silence from one end of the cemetery to the other, as far as the road, that you could distinctly hear the rustling of her silk skirt on the mound of earth, and the stifled sobs of the choir boys'.[3] Jambe-de-Laine was a nymphomaniac, but she was also a châtelaine, and she seemed, in the

[1] Editions de la Pléiade, pp. 1492–3   [2] Ibid, p. 1496   [3] Ibid, p. 1498

notorious degradation to which many of the bystanders had contributed, 'the victim abandoned to the appetite of one class by
another'. When she stands, with her head thrown back, beside the
coffin and exclaims with an ear-piercing shrillness: 'I will avenge
you', we are to understand that the little cowherd, like so many
others, had probably ministered to her satisfactions.

As she tries to place her hands, a second time, on the coffin, the
gravedigger strikes her with his spade, and the blood spattered on
the pallor of her cheek turns her from a Pierrot into a clown. Then
a clod of earth hits her on the chest, and when a villager tries to
persuade her to leave peacefully, she sinks her nails into his face,
leaps away from the infuriated crowd, escapes through the gate of
the cemetery, jumps into her carriage, and with no more than a
click of the tongue sends the great mare upon its way. But the
crowd has caught up with her, and a young man, attempting to
seize the reins, is kicked to the ground. The carriage is overturned
at a bend in the road, as the wheel loses its axle, and Jambe-de-Laine,
breaking free of the debris, is last seen silhouetted against the sky,
'the rags of black silk falling to her knees in long tatters hardly lifted
by the wind. When they all reached the slope, stumbling together,
she lifted her arms without a word.'[1] She will have, however, one
more word before the crowd has finished with the lynching.
'Philippe!' she cries out twice. One of those who had tried to restrain
her was called Philippe, but it was of another Philippe that she was
thinking. Magnificent and mad, Jambe-de-Laine, and the great
mare that she alone can master, stands for the life that cannot find
its proper outlet in the *paroisse morte*, just as Monsieur Ouine stands
for the death that seeks no outlet beyond itself. Both have fed – the
one with a ferocious gluttony, the other with a passive absorption –
upon the adolescent who is their prey.

If, as many believe, *Monsieur Ouine* is the masterpiece of Georges
Bernanos – though the judgment seems to me open to question –
the scene recalled here in some detail certainly shows his imagination
working at its fullest stretch. To have organised the inorganic in a
kaleidoscope that leaves confusion clear, is a triumph that has few
parallels in contemporary writing. *Monsieur Ouine* will always be an
enigmatic novel, and Claude-Edmonde Magny, in the article already
referred to, explains the reason why.

[1] Ibid, p. 1502

One can say that *Monsieur Ouine* is a novel wholly devoted to the description of the mystery of Evil. The mystery is visible and tangible, though it cannot be understood. It is evident to the senses and to the soul, composed of something negative, a reality which simply *does not exist*. That is why the death of the little cowherd – the enigma which lies at the heart of the book – will never be explained. Like the many ambiguities in the behaviour of the different characters and their relations with each other, it symbolises in some way the fundamental and irreducible opacity of Evil for the human spirit.[1]

[1] *Poésie 46*

CHAPTER 13

VANISHING ILLUSIONS

I

GUY HATTU had returned to Brazil after the French capitulation, but left again to join a commando of the Gaullist army. Michel was on board a submarine chaser, and Yves was now well enough to follow his military inclinations. Bernanos was alone with his wife – whose delicate health was a constant anxiety, two of his three daughters – for Chantal was in Rio – and Jean-Loup. Occasional visits to Rio, where he could now afford to rent a *pied-à-terre*, relieved the solitude of Barbacena. The house at Cruz das Almas was pretty, with stabling for four horses and two horse-carts, and further accommodation for saddlery and grain.

Bernanos had now given up smoking, but his wardrobe – never very ample – was considerably the worse for wear. He was missing his sons and nephew, and thought of them as he read the Psalm 90 from Compline, which Dom Besse had asked him to read during the 1914–18 war.

It is arguable that he served the causes he had at heart better by his imaginative than by his polemical writings, for here neither facts nor controversy could refute him. As if in relief from the daily see-saw of hopes and fears, he turned aside, in 1943, to compose his wonderful meditation on Martin Luther, which finds no place in his collected writings. The heresiarchs were very close to the saints, and Bernanos was naturally attracted to the temperament of Luther – where maybe he caught a glimpse of his own reflection – rather than to the cold logic of Calvin. He saw in Luther a man

made for joy, the rough joy of daily work, with a bundle on his shoulders or heaved off them with a twitch of his loins. A man who didn't drink out of a fine decanter, but out of a peasant's jug, one of those jugs of coarse and honey-coloured pottery, which they fill with anything from the barrel – beer or cider or *eau-de-vie*.

Bernanos was tempted to a comparison with another great

heresiarch, Félix de Lammenais, for whom Pius XI had expressed a
sympathy almost amounting to devotion – for Lammenais had been
the scourge of the Church in the nineteenth century, as Luther had
been its scourge in the sixteenth. Luther had not lasted any longer
than Lammenais.

He, too, had become maddened, and taken the bit between his teeth, like
a farm-horse putting his great foot into a wasp's nest. He rushed off
clumsily on his four hooves, and when he stopped – not because he was
tired, to be sure, but to see where he was, recover his breath, and examine
his wounds – the old Church was already a long way behind him, at
an immense, incalculable distance, separated from him for a whole eternity.

The words that Bernanos imagined in the mouth of God, as He
speaks to Luther, reveal not only an insight into the character of the
great reformer, but into that of the Church which he set out to
reform.

'Son Martin, take care – it is I who have sown in you this bitterness. It is
with me and in me and by my ordinance that you suffer from the
wretched state of my Church. Don't presume upon this suffering to my
face. Others who love me a thousand times better than you are capable
of loving me, don't feel it to the same degree, or hardly feel it at all.
What revolts your conscience seems to them no more than a dream, a
bad dream, and they turn their thoughts away from it whenever they
want to, because they are living in another world. But your place is
firmly marked out in this world – I have seen to that – and I have made
you a carnal man, solid and heavy. I shall pit you against other men, just
as carnal as yourself, formed of the same matter, so that they shall feel the
force of your blows, because it is through you, if you keep faith with me,
that I have decided to break their pride and to avenge my people, whose
souls they are putting up for auction. But don't deceive yourself, brother
Martin; this is neither the greatest nor the noblest task I could give you;
it is simply a task made to your measure – that is all. I have given you
health and strength and popular eloquence and a genius for controversy
almost equal to that of my son Augustine. But these are not the favourite
weapons of our saints – make no mistake about that – you will only find
them good for tearing up, sweeping away, and uprooting the corrupted
stocks. Think of my apostle Paul, whom you're so fond of. He, too, was
a carnal man, violent, rash, and argumentative. What a business I had to
soften and unstiffen his soul . . .'

The voice pursues the comparison with St Paul before moving to its superb conclusion –

'From the beginning, my Church has been what it is today, and will be until the end of time, a scandal to the strong, a disappointment to the weak, the ordeal and the consolation of those interior souls who seek in it nothing but myself. Yes, brother Martin, whoever looks for me there will find me there; but he will have to look, and I am better hidden than people think, or than certain of my priests would have you believe. I am still more difficult to discover than I was in the little stable at Bethlehem for those who will not approach me humbly, in the footsteps of the shepherds and the Magi. It's true that palaces have been built in my honour, with galleries and peristyles without number, magnificently illuminated day and night, populated with guards and sentries. But if you want to find me there, the clever thing is to do as they did on the old road in Judaea, buried under the snow, and ask for the only thing you need – a star and a pure heart.'[1]

It was in a similar mood, on the 8th of September 1943 – the Feast of the Nativity of the Blessed Virgin – that Bernanos wrote the first, and only, pages of the *Vie de Jésus* on which he had brooded for so long. He worked at it for only a few days, filling five pages of a notebook with his close handwriting and multiple corrections. They tell us little of what the book would have become, because they scarcely touch upon its central character.

I should like to write this book [Bernanos began] for the most miserable of mankind, and I should also like to write it in their language, but that is forbidden me. One can imitate neither misery, nor the language of misery. To share without sacrilege in the sacrament of misery one has to be miserable oneself.

Christ came into this world, and He came into it for everybody, not only for the miserable. Around His crib were the shepherds and the Magi, but neither the shepherds nor the Magi were miserable. Perhaps the good thief was miserable, but we cannot be sure. Contrary to what the moralists generally suppose, true misery does not lead to crime; it ends up neither in good nor in evil; it leads nowhere. The true misery of the miserable has no issue but in God.

Bernanos was evidently intending to develop the distinction which Péguy had made between *pauvreté* and *misère:*

[1] *Bernanos par lui-même*, pp. 182–6

The poor man is not a man whose state of life deprives him of what he needs. He is a man who lives poorly, according to the immemorial tradition of poverty; who lives from day to day by the work of his hands; who eats out of the hand of God, as the old and popular expression has it. He lives not only by what he makes with his hands, but by his brotherhood with others who are poor like himself, by the thousand and one little resources of poverty, by what he can foresee and what he cannot foresee. The poor possess the secret of hope . . .[1]

At this point the manuscript stops. The daily preoccupation with the foreseen and the unforeseen, the daily and difficult renewal of hope, distracted Bernanos from the book which he never lived to finish.

2

In the summer of 1940 high officials of the Quai d'Orsay were telling their Brazilian friends that 'Bernanos has not ten Frenchmen behind him.' He replied, when the estimate was repeated to him, that they were not behind him but in front; and by 1943 they were more than ten times ten. He had little contact with the men of the French Resistance, but he placed his hopes in them. It was they, if anyone, who would 'take up once again the great work of 1789'; and the difference, he affirmed, between 1789 and 1793 was the difference between Péguy and Maurras. The work of 1789 was the work of Christian men, even if they imagined they were unbelievers. Bernanos would have said the same thing of the Communists, who were the strongest arm of the Resistance. The difference, again, was the difference between Robespierre and St Just, whose ambition was no more and no less than to 'create in Europe the possibility of happiness'. But the cold dogmatism of Robespierre had fathered the dictatorships of Left and Right, where all men should be equal and the dictator more equal than the others. Bernanos had no sympathy for 'egalitarian pride'; and he allowed his nostalgia to play with the picture of some rather dilapidated château where the gardener would screw his gnarled hands into a pair of white cotton gloves in order to serve the châtelaine.

In the 500 pages of Bernanos' polemical writings from Brazil[2] the reader is surprised to find how relatively infrequent is the name of

[1] *Bernanos par lui-même*, pp. 186–8   [2] *Le Chemin de la Croix des Ames*

Adolf Hitler. When he is mentioned at all, it is with a kind of compassion – for Hitler, too, had been an *enfant humilié*. As the balance of forces shifted, with Britain essaying the role of honest broker between America and the Soviet Union, the stature of de Gaulle increased and Bernanos' recognition of his role became more vocal. His revolt against the armistice was 'one of the few political episodes of this war capable of stirring the popular imagination. A legend was created around the man and the event. Be careful how you lay your hands upon the event and upon the man.'[1] Only the 'hammer strokes of that great voice' had consoled Bernanos during the summer of treason and catastrophe. It mattered little that the people of France had not chosen de Gaulle, since history itself had chosen him; and when the rumour reached Brazil that he had resigned, Bernanos sent him the following telegram: '*Avec vous sans réserves*'.[2]

Now that so much of North Africa was in Allied hands, and that his sons and nephew were fighting under the Cross of Lorraine, he sometimes thought of moving camp to Morocco. Meanwhile he kept in close touch with Gaullist circles in Rio. Writing so far from the men and the events, he did not always judge them with equity. The democracies could have had the Russian alliance for the price of the Baltic states, and no doubt a large slice of Poland – but would Bernanos have had them pay it? He was as impatient as Stalin himself for a premature offensive in Europe, but the ghost of Munich walked again with the sacrifice of the Poles to the necessities of *Real-Politik*. Increasingly, as victory became certain, he feared that it would be a *victoire manquée*, and, like the victory of 1918, a *victoire muette*, yet speaking as loudly as the martyrs of the Warsaw ghetto while the Soviet tanks waited cynically beyond the walls.

On more than one occasion he opened his flank to controversy. A certain critic of some eminence, M. Carpeaux, accused French culture of 'sterilising the intelligence'; and he belauded in its place the culture of Germany, from which he had escaped to the hospitable exile of Brazil. For M. Carpeaux was a Jew, and Bernanos was quick to inform his readers that his real name was Karpfen. He had taken instead the patronym of an illustrious French sculptor, and his polemical manner was such that 'if he persists in employing the style of a musketeer, he will be obliged to modify his civic status a

[1] Ibid, p. 359   [2] 18th June 1943

second time, and substitute for the name of Carpeaux that of
d'Artagnan.'[1] Bernanos had an old-fashioned prejudice in favour of
people calling themselves by the name they were born with. In
replying to M. Carpeaux he analysed a pessimism which

has in no way the character of an impiety or a revolt; it is the sacred and
religious pessimism of Ecclesiastes. But it is also the metaphysical
pessimism which is so deeply stamped on the German soul, whenever
its pride is wounded. And perhaps these two pessimisms are one and the
same, for in spite of the hatred – or maybe because of it – which sets them
at odds, like brothers at enmity with each other, the Jewish people and
the German people are linked together in a mysterious affinity.[2]

Of this affinity both the personality and the writings of M.
Carpeaux seemed to Bernanos an example, but he was reproached
by several Jewish compatriots for drawing attention to it. This
enabled him to express his mind on the Jewish question, and it
enables us today to see how far he had moved from the crude anti-
Semitism of *La Libre Parole*. He was not immediately attracted to
Jews, as others, maybe, are not attracted to Frenchmen, but there
were two Jews whom he counted among his best friends in Brazil.

One is a young religious, a converted Jew, and even a German Jew. The
other, whom the service of France has taken away from us, is neither a
religious nor a Catholic, but he will remain for me an example of fidelity,
sincerity, modesty, and grandeur – an admirable specimen of humanity.
Converted or not, I am sure that the gentle mercy of God will not place
him too far away from me in Paradise, always provided that I succeed one
day in getting there.[3]

This was Georges Torres, the stepson of Léon Blum; he was afterwards to be killed fighting in Alsace.

But Bernanos would not admit that the Jews were just like anybody else. The Jews were a race, as the Germans were a race;
neither were a nation in the sense that the French were a nation.

If there is a Jewish race, there is a Jewish sensibility, and a Jewish thought, a
Jewish sense of life and death, wisdom and happiness. I willingly agree
that these social and mental characteristics which they have in common
are more strongly marked in some cases than in others. All I say is that
they exist. I neither despise nor condemn them. Some of them are out of
tune with my own sensibility, but I know that they belong to the common

[1] *Le Chemin de la Croix des Ames*, p. 416   [2] Ibid, pp. 419–20   [3] Ibid, p. 422

patrimony of mankind, and that in the world they maintain the spirit and the tradition of the oldest spiritual civilisation that history records.[1]

Bernanos paid his tribute to the French Jew, assimilated to the nation, contributing to its genius, and often heroically at its service; whereas east of the Rhine

the German soul and the Jewish soul share the same pride, the same heartrending inferiority complex, and also the same bitterness – for a superior race, a race of the elect, is necessarily aware of its solitude among the nations. It believes itself to be hated and envied by everybody. When I wrote that the genius of the Jews was in deep accord with the genius of Germany, I meant that the German milieu, so far from tempering certain characteristics of the Jewish race, welcomes and exaggerates them.[2]

These conclusions may be criticised as oversimplified and summary, but they cannot be condemned as anti-Semitic. Bernanos told Dom Gordan that he would 'rather be whipped by a Rabbi than cause suffering to a Jewish child or woman.'

The opening of a second front in Europe, with the liberation of Paris and large tracts of French territory, brought thanksgiving rather than euphoria. Bernanos would have been happier if France had liberated herself, although, from within as well as from without, she had acted with courage and efficiency according to her means. She still had the power, however, to free herself from the servitude of cowardice and corruption. Bernanos lacked the 'Anglo-Saxon' respect for the due process of law, and the execution of Pucheu in Algiers had caused him no qualms of conscience. In 1942 the Comte de Paris had sent him a message through a Swiss friend that he was wholly in agreement with him as to the rôle the Royal House of France should play in the unlikely event of its restoration – although there were moments in Algiers when anything looked possible. It should be no part of their policy to serve the vested interests; they held their mandate from the people; the doctrine of Divine Right was an invention of 'servile theologians' wishing to freeze the Spanish throne in what proved to be a fatal immobility. The Comte de Paris excused himself for 'appearances', but these appearances were sufficiently evident to stimulate a report, in November 1944, that he had been arrested on orders from de Gaulle. If the accusations

[1] Ibid, p. 423   [2] Ibid, pp. 423–4

brought against him were true, Bernanos had no doubt that he should be welcomed by a firing squad wherever he happened to present himself. In fact, both the report and the accusations were unfounded.

Accusation was flowing very freely, and from suspicious quarters. Three months later Bernanos entitled an article *Le Saint-Office Communiste*. This was a reply to Aragon who had demanded that André Gide be expelled from the National Committee of Writers. Bernanos – *Monsieur Ouine* notwithstanding – did not share the belief of Mauriac and Claudel that Gide was possessed by the Devil, but he admitted that he found it difficult to be just towards 'one of our greatest writers, who does honour to our language'.[1] Aragon's inquisition came under four heads. Gide had employed himself during the occupation in a study of the German language, a charge that was obviously not worth refuting. He had written – without approval or dissent – that nine Frenchmen out of ten were prepared to accept a German hegemony provided it gave them material security. Since Bernanos had heard a similar resignation preached by the French Ambassador in Rio, and by one of his colleagues who was still *chef de protocol* at the Quai d'Orsay, he did not see why André Gide should be singled out for particular victimisation. Thirdly, Gide had written that to '*composer* with the enemy of yesterday was not cowardice but wisdom. What is the point of bruising oneself against the bars of the cage?'[2] Bernanos admitted that these words might be taken as an expression of 'moderate Pétainism', but he argued that to *composer* was not the same thing as to collaborate. Moreover Gide had seen 'unlimited possibilities of acceptance which in no way engage one's deeper self. The far greater risk is to allow one's thought to be dominated by hate.'[3] This – Bernanos argued – was no more than 'practical submission to an illegitimate authority that one's conscience refuses';[4] and not to 'bruise oneself against the bars of one's cage' was to refuse the domination of hate. 'The intoxication of hate, like any other intoxication, seems to me a useless dissipation of energy.'[5]

The fourth accusation was based on what André Gide had written on the 28th of September 1940:

If tomorrow, as I fear, all liberty of thought or at least of expression is

[1] *Le Chemin de la Croix des Ames*, p. 479   [2] Ibid   [3] Ibid   [4] Ibid   [5] Ibid

forbidden us, I shall try to convince myself that art and thought itself will lose less than by an excessive liberty. The best are immune from the debasement of oppression – and the others don't matter very much. So long live the repression of thought![1]

Such words were undoubtedly damaging, but Bernanos reminded his readers that to wish long life to the oppression of thought was not to wish long life to its oppressors. In a similar sense he had himself written that persecution revived the faith and charity of Christians, but not even his worst enemy had accused him of wishing to rehabilitate Nero. What disgusted him in the Communist inquisition was its hypocrisy. At the very time when André Gide was trying to make the best of a situation, uncomfortable to say the least, its press could write as follows:

The party, which fought against the treaty of Versailles, for the brotherhood of the French and German peoples, and against the imperialist war, holds its head high ... the party is showing you the way of salvation. And the way of salvation is not the way indicated by General de Gaulle, who wishes France to be tied to the wavering fortunes of British imperialism on its decline; and it is not the way which would end in the enslavement of this country to the profit of ferocious colonisers.[2]

With the entry of Russia into the war the tune had changed. Now, on the eve of Yalta and on the morrow of Teheran, no one could mention the Poles without a blush, if they mentioned them at all, for fear of being denounced as reactionaries by the same *petit bourgeois* intelligentsia who had once been so prodigal in their flattery of André Gide. Bernanos had nothing but contempt for those 'whom we see rubbing themselves against the Muscovite bear in the hope of reviving their impotence, and who talk among themselves, with their greedy little faces, of *épuration* and executions *en masse*. But when the day arrives, they should be made to drink the blood in a bib, as you give milk to a new born kitten.'[3] Bernanos had not forgotten his conversation with Malraux before Malraux had rejected the Communist recipe for salvation. His defence of Gide may be read as an exercise in casuistry by one who generally did not spare his scorn for casuists; and he was on all the stronger ground since his own inquisitions, however unsparing, had never been selective. Moreover Bernanos was in some way obsessed by

[1] Ibid   [2] Ibid, p. 484, quoted from Les Editions Communistes   [3] Ibid, p. 481

Gide; once he picked up his *Journal* he was unable to put it down. He would have liked to know what Gide thought of his own writings, but there is no mention of Bernanos in the *Journal*. Piqued a little by the vanity, of which he was not entirely innocent, he confessed with a wistful simplicity: 'I should very much like him to say something about my work.' For the moment it was enough that, once again, he had seen 'one man being set upon by many', and once again his 'sympathies were with the underdog'. They were always to remain there.

So far from releasing new energies, the effect of the Liberation was to leave Bernanos exhausted in mind and body. For some weeks nothing came from his pen; and he remained plunged for long hours in prayer. Since his piety was at once so robust and so unobtrusive, it is interesting to record its punctilio. He said his rosary every day, read the liturgy of the Mass if he were unable to attend it, and always recited Compline before going to bed – generally at 10 p.m. His faith was the faith of Pasteur's 'Breton peasant' – or 'Breton peasant's wife'. Meanwhile the horses' hooves clattered on the single paved street of Barbacena, while the priest and the doctor, the chemist and the notary, the cowherd and the digger for gold in the Rio das Velhas went about their business which varied little from one day to another. It was true that Brazil was now at war, but long before the conference of Rio de Janeiro, the gold-digger had asked Bernanos: 'Well, sir, how is *our* war going?' – and this was the question that he never ceased asking himself. The talk was more and more of the Big Three, although only two of them were really big; and the chance or the option of the future would lie between domination by one big trust or by many. Whichever way he looked Bernanos could see only the restriction of liberty; machines doing the work of men, and men reduced to robots. He talked no more about the revolution of order; he did not care in whose name the revolution was made, provided the men were free who made it. The French genius for spontaneous organisation had been shown in the Resistance, as it had been shown in 1789; but would it survive the emergency which had called it into being? The men of 1789 had looked forward to something other than a planners' paradise.

It may be objected that Bernanos abused the freedom of his solitude, as he sent his prophecies over the air or through the press with only his wife, his younger children, a single cow, a score or two of detective novels, and the portrait of Winston Churchill over the mantelpiece for company. Denunciation was easy for one who had no remedy or responsibility for reconstruction. To write in terms of the absolute was all very well, but the absolute implies the relative as light implies shade, and height depth. Even those who have their eyes fixed on the summit have to struggle with the boulders at their feet. Elsewhere, in a world still at war, men were planning for the future. No doubt their plans would go awry. The preliminary palavers at Dumbarton Oaks did little but prepare a forum in which the disunited nations could fight with words instead of with weapons. In the meanwhile Bernanos would have fought with weapons if he had been able to; he had not long to live, and he would have been a happier man if the chance had been given him to die with them in his hands.

3 [1]

Once the Provisional Government was firmly established, belatedly recognised by its allies, General de Gaulle urgently invited the eminent exiles to return home – Teilhard de Chardin from Peking, Maritain from New York, and Bernanos from Brazil. They obeyed, some more speedily than others. For Bernanos this was a call of duty, not altogether of desire. For nearly seven years he had preserved *une certaine idée de la France*, no less idealised than the *idée* of de Gaulle; soon he would be obliged to confront the idea with the reality – and he had few illusions in his luggage. He was now spending a good deal of time in Rio, generally staying at the Pax Hotel, since he had given up his *pied-à-terre*. He was suffering both mentally and physically, eating very little, and it is possible, as he himself suspected, that the first symptoms of a fatal cancer of the liver were now declaring themselves. Lassitude and an almost visionary power alternated in his conversation. He seemed to be 'observing himself, registering and analysing his sensations with a lucidity that only increased his suffering. Nothing and nobody could help him; his only comfort was the patience with which others put up with him. He accepted this without any false shame; he was

[1] For much of the information and most of the quotations in this section I am indebted to the Diary of Fernando Carneiro da Cunha: *Bernanos no Brasil*.

simply grateful for it.'[1] One day Dom Gordan took him to his abbey, knowing how much he valued the peace which he found there; but on this occasion he stayed only for a few hours. 'He felt himself a prisoner; the silence, solitude, and solemnity of the enclosure caused him an almost physical suffering. He broke out into bitter words, and gave himself freely to the thoughts which were tormenting him, and I could do nothing else but take him back to his friends the same evening.'[2] He described how he had suffered like this before, when he was writing *Sous le Soleil de Satan*, and now he was struggling with a reluctance to accept a second invitation from de Gaulle, conveyed to him by Gaston Palewski. To this he only resigned himself on the advice of his spiritual director. Perhaps he was haunted by a presentiment of death which was closer than anyone supposed, and by the *Vie de Jésus* of which the solitary fragment lay abandoned in a notebook at Barbacena. On the 1st of December his decision to leave within the next three weeks was communicated to Paris.

Sometimes the children would come down to Rio. Claude, who looked after the *fazenda* when her father was away, had no wish to leave it. She was already over twenty, 'quite a hot number, with the aquiline profile of her mother, fierce, slanting eyes, long, almost straight hair, and upthrust breasts . . . a beautiful savage'.[3] For her brothers, too, the freedom of the fields was threatened by a return to the world of politics, of which they had already heard too much. Claude remembered the discussions in France before the war – how the friends would fill the house, arguing at the top of their voices until daybreak, while the children, understanding not a word, fell asleep with their heads on the table. In Rio she escaped from politics into the sea, with her hair streaming in the wind; and on land there were picnics and rides in the forest. One night, at Alto da Tijuca, they met a man with a guitar whom they took along with them in the car as they drove slowly down the wide avenues and the mysterious forest roads. These were the songs of an older France, *Sur les marches du palais* being, as always, a special favourite. They would also talk a good deal about *The Threepenny Opera*, by Brecht-Weil, which Bernanos himself seems to have much appreciated. When they had shed the guitarist, a mouth-organ bought in Petropolis had to do service instead; and back in Barbacena, after the long and

[1] Dom Gordan: *Bulletin* 6, pp. 3–6   [2] Ibid   [3] *Bernanos no Brasil*

tiring drive, Claude resumed her responsibilities – 'when I do something I do it thoroughly' was a justified boast – and Dominique had the *entrée* to the humblest cottage of the peasants who lived near by. The children dreaded the return to France because it had become so foreign to them; Bernanos because it was so familiar and because he, too, was afraid that it might now appear so foreign.

In Rio he would sit, his game leg crossed over his good one, in the Café Brasiliera, or the Club dos Caicaras, or another club which he ironically christened the 'Salazar', and talk incessantly with his friends. He was something of an actor, and he needed an audience. He was haunted and irritated by Maritain, admiring his intelligence, criticising his politics, and occasionally poking fun at the plane of contemplation on which he maintained his private life. But there was a deep affection beneath the badinage. He prayed daily for Maritain, and seemed to have a special feeling for Raïssa, fearing only that Maritain would be manipulated by democratic circles in France, and wished him to remain on the heights of philosophic speculation. Once he had descended from them, he ran the risk of being rejected *en bloc;* and in fact many people who have admired Maritain as a political theorist have disagreed with his philosophy, and vice versa. Bernanos would quote Dom Gordan in affirming a resemblance between Calvin and St Thomas Aquinas; and when Dom Gordan stubbornly asserted that Bernanos' way of thinking was unconsciously Thomist, Bernanos improvised the fantasy of a newspaper story that 'an old man has been fished out of the Seine who, just before he died, gave his name as Georges Bernanos, and realised that he had thrown himself into the river when he discovered, at almost sixty years of age, that he was a Thomist!' Bernanos envied Maritain the consolation of his ideas. 'I have no doctrine except my catechism. All I see is my fellow men.'

He was haunted, equally, by the mystery and scandal of the Church. Every church, he would argue, tended to crystallise into a synagogue, and if Christ came back to earth He would be crucified by the cardinals. All the forces of nature combined to turn the Church into a synagogue, and she was only saved by the saints who pulled her back from the abyss. The saints – and the saints alone – were the proof of her divinity. But there was one thing she lacked, although it was a lesser thing than sanctity – and that was the sense of honour. Bernanos was always apprehensive that some book of his would be formally condemned, and if it had been he was ready to submit. Many things might have been different, he maintained, if Lammenais had possessed the grace of submission as well as the gift of prophecy. But it was the deepest tragedy in the life of Georges Bernanos that he looked for honour in the Church to which he belonged, and did not find it.

Where politics were in question, it was very different. Here he looked for a revolution of the Christian conscience 'with a strong dose of anarchism'; and he wondered why the English were so submissive to the punitive taxation imposed upon them. The profile of Sir Stafford Cripps inspired in him a particular repugnance; it reminded him of a 'primary schoolmaster'. Why did the young, everywhere, surrender to the extortions of the state? 'The state will never leave go of what it once has taken.' He opposed the idea of legitimacy which he venerated, to the idea of legality for which he professed a Maurrasian disdain, imagining a loyal adherent of the Stuarts arguing as follows: 'Obey our king, be faithful to him, he's thoroughly bad on occasion, and doesn't always recognise our devotion. But what will you have? He's our king, God made him the way he is, our duty is to serve him, and that's how we serve our country, and his son will surely be better than he is!' And then, as if he anticipated an objection, Bernanos would distinguish between legitimacy and absolute power. No earthly power was absolute; the king reigned by natural and hereditary, not by Divine, right. Monarchy was not perfect; it was based on a relativity in time, for the first king of a legitimate line was illegitimate. But personal power, embodied in the tradition of a family, conferred a dignity and imposed a duty on the man who held it, whatever his personal defects, and a responsibility which itself created a respect for the people he served.

It was a far cry from this historical nostalgia to the harsh and noisy realities of the hour. The Allied victories had brought a sudden return of civil liberty to Brazil, and a consequent upsurge of democratic sentiment. Bernanos viewed this with his habitual distrust. As for Sicrano, its principal spokesman, it was 'enough to look at his face'. A new French ambassador had come to Rio, who 'has many of my ideas, but he doesn't love the things that I love. I can only talk to someone who loves what I love myself. And then,

The hut at Vassouras where he wrote
Nous autres Français, 1939

At Cruz das Almas

In Rio de Janeiro, 1944

you see, people who have a profession are so self-assured. I have no profession.'

On the other hand he was on excellent terms with Sir Noel Charles, who had replaced Sir Geoffrey Knox at the British Embassy. Bernanos had never ceased to proclaim that, historically speaking, England had won the war at Dunkirk, and as it moved to its finale his prophecy that the fall of Hitler would be like a Beethoven symphony, was being fulfilled to the letter. On New Year's Eve (1943) he sent to Sir Noel Charles the following good wishes:

May it please God that everyone should soon be put back in their proper place, the apaches on the pavement, the thieves in prison, the servants in the servants' quarters, the lunatics in the asylum, and the cowards be consigned to the devil, so that your noble country and mine, like two old neighbours in the country, may start quarrelling again from time to time, just to prove that they can't do without one another.[1]

Not all the French resident in Brazil were immune from the mystique of Vichy, and Bernanos had no patience with them when they complained of trouble with their servants. He was heartened, however, by a meeting with two members of the *maquis*. He refused to attend a congress of Brazilian writers in São Paulo because he feared that it would be dominated by a 'band of hypocritical and fanatical Marxists'. It was more amusing to sit in the Brasiliera and talk about Funck-Brentano's *Ancien Régime;* to wonder if Cardinal Spellman would be appointed Secretary of State; and to contemplate the end of the world with equanimity. 'It can all happen quite simply. Just as if everything were going on as usual, but in the Father's house.' These sessions at the Brasiliera could be stormy. A French interior decorator, snobbish and manifestly homosexual, did not endear himself to Bernanos by observing: 'We must have many friends in common.' He went on to describe with appropriate gestures the shape of a table that he wished to make out of a particularly delicate wood. Did not Bernanos think that this would look well in the salon of a marquis or an ambassador? 'Yes,' thundered Bernanos in reply, 'provided they were pederasts like yourself.' Another interlocutor took it upon himself to attack Proust for exactly the same reason, but Bernanos – impetuous, as ever, in defence of the injured party – launched into an endless

[1] 31st December 1943: *Correspondance* II, pp. 529-30
G.B.–Q

apologia, pretending that he spoke from personal acquaintance.[1] Sometimes he would talk of literature – of his admiration for Julian Green, whose fiction he described as a 'cold nightmare', and of D. H. Lawrence whom he dismissed with contumely. 'It's the English prudery in reverse.' If one objected that his picture of Lawrence was a caricature, he replied that Lawrence himself was a caricature. He had read *Lady Chatterley*, but not Lawrence's defence of it.

As the day of departure drew near, he became more and more restless, unable even to write in a café and perambulating the streets. The heat and humidity oppressed him. 'If you stay for a single moment with your mouth open, the mould accumulates on your tongue.' He toyed with writing an article on the German army – a tribute to the last of the great armies – but abandoned the idea, fearing no doubt that it would be misunderstood. Once he tried reading to a friend what he had written, as he had once read *Sous le Soleil de Satan* to Vallery-Radot. The session was a failure, however, and broke up in mutual irritation. When he had the thread of an idea it was easily broken, and it was the thread that he followed, never quite sure of where it would lead him. In March 1945 Maurras was standing his trial, and escaped the death sentence through a clever trick of the *camelots du roi*. Bernanos spoke of him, without hatred, as if he were already dead, imitating his hoarse voice and maintaining that if Maurras' theories had carried the day, Hitler would never have come to power. The disciple had quarrelled with the master, but there was much in the master's teaching that he would never reject. Here, again, was one man being set upon by many, and Bernanos refused to join in the hue and cry. Although he placed all his faith in the young, they were timid in approaching him. As they eyed him admiringly in a café, he remembered the day when Maurice Barrès had passed close by him and he had been too nervous to accost the *cher maître*. Maurras had equated liberty and power, and there was a disquieting parallel between those who thought they had found liberty in submission to the power of Hitler and those who now sought the same liberty in submission to the power of Stalin. If liberty was only to be found where Bernanos found it, he had reason to describe himself as the *dernier des hommes libres;* and if the young had ventured to approach his table, their starry-eyed

[1] Recorded by Albert Béguin: *Correspondance* II, p. 559

repetition of the fashionable nostrums would have met with a rude shock.

At times the beauty of what he was leaving behind moved him to tears. He had stayed for a few weeks, earlier in 1944, at Paquetá, and wished he could have remained there, like John VI of Portugal. Now as he watched the sun go down over the curving outline of the bay, the fire softened in the large, blue eyes which were so often wild with rage – the *saeva indignatio* that he shared with Swift – and he remarked how impossible it seemed to him that in the future life there should not be something which prolonged the pleasure one had taken in the earth, and justified one's attachment to it. It was the same thought which prompted his famous: '*Quand je serai mort dites au doux royaume de la terre que je l'aimais plus que je n'ai jamais osé dire.*' Another moment of short-lived exaltation he had enjoyed when Germany capitulated on the 15th of May 1945. 'Whatever ordeals are in store for me tomorrow I shall rediscover in their sadness, like a diamond beneath the ashes, the memory of these glorious hours.'[1] His *Adieu to Brazil* was written in the Café Brasiliera; henceforward he would be continually changing his address, but he was constant in his habits.

There were many personal adieux. Franco de Lima was drinking his beer on the balcony of the Brahma Hotel when the waiter told him that someone at another table wanted to speak to him. It was Bernanos. They had not seen each other for a year, but Bernanos was so dispirited that Franco de Lima was almost sorry they had met. 'Watch what they say or write about me, here in Brazil. Many people are going to call themselves my friend, and attribute to me phrases I never used or ideas I never had.' On the 1st of June the whole family were in Rio, the children loud in argument about this and that. Bernanos, seated in the car under the tall trees of a familiar square, looked around him and exclaimed: 'To think that this is probably the last time that I shall see the light at this hour. It's a fearful thought.' Never before, he said, except at school when the holidays were over, had he felt so strongly that he was doing something entirely against his will ... returning to France. He embarked on the following day, and as he paternally kissed the many friends who had come to see him off, they noticed the cold sweat on his face.

[1] *Le Chemin de la Croix des Ames*, p. 494

After disembarking at Liverpool, Bernanos arrived in London on the 27th of June. There he met his friend André Rousseaux. It was seven years since they had said goodbye to each other on the terrace of the Brasserie Lipp, and they spent the whole day together. Rousseaux gave him a picture of the situation in France which did not exactly correspond with the picture he had presented at the French Institute in the afternoon. He had drawn a parallel between Péguy and the *maquisards*, but the parallel was already a year old.

He questioned me about the France that he was to see once more in a few days' time, and he awaited the meeting with infinite tenderness and immense anxiety. I told him all that we had experienced, over the last nine months, of stupefaction and disappointment. It was fairly imprecise and in naïve contradiction with the proclamations of a renewed and revolutionary future which I had launched in public an hour before. We spoke very frankly. It was understood that this revolution, this rebirth of France, burnt us to the soul, like a fire that nothing should extinguish. As for the moral collapse in which its flame ran the risk of wavering, here what I said described only very vaguely a confusion that I still did not perceive clearly for myself.

I can see Bernanos sitting opposite me at the table of the restaurant where we dined that evening, close to Buckingham Palace. 'I was afraid of it,' he murmured. 'I was afraid of it.' He spoke these words in an undertone, as if he were weighed down by a fearful weariness. The great anger to which he was to give vent a few weeks later, and which was to thunder until his death, had not yet exploded. But it is true to say that he already had a deep perception of what only a very few Frenchmen felt as an obscure uneasiness. No doubt we could already have realised that what Paris had prepared, for more than six months before the 25th of August 1944, was not so much its liberation – which was a farce – but the replacement of those in occupation by the occupation of those who had arrived. We should have had the courage to admit that from that moment the moral bankruptcy of the Resistance had marked the lowest point of resignation to which France had descended. We shut our eyes to a truth which would have broken our hopes of a marvellous resurrection, like a body broken on a wheel. Bernanos, I now realise, kept his eyes open as he waited for the atrocious truth to become clear to him. That is what I gathered from the distant look in his eyes, as he murmured in a low voice: 'I was afraid of it.' He foresaw the blow which would strike him to the heart when his emotion at seeing the cliffs of Dieppe smile on his return had passed away, and when each step he took on his native soil would plunge him deeper into this bankruptcy and this sham. . . . The reality of contemporary France, which no genuine victory had effaced, was the capitulation of 1940. That is why, on the day when Paris was liberated, Bernanos remained silent.[1]

The root cause of what Rousseaux obscurely perceived, and Bernanos divined more clearly, was the equivocation at the heart of the Resistance. The Communists, spiritually enslaved to Stalinist Russia, were preparing for their own revolution which they hoped their merited prestige would facilitate. Others, less numerous and less strictly organised, were preparing for a revolution which would ensure the liberty of man, preserving it from the anonymous dictatorship of money, and also from other dictatorships which were anything but anonymous. They had no wish to see the Gestapo replaced by the OGPU. Nor did they forget that some of them had been, openly or clandestinely, in the field at a time when the Communist voices now calling the tune were still taking their orders from Moscow. The *parti des fusillés* had the right to celebrate its martyrs; but there were other martyrs who did not identify their *parti* with their *patrie*, and who perhaps did not belong to any *parti* at all. Georges Bernanos was one of them.

De Gaulle himself was quick to observe that certain elements of the Resistance were more anxious to keep their arms in order to settle their private and political accounts than to use them against an enemy that had not yet thrown in the towel. Former sympathisers with Vichy lost no time in changing their coats. Only the authority of de Gaulle prevented the worst injustices of the *épuration;* and against the abuses of the black market it was powerless. Between the repentant Pétainistes and the Communists biding their time, with the new party manoeuvrings only too reminiscent of the old, the revolution in which Bernanos had placed his hopes vanished like a mirage. The French people, as a whole, were content to relapse into the facility which had been their undoing. They were grateful to have come to the end of one road; they had no stomach to set out upon another.

[1] *Démission de la France: Cahiers du Rhône,* pp. 321–3

CHAPTER 14

CONTROVERSY AND
CONTEMPLATION

I

BERNANOS returned to Paris on the 29th of June, having confided
to a friend on arrival that he had 'spent the night outside the door in
order to learn about this country all over again.' He was welcomed
by the Manificats, a number of other friends, and Michel in naval
uniform. He went straight to Avallon with the Manificats, made
several visits to Paris in July, and was very soon contributing articles
to *La Bataille*, a weekly journal which had already published one of
his texts in its first number (30th November 1944). Paris was
suffering from a severe bout of literary inflation; reputations, as
well as newspapers, sprang up overnight. On the 14th of July *Le
Figaro* published an interview with Bernanos by Luc Estang, a
brilliant young critic and novelist who had been active in the
Resistance. He was also the author of *Présence de Bernanos*, the first
full-length study of Bernanos to appear in France. This had not yet
been published, but Bernanos was naturally delighted to see him,
and he would not have objected to Estang's summary of their
interview: '*Georges Bernanos reste non-conformiste.*' There was talk of
his election to the Académie, and Bernanos liked to imagine the
scene he might have played if he were younger, the sword at his
side and the three-cornered hat on is head, creating a scandal in
the nearest *bistro*.

'Can you see me, Dominique, with my sword across my stomach, in one
of those bone-shaking little trains in Brazil? The idea doesn't interest me
at all, in spite of the pleasure it might give my family if . . . look at him
laughing over there' – as he pointed to Michel in his *matelot's* uniform. 'I
have come back to my country with the firm intention of saying everything I think.'[1]

He certainly said it. Many of his admirers thought he said it too

[1] Milner, pp. 337–8

strongly, too persistently, and too soon. The France of the *après-guerre* was not to be 'learnt all over again' so quickly. Bernanos had suffered in his way, but not as the French had suffered. Where he had imagined, they had experienced. '*Présence de Bernanos!*' François Mauriac exclaimed when Luc Estang's book appeared. '*Absence de Bernanos avant la guerre, absence de Bernanos pendant la guerre,*' and soon he would have reason to add '*absence de Bernanos après la guerre*'. Mauriac had caught, most unjustly, the rough side of Bernanos' pen. Bernanos was right to call in question certain injustices of the *épuration*, but Mauriac had done all he could to mitigate them. He had behaved with courage under the occupation, and resigned from the National Committee of Writers – many of them avowed lackeys of Stalin – for the same reason that Bernanos would have resigned, if he had found himself in the same position. The fact that Mauriac was descended from the Sillon did not justify Bernanos' denigration of one who stood, essentially, for the same things. If the posterity of the Sillon like Georges Bidault and Françisque Gay, François de Menthon and Henri Teitjen, were now in positions of power, it was because they had proved themselves better patriots than the *camelots du roi*. The Maurrasians had had a unique opportunity to strike a blow for the *pays réel*, and had missed it. These truths were unpalatable to Bernanos, and he did not swallow them easily. But when Mauriac, through André Rousseaux, invited him to stand for the Académie, where his election would have been a foregone conclusion, he declined with dignity. He believed that Richelieu, who had founded the Académie, would have appreciated his reasons for doing so.

At about the same time Bernanos read in the newspapers that he had been promoted to the Order of the Légion d'Honneur. He had already refused it on three occasions; now his acceptance was taken for granted. After requesting the cancellation of the appointment in a letter to the Grand Chancellor of the Order, he wrote to General de Gaulle, explaining that if he were to accept the honour, he would have preferred to win it on the battlefield, and under the General's command. De Gaulle accepted the refusal in a gracious letter, written in his own hand.

It was as a result of 'learning one's country all over again' that new friends took the place of old. Of these the most important was Albert Béguin. Born in Switzerland of Protestant parents, Béguin had been converted to Catholicism and naturalised to France. During the war he had edited the *Cahiers du Rhône* from Geneva – a collection of essays and verse which expressed the spirit, and fortified the morale, of the Resistance. Pierre Emmanuel, Pierre Jean Jouve, and Loys Masson were notable contributors to it. Béguin moved to Paris at the Liberation and was now assisting Mounier in the editing of *Esprit*. He was a critic of extraordinary erudition and discernment and fastidious style, standing far to the left of Bernanos in politics but wholly – some would have said uncritically – under the spell of his personality and genius. Like Bernanos, he was an extremist, and this was a case where extremes met. It would have been tempting, before so many people had changed their colours, to imagine Béguin as an adherent of the Action Française; but no one would have ever described him as a Christian democrat. Bernanos was particularly grateful for Béguin's review of *Monsieur Ouine*, for Béguin was among the very few critics in France to appreciate that essential, but perplexing, work.

In a letter explaining an article on Estang's *Présence de Bernanos*, Béguin tactfully interpreted the feelings of those who were disconcerted by Bernanos' inveterate polemic.

I hope you will not be shocked by the conclusion of the article. I wanted to say why I wish, in common with many of your friends, known to you or not, that you would return to the novel. People will understand, I think, that I am not trying to divert you from your role in temporal affairs, but because, on the contrary, I am more and more convinced that it is by the novel that you can most actively play this role, and play it in the greatest depth. In the vital debate where you stand almost alone against the spirit of this appalling century, right is on your side in face of the whole world. You are right, I have no doubt, even where I sometimes find it hard to follow you. But what we need, and what only you can give us, is the presence of a soul running the ultimate risks, and this can only be truly communicated by your characters. The two Mouchettes teach me more about the condition of the French soul than the most vehement of your articles – and they can do more to arouse and cure it.[1]

When Bernanos took this advice, it was to drama, not to fiction, that he turned.

Meanwhile in his articles for *La Bataille*, *Le Figaro*, *Carrefour*, *Témoignage Chrétien*, *Temps Présent*, and *La Plume*, in lectures for the

[1] *Bulletin* 7, pp. 13–14

Rencontres Internationales in Geneva, and in Belgium, and in conversation with his friends, he continued to hit out right and left. On the 28th of March 1946, a young visitor showed him a book of press cuttings. Suddenly Bernanos lighted on the following phrase written by a friend: 'The Communists, whether they are right or wrong'. What did that mean? he thundered. 'Either they are right or they are wrong. He too . . .' It was in vain to excuse the writer.

I did not realise that I was a Sancho Panza, who had placed in the saddle the intransigent Don Quixote that slumbers in Bernanos. There he was, launched into a frightening gallop and I was out of breath following him. Writers, Generals, Ministers, Academicians, Heads of State, leaders of education, churchmen, and political parties – the thunderbolt fell without pity on them all.[1]

In the same month Henri Guillemin ventured to speak to him about the Catholics of the Left. 'They disgust me,' exclaimed Bernanos. 'They make me sick. Tartuffes! They groan about the way the Catholics behaved during the Dreyfus affair, and now that the Russians and the Communists are responsible for nameless horrors, they keep quiet. Their lips are well and truly sealed about all that.'[2] His fury did not even spare Claudel. 'If his appetite were only satisfied with women – but it's the shekels. He says that he was behind a pillar in Notre-Dame? Very well, for once in his life this Pharisee was behind something, and not in front so that we could see him. It's time the good God economised his production of converts.'[3]

De Gaulle had expressed the fear that if Bernanos returned to France, he would go into opposition. This was true in the sense that he was opposed to practically everyone – except de Gaulle; and de Gaulle could not lead where France refused to follow. *'C'est la Jeanne d'Arc de la merde,'* exclaimed Bernanos on his return from Colombey-les-deux-Eglises, where he had prophesied that the General would be forced into retirement. Anger had become a psychological, and perhaps also a physiological, necessity for Bernanos, alternating with deep fits of depression:

His anger was irresistible, and then he would invent a vocabulary of insult, usually falling upon his interlocutor with flaming eyes. One

[1] André Laugier: *Cahiers du Rhône*, p. 309   [2] Milner, p. 337   [3] Milner, p. 337

couldn't look at him. One had the impression of swords shooting from his eyes.[1]

But this was only one side of the portrait: Béguin goes on to give the other:

People imagine that there was nothing but tragedy and sadness in Bernanos. In fact, apart from that, no man was ever more in tune with life. His laugh was magnificent – the laugh of a child which he kept right up to the end. He was passionately in love with life, and the little pleasures of life meant a great deal to him, and the great joys of the interior life he felt as strongly as, at other times, he felt the force of anger.[2]

If he were convicted (and convinced) of injustice, he was ready to make amends. Cardinal Suhard had certainly acted as a spritual buttress to Vichy, and Bernanos did not spare him. But Suhard acknowledged his mistakes and placed himself at the head of the most promising Catholic revival that France had known. It is not too much to say that the second Vatican Council was anticipated in Paris. Realising that he had been unjust to Suhard, Bernanos sent him his apologies through the abbé Pézeril, and the Cardinal replied with his blessing. Mauriac himself admitted that the 'invective of Bernanos was bound up with a substratum of charity in which his whole life was bathed and glowed'; and once again we have the testimony of Béguin:

Apart from the moments where he was a prey to the demons of anger, he was more capable than anyone I have ever known of tenderness to the other person. When his eyes fell upon a human being, they were the perceptive eyes of the novelist which see into its depths, but at the same time the eyes of someone so penetrated with love that you couldn't help feeling it. It started out of the look he gave you, and there was no resisting it.[3]

The hatreds of Georges Bernanos were the counterparts of his loves – and neither were sensitive to mitigation. On the one hand he pursued his vendetta against the men of Vichy – more particularly against Weygand – but he saluted, with his friend Brückberger, the courage with which Joseph Darnand had met his death. The execrated head of the *milice* had shown an equal courage in the field, and in his subsequent actions he had merely followed his oath to

[1] Albert Béguin: *Bulletin* 31, p. 6   [2] Ibid   [3] Ibid

Pétain to its logical and criminal conclusions. When Bernanos proposed to write an article on this for *Combat*, it was refused by Albert Camus, and Bernanos wrote no more for a paper whose editor, Claude Bourdet, had been among the first to welcome him. More significant were his disputes with the Catholics of the extreme Left. Among these Loys Masson was prominent. Writing in *Les Lettres Françaises* he could see no future for liberty except in Communism. 'If you had seen the Communists die under the occupation! If you had seen them live, denying with their love the four walls of death which encircled them! If you could only look into the future!' Bernanos had demanded space for liberty to expand, but for Masson 'the desire for space is a malady and a temptation. And contrary to what you think, I believe that today space is the negation of liberty.' Bernanos had counted Communists among his friends in Brazil, and they knew as well as he did that the Marxist and the Christian conceptions of man were irreducibly opposed. He was not concerned to refute the former; he merely refused it, and he was exasperated that men who professed his own faith – the *petits abbés communisants* – should not recognise the contradiction. He knew very well the contempt with which the Stalinists – nowhere more servile than in the French Communist party – regarded their Christian fellow-travellers: and he pictured the Marshal with the benevolent moustachios saying to his aide-de-camp, standing stiffly to attention:

Comrade aide-de-camp, there is a little Christian here on my shoulder. He does nothing but weep, and there is a risk he may tarnish my gold braid. Please get rid of him, wipe his cheeks, and put him to bed.[1]

For the publicists and militants of the party – with one or two exceptions – Bernanos had the same feelings that he had always entertained for their clerical opponents.

Were they a hundred times more sincere than I believe them to be, they would still be only sincere towards themselves, and not a whit less insincere towards other people. They conceal what is in their interest to hide, and show what is in their interest to reveal. They fake the rest, and despise the imbeciles. We shall see them tomorrow treating Gide as the *dévots* still treat Voltaire. They will say that the author of *L'Immoraliste* died devouring his own excrement. Why cannot M. Masson see that he is the dupe of the same kind of people who tell us that the only reason

[1] *Français, si vous saviez* (Gallimard, 1947), p. 40

why Luther set Christianity on fire was because he wanted to marry his mistress?[1]

No one had deserved better of the state than Stanislas Fumet. After courageous action in the Resistance he was now editor of *Temps Présent*, the weekly journal of the Catholic Left which had risen, phoenix-like, from the ashes of *Sept*. Bernanos had known and admired him since the days of *Sous le Soleil de Satan;* their options and antipathies were very much the same; yet Fumet reminded Bernanos that recent events had given to democracy a meaning at which it was sacrilegious to sneer. Having spent some months as the guest of the Gestapo, he knew what he was talking about.

We know very well that democracy is a word which irritates you and that you find it easy to sniff out in it the kind of speeches that one hears at all the agricultural gatherings. But what would you have? You stayed for a long time away from France, and even if you *knew* certain things that were happening – things that taught us to give a very precise, a very humble, and at the same time a very essential meaning to the word 'democracy' – you didn't *experience* them. Not to be arrested at anyone's sweet will, not to be executed without trial, not to be forced to choose, by a permanent system of government, between death and abjection – these are some of the things we mean when we speak of democracy. . . . You are pleased to proclaim from the housetops your disgust with the passivity of the French. We, on our side, are trying to teach them once again the meaning and the practice of activity, and this is the 'work of white ants' to which the 'good fellows' of *Temps Présent* are devoting themselves. Evidently you are far above all that. Space and the virgin continents await you. Since you have returned to us – very provisionally as you never stop warning us – you have gone about chewing over your nostalgia for the desert. In the dismal conformity of public opinion, we don't deny that you have acted as a useful exhaust-valve for our anger and disappointment. But for how many months have you been back, and for how many months have you enjoyed this little game of breaking the crockery, telling us every day that you have had your fill of disgust, and that you are going to take to the high seas once more?[2]

For Bernanos 'no word in any language' was 'so prostituted as democracy'. These were waters in which he 'could not swim as well as Georges Bidault';[3] and a man who believed that France now 'ran

---

[1] *Français, si vous saviez*, p. 42   [2] Ibid, p. 347
[3] *La Liberté pour quoi faire?* (Gallimard, 1953)

the greatest risk and had the greatest chance in her history'[1] was not likely to forgive Aragon for his words in the *Révolution Surréaliste:* 'What repels us even more than patriotism, which is like any other hysteria – only more hollow and deadly – is the ideal of the fatherland.' But it was felt by Fumet, and many others, that if Bernanos had borne the heat of the desert, they had borne the heat of the day; and the self-regard, if not the downright egotism, of his polemic gave them an opening which they would have been less than human if they had not seized. Where he was trying to get the country on its knees, or into the front line of battle, they were trying to get it on its feet. In doing so they were reluctant to break with their Communist allies. What was charity and common sense to them appeared cowardice and compromise to him. Certainly the Catholics of the Left leaned over backward in trying to preserve the *union sacrée* of the Resistance. They were shamefully indifferent to the inclusion of Poland in the Soviet system, and the fate of Mihailovitch – 'the first of the *maquisards*', as Bernanos termed him – left them unmoved. Indeed there were not many people, anywhere, to trouble their heads or their consciences about Drazha Mihailovitch.

As I write these lines, in the early morning, with the dawn suddenly gilding a motionless sea, I remember that Mihailovitch is facing the firing-squad. Innocent or guilty, what does it matter? The world couldn't care less – and I couldn't care less about the world. No cowardice can secure its salvation or arrest its doom. Crouched on the atom bomb, bilious with hate, its heart absolutely empty of love and its mouth full of social justice, it has become an object of derision. In any case I shall not pray for it.[2]

Here we catch the bitterest dregs of the Bernanosian disgust; and it was François Mauriac who reminded the readers of *Le Figaro* that disgust can be a temptation just as insidious as despair; that the one, pushed to an extreme, is a manifestation of the other. Where Bernanos had seen in the splitting of the atom 'the decisive triumph of technique over reason',[3] Teilhard de Chardin had saluted it as a new conquest of man over nature. But Bernanos had no desire for man to conquer nature; he only wished him to live in accordance with it. Teilhard had returned to France only a little later than Bernanos and he described the months which plunged Bernanos

[1] Ibid   [2] *Français, si vous saviez*, p. 178   [3] *La Liberté pour quoi faire?*

into a nadir of pessimism as 'the most exalting of his whole existence'. Fortunately, perhaps, the two prophets never met; and Bernanos thought it was frivolous to preach the gospel of evolution when the world was so obviously evolving to its doom. He was not surprised when a publicist of the Communist party like Pierre Hervé described him as a 'frog asking for a king', and went on to say that 'if certain persons feel the vocation of a courtier, they will see that our people are not impressed by this kind of talk.' Bernanos was not so naïve as to anticipate an early restoration of the monarchy. Nor could he be surprised if Mauriac, without descending to personalities or venting an intelligible spleen, replied indirectly to his denigrations. The article spells out what many Frenchmen were hoping from Bernanos, and why they were disappointed.

Is Georges Bernanos in any doubt of what he represented for us during the four abominable years? How we awaited his return, as we awaited the return of Maritain? . . . Before the Liberation, at the darkest moments of a night in which many of those we believed in went astray, and in which the best perished, our hopes turned to those few writers beyond the sea who would one day disembark. Bernanos came back. From the first words he spoke the picture we had formed of him was effaced by the man as he really is; the old, implacable angel, his pen already bristling in face of such traces of mud as the filthy tide had left behind, as it receded from us. We didn't ask for sympathy, but for comprehension. It is an understatement to say that he has made no effort to avert his gaze from the scars which our fetters, scarcely broken, have left upon us.

The heroes are never more than a handful. To the vast crowd of collaborators, traffickers, cowards, and dodgers Bernanos has fiercely opposed his own idea of honour. How should he have pardoned them when even the best have not found favour in his eyes? For his disgust leads him to over-simplify. He reduces Claudel to certain comic and horrible features, as if the universe of Claudel did not render homage to the man who created it. In the same way he eliminates the noblest reasons which impel some of our people towards Communism, and attributes to them only the basest motives. When he insults 'the little crabs of *Esprit*', he outrages those who hunger and thirst after justice – instead of blessing them, as the Lord would have done. For it is the hunger and thirst which create the mirage.

And yet if we bear no rancour against Bernanos, it is because we realise that the refusal of this sombre world in which we struggle can only be total. One must either reject or totally accept every aspect of one's time.

If Bernanos did not harass us, we should perhaps forget that we inhabit a universe where hardly anyone is honest, except the saints; and Bernanos invents them to take the place of those who do not exist. His mission is to remind us, incessantly, that we all collaborate in the same imposture, whether we want to or not, and that we are all of us its accomplices.[1]

These words were both generous and candid; and Mauriac would have been comforted to know that Bernanos still had one or two saints up his sleeve. But when every allowance has been made, it must be admitted that no man ever returned from exile with a richer capital of good will, and that none spent it more recklessly. 'What has struck you on coming back to Paris?' de Gaulle had enquired of Malraux. Bernanos would have echoed Malraux's reply: 'Le mensonge.' In ten seconds, Malraux admitted, Bernanos said 'what would have taken me ten minutes,' and he remembered the droop of Bernanos' heavy eyelids when he told him that 'with the concentration camps Satan had visibly reappeared over the world'.[2]

Nevertheless, for defeated Germany Bernanos had nothing but a deep pity in which sentiment played no part whatever. In reply to an article by Karl Barth he declared that 'the silent prayer of the heart' was all one could give to a nation which 'though defeated, was still committed to its formidable adventure . . . please God that we may not thoughtlessly involve ourselves in a matter which only concerns His implacable and inflexible compassion.' He prayed that 'having paid its own debt' Germany 'might be given the grace to discharge ours as well, in expiation for those who have conquered, but are not worthy to sit in judgement on her.'[3]

2

To all who knew him closely Bernanos was evidently at the end of his tether. One indication of this was his nomadic life. Nostalgic, as ever, for the *midi*, he moved in August 1945, to Briasq, near Sisteron in the Basses-Alpes. The house had belonged to a rich collaborator, furnished in a bastard style of 1880, but it had neither water nor light, and was practically without windows. By 4.30 in the afternoon

[1] 17th July 1946: *Français, si vous saviez*, pp. 356–8   [2] *Anti-mémoires*
[3] *Français, si vous saviez*, p. 81

the sun had disappeared behind the mountain.[1] In writing an inscription for Jean-Loup's copy of the *Journal d'un Curé de campagne*, translated into Portuguese, Bernanos referred to the place as the '*château de la misère*'. By the middle of November he had moved to Bandol, and Toulon, as he passed through it in December, stirred intolerable memories. The bright morning in June when he had embarked for Majorca; the deserted streets and the closed shutters; the pavements still moist with the dew; the great awning of the café where he had sat writing with Michel Dard not yet erected against the sun; the *matelots* and their girls; the bay and the ships at anchor. He had left it when France was still a great nation with its armies and its squadrons intact; now it spoke, with a mute and heartrending eloquence, of what the Germans had destroyed and of what the French had destroyed themselves. He had come back to it on a cold and sticky December day, walking 'mechanically down the rue d'Alger to the Bay, like a prisoner between two gendarmes, looking neither to left nor right'. When he reached the Bay, he stood there 'shivering with cold and fatigue, leaning on my two sticks, suffering from my injured leg, but also from another deeper wound – from a certain mutilation of the memory, of the deepest memory, the memory of flesh and blood.'[2] The Café de la Rade was no more, and he fled its discoloured rubble as if it were a ghost, to the furthest extremity of the quays.

It was at moments like these that Bernanos thought seriously of returning to Brazil; and indeed the idea had never quite left him. In the room which served him as a study there hung the photograph of the Abbot of São Bento, on whose advice he had decided to come back to France. He dreamed of forming a colony of young Frenchmen, who would recreate his own '*idée de la France*' among people who themselves had never lost it, and he wrote in this sense to a number of his Brazilian friends.

His big idea was to create a sort of French village. He would get young lads to come out there, paying their expenses with the royalties from his books. This would allow them to live off the immense tracts of land where they would build their own houses with bricks of dry mud and the leaves of banana trees, in a country where the name of France is still a symbol of liberty and honour. Afterwards they could return home, aware

[1] To Guy Hattu, mid-November 1945: *Correspondance* II, p. 581
[2] *Français, si vous saviez*, p. 330

With André Rousseaux
in Geneva, 1946

In Paris, 1947

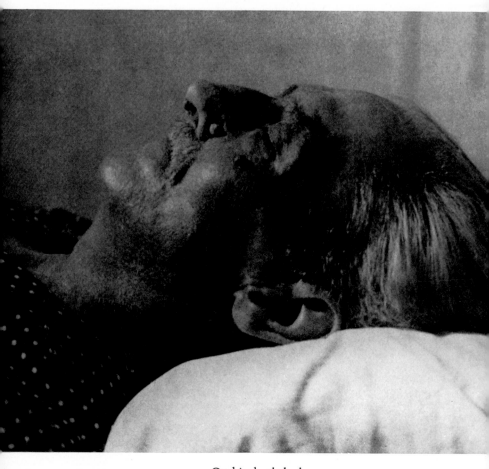

On his death-bed

of this enormous influence and anxious not to disappoint the trust it had inspired, with a deep understanding of the civilising mission of France and what it meant.[1]

What lent colour to Bernanos' vision was no longer the spirit of adventure which, all those years ago, had sent Maxence de Colleville to Paraguay, nor even his own dreams of a patriarchal existence in the *sertão* with the cattle roaming around him. It was rather the weight of an immense fatigue. He had gone to Brazil to discover a new life; if he returned there it would be in the hope of a death free, at last, from bitterness. For he, too, was aware of the 'temptation of disgust'. As Max Milner has pointed out, the parallel with Péguy is very close. The following passage is the only place in all his writings where Bernanos seems to be unconsciously parodying another man's style, and yet nowhere else does he speak so intimately in his own person.

I am in one of those states of extreme fatigue – 'dead beat' – which Péguy never stopped complaining of for several months before the war, and from which the war delivered him. I say the war rather than death, because the death came only after the deliverance – one peace followed upon another. I, too, know this fatigue: this dead tiredness, this harassment, this disgust, this concentration of disgust at the root of the soul, this impurity, this stain from which only the pity of God can absolve me. The shame and the remorse of this fatigue weigh more heavily upon me than the fatigue itself. The fatigue without and the fatigue within; the immersion of it, the sin and stigmata and malediction of it . . . a kind of poisonous discolouring of one's whole being. The remorse for all the sins one has not atoned for . . . the sins of one's own life and the sins of all those lives now over and done with which have left their scum upon us, incessantly thickening the air we breathe, and even tainting our dreams. Surely prayer is the only remedy for this filthiness, and even prayer is infected by it! Have pity on us! Forgive us our fatigues! Purify them! Cleanse us from this dirt! We do not want to roll dead with fatigue before your Face.[2]

This was neither the last prayer, nor the last confession of Georges Bernanos, but it is not altogether misleading to read it as such.

Chantal Bernanos had remained behind in Rio, where she had married an officer in the Brazilian air force. She had two children and was expecting a third. Yves had also married a Brazilian, but he was now seriously ill with tuberculosis in a military sanatorium. His wife and two little girls were also living at Bandol. In June Bernanos spent three weeks in Morocco, and he was hoping to rent a house at Bourgueil, in Touraine, for the *grandes vacances*. But this plan fell through, and at the end of September they went instead to Thoisy, La Chapelle Vendômoise. Apart from short visits to Algeria and Switzerland in September, and to Belgium with Albert Béguin and his wife in November, Bernanos made this his headquarters until the end of the year. In December he moved with his wife to Paris, living at the Hotel Cayré, the Hotel Montalembert, or sleeping on a sofa at Luc Estang's apartment in the rue l'Université. The cat had a curious habit of walking over the piano whenever he was there. At the Cayré

he looked sadly at the armchairs and carpet in the hall, witness to a comfort which he claimed to have sought for unsuccessfully all his life. He made fun of himself, and was not particularly proud of his incapacity to manage the ordinary details of his daily round. As to the extraordinary ones, there we didn't think he did too badly.

You could not see him without realising immediately what he was – a colonel of the dragoons, wounded at Waterloo, and supporting himself on two sticks. He was dressed with a mixture of austerity and negligence, worthy of an officer on half pay or a Spanish nobleman in exile. Everything about him told you that this was what he was – a Grandee of Spain: the nobility of the way he looked at you, the black circles round his eyes, and that astonishing voice, hoarse and loquacious, with an accent that seemed to echo from the old courts of Europe. He would sit down, bury his head in his hands, shake his mane of hair, and then he would come alive. Dreaminess and rage were in his eyes, and a good deal of both. He launched into a monologue, as one breaks into a charge. Then, suddenly, he would pull himself up with a mischievous laugh, youthful and charming; and it was on these occasions that he complained indignantly that the hearts of the French had gone soft: 'What!' he would exclaim, 'not a single madman, not a single fanatic, among the lot.'[1]

There was one, however. It was now, in this winter of 1947, that Bernanos made his single friend among the important writers of his own time. André Malraux and Bernanos were each moved by the same indignations and the same hunger for the Absolute, although

[1] Roger Nimier, *Le Grand d'Espagne*, pp. 15–20

with Malraux it found different satisfactions – if indeed it was ever satisfied completely. A conversation between the two men is difficult to imagine, because each was a master of the monologue. But conversations there were; and the man who had fought with the Communists and the man who had fought with the *camelots du roi* were now in the dwindling ranks of a general who had just resigned for want of an army to follow him.

It was therefore to Vincent Auriol, who had succeeded de Gaulle as Head of State, that Bernanos – who had threatened implacable vengeance from Barbacena – now addressed his last appeal for clemency, not because he thought that certain people should go unpunished, but because so many of those morally and materially responsible were allowed to go scot free. The case in question concerned a certain pamphleteer, Lucien Rebatet, who had been associated with Robert Brasillach on the collaborationist journal, *Je suis partout*. Bernanos contrasted the punishment meted out to writers with the immunity allowed to the economic collaborators, to the admirals who had scuttled the fleet, and to the prelates whose connivance with Vichy had done so much to mislead public opinion. This was not the only occasion on which he protested to authority against what he regarded as a selective miscarriage of justice.

On his return from Switzerland in February – seventeen lectures in eighteen days – Bernanos gave his celebrated oration at the Sorbonne: *Démocratie et Révolution*. Speaking at very short notice, he was obliged to improvise it, and was annoyed that the organisers had changed his original title: *Révolution et Liberté*. The following day Jean de Fabrègues was waiting for him in the vestibule of the Hotel Montalembert, with a crowd of American reporters armed with cameras and notebooks. Bernanos entered, and with his volcanic laugh exclaimed, pointing at himself, 'I present to you the last defender of the democracies in peril.' Then his tone changed, the gleam of anger came into his eyes, and he broke into a characteristic diatribe.

But it is not I who have changed; democracy has been the death of us. The totalitarian systems have been fathered by democracy. To hell with democracy!

This was not the gospel that the American journalists had come to hear, and they departed, sullen and stupefied, with their notebooks. The blank pages symbolised the blank space between the mind of Georges Bernanos and the 'Anglo-Saxon' mentality.[1]

At the beginning of March he answered an appeal by the Alliance Française to lecture in Tunisia; but the lectures were no more than a convenient excuse. He had no wish to come back, and he soon persuaded his family to join him – his wife, Dominique, Jean-Loup, Yves' wife Elsa and her two children. They established themselves at the Hotel de France in Hammamet, and to a local audience he compared the Church to the *chemins de fer*. 'It has three classes – the third, in which I travel myself, the second, and' fixing the Archbishop of Carthage with his basilisk eye, 'the first'. He radiated to the island of Djerba, and as far as Morocco, speaking at Rabat and Casablanca – always on the same subject: *la France, patrie universelle*. Perhaps he would finally settle in Morocco; it was that much nearer the Southern Cross, his daughter Chantal, and Michel who had gone back to Brazil, and so many friends. If only he could see the dark Sierra rising from the sea, and the great white city, which had seemed to him as beautiful as a woman. Or, if he did not stay in Morocco, he might wander south to one of the lost cities of Tunisia where there was a garrison, approachable by good military roads – for he had now bought a powerful BSA motor-cycle. Anywhere so long as he did not end his days in a *sous-préfecture;* and could live as far removed as possible from what he might be tempted to hate or to despise.

He returned to Hammamet on the 11th of May, and by the end of June had been able to rent a house – Villa Equem. He was now invited to contribute to a collection of essays entitled *L'Avenir de l'Homme*. The title had a Teilhardian ring, and Teilhard, with Malraux and a Communist, had received similar invitations. Bernanos was ill at ease with this brand of intellectual ecumenism, and he did not mince his refusal. He did not think that Teilhard's 'acrobatics' would carry conviction to a single Marxist, and a Christian who believed in the doctrine of original sin would have no need of them.

Too many rich people had built their villas on the shore of Hammamet for Bernanos not to feel that he had fallen among thieves, although he described the light to which he awoke every

[1] Jean de Fabrègues, *Bernanos tel qu'il était*, p. 258

morning as 'la lumière de Dieu'. He played with the idea of going
to Italy, and was in correspondence with a friend over the renting
of a house on the west coast of Sicily. In the event, however, he
moved with the family to the Hotel Atlantica at Gabès on the North
African shore. It was the last but one of his migrations. They were
installed there shortly before Christmas. The girls – for Claude had
now joined the party – had persuaded their father to buy a gramo-
phone, and to escape the unrelenting cacophony of jazz he took to
rising early in order to write for three hours without disturbance.
He sat there, draped from head to foot in his *gandourah*, sending
inflammatory articles to various papers – *Carrefour*, *Le Figaro*, and
L'Intransigeant. His style had lost nothing of its fascination and
ferocity; he was a man whom it was always a pleasure to read and
with whom it was a privilege to disagree. But the great rage of
polemic was soon to be exhausted, and the genius of Bernanos was
free to fulfil itself in a work innocent of anger and prophetic of the
death whose approach was at once masked and foreshadowed by
fatigue.

There had been much talk of making a film based on the *Journal
d'un Curé de campagne*, in which Jean-Louis Barrault was eager to
play the principal part. Bernanos had admired him in *Les Enfants du
Paradis*, and warmly seconded the idea. But the project came to
nothing, and in the meanwhile another idea proved more fruitful.
No one had been closer to Bernanos in the years immediately
preceding his exile than the young, ardent, and attractive Dominican,
Raymond Brückberger. 'Brück', as he was commonly known, had
fought with Darnand's Franc Corps during the brief campaign of
1940, and was among the first to rally to de Gaulle. He became in
due course principal chaplain to the *maquis* and escorted the General
into Notre-Dame for the Te Deum of the Liberation. His was the
responsibility of informing Cardinal Suhard that he would be wise,
on that occasion, to absent himself from his cathedral. Brückberger
was a man after Bernanos' own heart – a *tempérament de droite* in
every understanding of the word, inflexible in doctrine and incapable
of compromise. Those who found him too combative – or too
clear-sighted – would compare him to some *ligueur* priest during
the Wars of Religion; and he would have agreed that the war in
which he had earned such distinction and exercised such authority
was as religious as any that history had known. Bernanos used to

say that he was 'a man to go tiger-shooting with', and he willingly collaborated on the short-lived *Cheval de Troie* which Brückberger was then editing. Bernanos, like Brückberger, was more an antique Trojan than a Greek.

In February 1938 Brückberger had lent Bernanos a copy of Gertrud von le Fort's novel, *The Last on the Scaffold*, translated into French and published by Desclée de Brouwer. This was based on the martyrdom of the Carmelite Sisters of Compiègne in July 1794. She had found the story in the *Relation* by Mother Marie of the Incarnation, the supposed illegitimate offspring of a royal and aristocratic liaison, who was miraculously cured of an early paralysis and later entered Carmel. She was in Paris on personal business when her sisters in religion were arrested; lived in hiding until 1823 when she entered the Carmel of Sens as a paying guest; and died in 1836. The inventory of the convent was made on the 4th of August 1790; the sisters were questioned the following day; and were expelled on the 14th of September 1792. They continued to live in Compiègne, scattered in small groups, until their arrest on the 22nd of June 1794. They were sentenced to death; guillotined on the 17th of July; and beatified by Pope Pius X on the 27th of May 1906. They had all mounted the scaffold singing the *Salve Regina* and the *Veni Creator Spiritus*.

Brückberger, collaborating with Philippe Agostini, had composed the scenario for a film to be based on Gertrud von le Fort's novel, and on the 30th of May 1947 he wrote to Bernanos proposing that he should write the dialogue for this. On the 1st of October he visited Bernanos in Tunisia. Bernanos, with no experience of the medium in which he was to work, was hesitant but finally agreed. He had, in fact, taken *The Last on the Scaffold* with him to Brazil, but he did not now consult it. Certain passages of his text – notably the first interview between Blanche de la Force and the Prieure de Croissy – he kept for eventual publication, judging them too 'interior' for the screen. In January 1948 Brückberger visited him again, and on the 1st of March the first part of the *Dialogues* was sent off from Gabès. The second followed on the 27th, and the third on the 8th of April – although it only reached Paris on the 20th. On the 28th of May the impresario, apparently judging the dialogue unsuitable for a film, announced its postponement; the booking of the studios was cancelled; and on the 21st of May Bernanos was brought to Paris with only a few weeks to live. The *Dialogues* were discovered in a trunk among his papers after his death, and it was Albert Béguin who arranged them for the stage. They were published in 1949, and the first performance of the play was given in Zürich on the 14th of June 1951. It was afterwards presented in Munich, Cologne, Berlin, Vienna and several other German and Austrian cities. The French *première* took place on the 28th of May 1952 with a production by Marcelle Tassaincourt at the Théâtre Hébertot in Paris, where it was played for more than 300 consecutive performances to immense popular and critical acclaim. Other productions were seen in Italy, Spain, Sweden, Norway, Finland, Denmark, Belgium and Holland. Great Britain is one of the few European countries where the *Dialogues des Carmélites* has never been produced, but here the fault cannot be laid entirely at the doors of the English theatre. A public reading was in fact organised at the French Institute, with Albert Béguin in the audience, and the play came through with powerful and moving effect. Later it formed the libretto of an opera by Francis Poulenc. In 1960, Brückberger and Agostini found the capital necessary to make the film, but they retained only a part of Bernanos' text and inserted it in a new scenario. The result was not particularly well received.

The effect of the play owed much to the circumstances of its composition. Bernanos knew that he was writing against time and on the 1st of March, when he sent off the first batch of his manuscript, the symptoms of a fatal illness declared themselves unmistakably. He worked very freely to his brief, sometimes for eight or ten hours at a stretch, altering, erasing, and abridging as he thought fit. Two manuscripts of the *Dialogues* were made in his own hand, and the third, definitive version, filling ten small school notebooks, was copied out by his secretary. This was used by Béguin, his literary executor, in preparing for the stage, and for publication, a work originally destined for the screen. Just as there were no rules of the novel to meet the theme of *Sous le Soleil de Satan* or *Monsieur Ouine*, so in the *Dialogues des Carmélites* Bernanos took the conventions of the cinema and wrested them to his own use. He proved, as other masters of stagecraft had proved before him, that good theatre – or cinema – is of many kinds, and that it is the prerogative of genius to invent them. But Bernanos was more than a genius: he was a visionary. And it is his profound insight into the heart of the

Christian experience and his courageous acceptance of the Christian risk, which give the *Dialogues des Carmélites* a place apart in the contemporary theatre. Indeed it stands with Corneille's *Polyeucte* – Bernanos always preferred Corneille to Racine – and certain plays of Eliot and Claudel upon the summits of Christian drama. Where *Polyeucte* is a tragedy of baptism and *Le Soulier de Satin* a tragedy of marriage, the *Dialogues* is a tragedy of death; although each of these plays also celebrates a triumph – the entrance into Christian life, or the endurance and consummation of it.

The fear of Blanche de la Force as she faces the challenge of martyrdom was never far from Bernanos, and it was nearer to him than ever as he worked on the scenario during those early months of 1948 with the *Vie de Jésus* – never to be written – close to the surface of his mind, and the hand of death lying every day more heavily upon him. This was the fear of Gethsemane. Chantal de Clergerie had exclaimed: 'In one sense, I would have you understand, Fear is the daughter of God, and she was redeemed on the night of Good Friday. She is not pretty to look upon – far from it. She is sometimes mocked, sometimes cursed, and renounced by all. . . . Yet make no mistake, she sits by every death-bed, interceding for mankind.'[1] Bernanos would soon experience this for himself, and Albert Béguin has explained how the Carmelites of Compiègne came to assist him on his own death-bed and to ensure 'that his tormented life should end in contemplation and that the mystery which he had never ceased to regard so anxiously should vex his spirit no longer.' Through all his books and all his life, from his earliest letters as a child right up to this last work of his, the theme of fear constitutes a kind of centre to which his thought continuously returns. Fear had been the dreaded and familiar companion of his childhood, an inevitable presence at his side during the First World War. The characters of his novels had many of them lived under its sway, and he found himself face to face with it as he analysed the history of his own times, or now, in the *Dialogues des Carmélites*, a time when men and women were challenged, no less brutally, to stand up and be counted.

The *Dialogues* is thus the most deeply personal, as it is the most rigorously objective, of Georges Bernanos' writings. He is here

[1] *La Joie*

subdued to the bare exigences of his theme, and the exaggerations of his polemic have disappeared in the serenity of a final insight. Very significant are the ways in which his treatment differs from that of Gertrud von le Fort. There is a complete absence of political bias; the rôle of the revolutionary inquisitors is purely utilitarian. The unfrocked priest who tries to influence the Carmelites has gone; and so, too, has the discussion on the abdication of the aristocracy. For Bernanos the Carmelites are the reverse of an exclusive and unapproachable *élite*, and he suppresses a scene from the novel where Blanche takes the stage and describes the fashions of the day. Mother Marie of the Incarnation lacks the slightly pretentious grandeur of her prototype; her mind is more reflective and her strength more contained. In her and Mme Lidoine one sees not only the fusion of the old peasant and military classes, but the two faces of the Church; prudence and audacity; the conservation of good, and the challenging of evil. In the novel the Prieure de Croissy is an episodic character, but for Bernanos she traces the spiritual dimensions of the play in words characteristic of the author – 'The contempt for yourself will lead you straight to despair. Remember that God will take care of your honour.'

Bernanos had written in *Les Grands Cimetières sous la lune* of 'the mysterious fusion of human honour with the charity of Christ'. This is supremely exemplified by the Carmelites of Compiègne, in whom Urs von Balthasar has recognised 'the spiritual and ecclesial transposition of the world of honour and nobility, where the very notion of honour remains intact, but is placed at the service of higher ends.'[1] Blanche, Sister Constance, Mother Marie, and the Prieure de Croissy are all of nobler birth, and the instinct of honour is particularly strong in them. But where the Marquis de la Force in the novel is impatient of what he regards as Carmelite superstitions, for Bernanos he represents the military traditions of an older France, not outstandingly pious but certainly not Voltairean. With Gertrud von le Fort there is no question of Blanche's salvation, but for Bernanos she must run the Christian risk, and run it to the end. Only a miracle of grace can save her; and where in the novel her personality is dissolved almost to its roots, in the play her response to the Divine invitation is active and conscious. Bernanos had written in *Nous autres Français* that 'a Christian does not save

[1] *Le Chrétien Bernanos*

himself alone; he only saves himself by saving others.' Where the
Blanche of Gertrud von le Fort is abandoned by everyone, in the
play Mme de Croissy, Sister Constance, and Mother Marie of the
Incarnation all stand by her; and she in turn assists their sanctification
by drawing them more closely to the heart of the Passion which
they are all to share.

Perhaps the greatest originality of Bernanos was in developing, as
he did, the character of Sister Constance. As Luc Estang pointed out,
she is the sunshine where Blanche is the shadow. After a reading
of the play to a community of Carmelite nuns, one of the sisters
expressed the view that the spirit of Carmel was better illustrated
by Constance than by any other of the characters. The youngest of
the sisters sent to the guillotine, Marie-Geneviève Meunier, had
chosen the name of Constance, but was not able to take her vows
on account of the decree passed by the Constituent Assembly. When
her brother asked her to leave the Carmel she refused to do so. This
young novice was therefore the prototype both of Constance de
Saint-Denis and Blanche de la Force, and it is significant that in the
play Constance kneels by the side of Blanche as they take the vow
to offer up their lives, if they should be called upon to do so. Very
different is the Constance of Gertrud von le Fort who 'confessed,
half crying, that she would be very frightened to be the last on the
scaffold'. Not for nothing had Bernanos kept the *Novissima Verba*
of St Thérèse of Lisieux beside him while he was at work on *La
Joie;* twice lost and recovered the book; and throughout his sojourn
in Brazil it was always close to his hand. St Thérèse was closer to
him than any saint in the calendar, with the exception of Jeanne
d'Arc; and he was the last to be misled by the sentimentality which
had deformed her image. She can be found in Constance and
Blanche, and most notably in Chantal de Clergerie. In the course of
an interview at Juiz de Fora in February 1939 Bernanos had spoken
of the spirit of childhood which was 'the heritage of the saints and
heroines of our race, the supernatural youth incarnated by our little
St Thérèse, to the scandal and the trial of every sort of fanatic, even
of those who would like to turn the Church into an austere and
lugubrious cemetery, instead of a garden in bloom.'[1] Again in 1943,
at the christening of an aeroplane, the 'Jeanne d'Arc', he reminded
his Brazilian audience that

[1] Guy Gaucher: *Etudes Bernanosiennes*, 1960

since the beginning of this century our country has given two great saints
to Christianity, two saints of universal renown, and that these two saints
were both female saints, and that these female saints were both young
girls – you could almost call them two children – Saint Thérèse of the
Child Jesus . . . and Jeanne d'Arc.'[1]

Luc Estang had reason to point out that there was much of Sister
Constance and Sister Blanche in St Thérèse of Lisieux; there was
much of Jeanne d'Arc in St Thérèse; there was much of both in
Georges Bernanos.

In suppressing the historical anecdote or, more exactly, in distilling
its supernatural essence, he was not abstracting his theme from time
present or time past. He was merely placing it in time redeemed.
Gertrud von le Fort had written of Blanche:

Born of the profound horror of a time in which the shadow of presenti-
ments pointing to future events was falling upon Germany, this figure
rose up before me as the incarnation of the mortal anguish of a whole
period approaching its end.

Just as the Terror of 1794 was linked to the rise of Hitler in the
genesis of the novel, so was it linked to the confrontation of death
in the dramatic adaptation by Bernanos. The scenario was not, in
fact, submitted for Gertrud von le Fort's approval, and this led to
subsequent dispute. No doubt the arbitration of Julian Green was
equitable – that the 'spiritual significance of the work' belonged to
Bernanos. Brückberger and Agostini had wished to concentrate the
action on Blanche and her fear, and to double the interior conflict
by external events more easily to be understood by the general
public. Bernanos took considerable liberties with the scenario as it
was handed to him, omitting ten of the sequences, abridging others,
and reducing the external action to the barest minimum, so that

the destiny of Blanche becomes the destiny of the Christian caught up in
History. But, for Bernanos, History serves merely as the setting for the
interior tragedy, and the perspective he adopts is essentially spiritual. This
choice of the spiritual as the fundamental value implies a triple sub-
ordination; of History to the adventure of salvation, of the event to its
psychological incidence, and of psychology to the supernatural.[2]

Critics as different in their orientation as Henri de Montherlant
and Gabriel Marcel, Jean-Jacques Gautier and Thierry Maulnier

[1] Ibid [2] Michel Estève: *Etudes Bernanosiennes*, 1960

(whose wife had produced the play in Paris) were alert to recognise the unique quality of the *Dialogues*. Montherlant admired the combination of the simple and the extraordinary; Marcel remarked how the apparent theatrical defect of the work – a succession of scenes without any psychological progression – was turned into a virtue, so that the play came to have the suppleness of life itself with the supreme reality visible behind each episode, but never artificially imposed. In effect, the forty sequences of the original scenario had now been reduced to twenty-two, and it was this condensation at the service of a situation in itself dramatic in the highest degree, which enabled the unspoken dialogue between the soul and God to be heard behind the fears and exhortations of the characters. Marcel saw in this distant collaboration between a French and a German novelist (competitive as it may have seemed to the latter) a sign of hope for a devastated Europe and a divided Christendom; an inspired pointer to the only plane upon which the antinomies of political disorder could be reconciled. Indeed more than one critic found the cosmic terrors of the atomic age reflected, and poignantly refined, in the fears of a single Carmelite sister in the shadow of the scaffold. All the effort of Bernanos had been directed towards the raising of human suffering – his own and other people's – to the supernatural level. He succeeded in doing this because he understood more and more clearly that the dying of Christ gave a meaning to every mortal death-bed; or rather, as he said himself, that 'each separate dying of ours *is* the dying of Christ'. This truth, realised in act and not merely in conception, was the last and greatest of his conquests. 'At fifty-nine,' remarks Sister Constance, 'is it not high time to die?' Bernanos was fifty-nine years old; he had not long to wait.

CHAPTER 15

'A NOUS DEUX'[1]

READERS of the *Journal d'un Curé de campagne* will remember the episode in which the curé, shortly before his death, meets the *légionnaire*, and is taken for a ride on his motor-cycle. This was an extraordinary premonition on the part of Georges Bernanos, for in February 1948 he visited the military outposts in the southern part of Tunisia, warmly welcomed by General Dio who had succeeded to the command of Marshal Leclerc. He accompanied the motor-cyclist platoons on his BSA, travelling 300 kilometres in a single day, with his sticks strapped to the machine. The young lieutenants were astonished at his endurance and enterprise, as the *'grande route'* which had haunted his childhood in Artois flew past him in the scorching Saharan sun – an image of that other road whose limit he had so nearly reached. To more than one of his correspondents he copied out a quotation from Montherlant's *Maître de Santiago:*

There is nothing for me to do at a time when honour is punished, and everything great is mocked at and belittled; when everywhere I see the scum in occupation of the first positions; and where the triumph of the stupidest and most despicable is assured.

Here, at least, Bernanos had discovered honour intact among Frenchmen standing to arms.

Immediately on his return to Gabès he was taken ill with an infection of the bladder, the real cause of which the doctors were slow to diagnose. He spent most of the next three months in bed with a slight temperature and on a strict diet, working hard to finish the *Dialogues des Carmélites*. He wrote several letters to Brazil, for he was still longing to return there. He could have gone at any time for the Alliance Française, but if he stayed, how could he live with the franc devalued? The sense of a mission to fulfil possessed

[1] For the substance of this chapter I am indebted to the account of Bernanos' last days by Mgr Pézeril in the *Cahiers du Rhône.*

him: he would go from town to town and preach the vocation of France like a gospel.

Michel returned to Europe in March, and visited his parents in Gabès just as the Saharan summer was beginning to dry up the springs of the rare oases. On the 7th of May Bernanos was moved to a hospital in Tunis, where an operation was planned for the following week. It was decided, however, that this should be performed in Paris, and on the 21st of May his friend Henri Jacques arrived to take Bernanos back by plane.

He entered the Lyautey nursing home in Paris on the 22nd of May, and was transferred ten days later to the American hospital at Neuilly. The subsequent operation disclosed a cancer of the liver, and left the surgeons no hope of his recovery. But his hold on life was still tenacious. Wishing for the attentions of a sympathetic priest, he asked Luc Estang to find him one, and it was thus that the abbé Daniel Pézeril, then a curate at Saint Séverin, came to enjoy his confidence. Pézeril brought him the Blessed Sacrament every morning, and Bernanos insisted, for so long as he had the strength of speech, on reciting the Confiteor in Latin, declaring himself incapable of saying it in French, and hammering out the consonants of *et tibi pater*. When he could no longer say it in either language, he followed it with his lips. After he had made his thanksgiving the two men would talk, and the moment came when Bernanos addressed Pézeril as *mon fils*.

They spoke much of the *Vie de Jésus* which he still had in mind. 'I must get to work on it,' he said, and Pézeril lent him the *Vie de Jésus* of Cardinal Bérulle. But he found this too artificial.

'I want to speak about Jesus Christ very simply to people who no longer know Him, from the threshold or behind the pillar of a church – as a poor fellow like the others.' Bernanos insisted that the Apostles, too, were like the others – going forward, step by step, and never grasping the full significance of what they saw and heard. It was to be the same with the Blessed Virgin. He was much exercised to strike the right note of compassion and respect, seeing her as a little girl allowing herself to be guided along the way but never knowing where it would lead her. He cherished the belief that Satan had foreseen the Incarnation and in tempting Adam had perhaps imagined that he was tempting Christ. Without a belief in original sin, Bernanos declared that he would never have been a Christian. He was careful that his work should have the right scriptural and theological foundations, and wanted to know what the exegetes now thought about the Book of Genesis. 'Don't you think that with their abominable evolution they will reduce it to a vapid fairy tale? At the best, all they can do is to turn one sort of poetry into another. And their own isn't worth anything – whereas the other . . .'

But he had not yet abandoned hope of writing one last polemic: it was to be entitled *Encyclique aux Français*. Pierre Bourdan,[1] who was neither a Catholic nor a Gaullist but had more care for liberty than many who were, came to visit him. 'Bernanos, we need you,' he implored. When Bernanos read in a newspaper that certain people counted on restoring the greatness of France by the importation of American tractors, he wondered indignantly how that would benefit its soul. A visit from Malraux also encouraged him to re-enter the fray. 'If only I still had the health of Pétain!' he exclaimed – and then the old incredulity took hold of him. Laval was different; there had always been people like Laval in France; but Pétain. . . . Then an absent look came into his eyes; he raised his hand; and making the sign of the Cross he murmured: 'Pétain, Laval, I bless them both.'

He had asked Pézeril to be at his side when they brought him out from the operation, in case they should be bringing out a corpse, but when he returned to consciousness he was singing the *Marseillaise*. His high spirits persisted as long as the illusion of recovery. When he was forced to swallow a spoonful of Lourdes water, heavily dosed with iodine, he observed how the Blessed Virgin must be enjoying the sight of his grimace. By the 30th of June, however, he no longer seemed the same man, so weak had he become. He drew Pézeril close to him and explained with tears in his eyes that an inspiration had come to him during the night. He would devote what time was left to him solely to his *Vie de Jésus*. 'Don't you think that the Lord is asking me to give up everything else?' When Pézeril confirmed him in this, he said that he now had something to live for. The sacrifice was a hard one. 'I am a novelist. Do they realise that if I had not attached so much importance to my polemical work, I would have still sacrificed my novels? But I have

[1] Pierre Bourdan worked for the French Service of the BBC during the Second World War. He was deeply imbued with the spirit of English liberalism, and spoke English perfectly. He was killed in a motor accident shortly after the death of Bernanos.

made my decision. I shall speak of nothing any more but Jesus Christ.' Pézeril suggested that after his *Vie de Jésus* he might still write his *Encyclique aux Français;* but Bernanos was adamant. 'Nothing but my *Vie de Jésus.*' He had the plan of it in his head; it would take him two years. He could not foresee that he had less than a week to live.

He was not thinking only of himself, nor even of the country which he had loved with a passion so desperate and so disappointed. What would happen to his family when he had gone? Who would care for their material needs? He asked Henri Jacques to look after them, and to watch over the future of his works. The communion of sinners was a reality just as vivid for Bernanos as the communion of saints, and there were those for whose spiritual welfare he felt himself responsible. Some were known to him personally; others were not. He did not speak of Maurras, but it is inconceivable that Maurras was not in his mind. He implored Pézeril to say a word to this one, and to do what he could for another; and for a third there was nothing to be done at the moment, except to pray for him. But for his children he felt more responsible than for anyone else. He was dying alone, as he had always known he must, but in saving his own soul he was impatient to save the souls of others.

He had enjoyed the champagne they brought him after the operation – it had the racy flavour of the French soil – and later, the *cuisses de grénouilles* and the trout; but now there was little food that he could swallow. His physical self was in dissolution, and his sleep disturbed by idiotic dreams. He refused the morphia so long as he was able to, for he wished to remain in full possession and knowledge of himself. When he woke he struggled not to fall asleep again, for 'if I sleep, it will be the end'. He had asked for Extreme Unction, interrupting the hallowed words – *quidquid per visum, per gustum et locutionem . . . per auditum . . . per tactum deliquisti* – with 'Que c'est bouleversant! Que c'est admirable!' When he uncovered his feet, Pézeril signed to him that this was unnecessary, and that time was pressing. Bernanos seemed not to understand, interpreting the gesture to mean that his mutilated leg had adequately expiated his sins. Pézeril reminded him that his work would intercede for him, but he replied: 'I am not responsible for what I have created; I am only responsible for what I have not been.' A photograph of Corcovado stood beside his bed, and he wondered if he had been

right to leave Brazil. Yes, he had been right. De Gaulle had twice
renewed the invitation, and he remembered Dom Gordan's advice:
'Your duty is to serve your country.'

On Saturday, the 3rd of July, Jeanne Bernanos and two of her
daughters found him sitting up, with hands clasped, while Pézeril
was reciting the Lord's Prayer. On the words 'deliver us from evil'
he uttered a heartrending cry: 'Father, Father, by the merits of
your son, Jesus Christ, do not make me suffer any more.' He was
out of breath and regained his bed with difficulty. 'Do you think,'
he asked, 'that God will forgive me my sins?' When the priest had
reassured him he fell asleep. The following morning he was too
deeply under the effects of morphia to receive Communion. At last
he opened his mouth and the Host was placed between his lips; but
he fell asleep immediately, and it remained there, visible, until he
woke up and was able to consume it. Towards four o'clock in the
afternoon he told his wife that he was dying, and repeated the so
familiar words, 'la Sainte Agonie', a little later. When Pézeril came
in he asked for his blessing in that high voice of his that was more
like a lamentation than normal speech. After a quarter of an hour
he begged for it again, and then called out 'Maman, maman'. The
nurse replied, rather oddly: 'Very well, just wait a moment, and
I'll go and look for her in the corridor.' 'You certainly won't find
her there,' rejoined Bernanos, 'because she is dead.' 'You'll soon
find her in Heaven', replied the nurse. 'Of course I shall find her in
Heaven', came the answer, with all the certitude of a faith that was
now impregnable against despair.

His wife, with Michel, Claude, Dominique, and his nephew Guy
Hattu, returned at 9.30 in the evening and stayed all night. His eyes
remained closed, and he breathed heavily from the oxygen which
alone sustained him. He knew that his family were at his side, for
he begged them to go to bed – 'You will be so tired.' He was in
atrocious pain, and then, all of a sudden, the mysterious cry escaped
him, 'A nous deux!' Was he defying the angel of death or the angel
of darkness? Was he commending himself to God? Or was he
remembering from the days when he lay on the carpet at Fressin
devouring La Comédie humaine, the challenge of Eugène de Rastignac
from the cemetery of Père-Lachaise? Shortly after midnight he fell
into a coma, and remained thus until the first light of dawn filtered
through the window from which the curtains had been drawn

back. Towards 5 a.m. the muscles of his face moved and his mouth opened. Then he repeated, very distinctly, three times the name of his wife, and other names which those around him could not catch. Each member of his family kissed him in turn. Jeanne Bernanos leaned her face against his, and he clasped her head against his own. She recited the *Our Father* and the *Hail Mary*, and his lips moved with the words. He repeated 'Jeanne' and then again, more quickly, 'Jeanne . . . Jeanne.' Without any movement of his face, his eyes closed gently and he was dead.

Among those who came to pay their last respects in the chamber where he lay was Pierre Bourdan. The impression he took away was shared by all who gazed upon the mortal remains of Georges Bernanos:

The cause that Bernanos served was as wide as the universe. Such men will not have lived in vain, since their image is before our eyes to renew our confidence, when we are afraid to see humanity reduced to the law of numbers, of statistics, and of material gain. If I ever need a fresh assurance that the destiny and the glory of mankind is not to be contained within these dismal limits, it will be enough to recall the luminous vision of a face where the last act of a serene faith was able to wipe out sixty years of suffering and bequeath to mankind, in exchange for this long ordeal, a smile of victory and ineffable promise.[1]

The Requiem Mass was celebrated at the church of Saint-Séverin in the presence of the family and friends, a number of young people and seminarians, and a few writers, André Malraux prominent among them. Only the Spanish Republicans and two Latin American governments were officially represented, and there was little to suggest that the man they were honouring had marked the history of his time. Nevertheless, as Malraux was later to write in words that may serve as an epitaph on the life of Georges Bernanos:

Ce n'est pas le rôle qui fait le personnage historique: c'est la vocation.

[1] *Cahiers du Rhône*, p. 340

BIBLIOGRAPHY

The following books by Georges Bernanos have been translated into English and published in Great Britain:

The Star of Satan, trans. by J. C.Whitehouse. The Bodley Head, 1927.

The Diary of a Country Priest, trans. by Pamela Morris. The Bodley Head, 1937.

A Diary of my Times (Les Grands Cimetières sous la lune), trans. by Pamela Morris. The Bodley Head, 1938.

The Open Mind (Monsieur Ouine), trans. by Geoffrey Dunlop. The Bodley Head, 1945.

The Fearless Heart (Dialogues des Carmélites), trans. by Michael Legat. The Bodley Head, 1961.

Night is Darkest (Un Mauvais Rêve), trans. by W. J. Strachan. The Bodley Head, 1953.

Mouchette (Nouvelle Histoire de Mouchette), trans. by Veronica Lucas. The Bodley Head, 1966.

Joy, trans. by Louise Varese. The Bodley Head, 1948.

The Crime. Hale, 1936.

Plea for Liberty (Lettre aux Anglais), trans. by Harry Lorin Binsse and Ruth Bethel. Dobson, 1946.

Tradition of Freedom, trans. by Helen Beau Clark. Dobson, 1950.

Sanctity will Out, trans. by Miss R. Batchelor. Sheed & Ward, 1947.

In France a definitive edition of Bernanos' novels has been published in a single volume of the Editions de la Pléiade, Gallimard; and the two volumes of his Correspondence, *Combat pour la Liberté*, by Plon.

The following works are also available in separate editions:

Le Chemin de la Croix des Ames (Gallimard), *Les Enfants humiliés* (Gallimard), *Français si vous saviez* (Gallimard), *Lettre aux Anglais* (Gallimard), *Nous autres Français* (Gallimard), *La Liberté pour quoi faire?* (Gallimard), *Le Crépuscule des Vieux* (Gallimard).

*La Grande Peur des Bien-Pensants** (Grasset), *Dialogues des Carmélites†* (Editions du Seuil).

*Un Crime** (Plon), *Dialogue d'ombres** (Plon), *Les Grands Cimetières* *sous la lune** (Plon), *L'Imposture** (Plon), *Jeanne—relapse et sainte* (Plon), *La Joie** (Plon), *Journal d'un Curé de campagne** (Plon), *Le Lendemain, c'est vous* (Plon), *Un Mauvais Rêve*§ (Plon), *Monsieur Ouine** (Plon), *Nouvelle Histoire de Mouchette** (Plon), *Sous le Soleil de Satan** (Plon).

Available in a pocket edition: *Librairie Générale Francaise, †Livre de Vie, § Guilde du Livre.

For critical studies of Bernanos, containing much biographical material, the reader is referred to the following:

Bernanos par lui-même, Albert Béguin (Editions du Seuil).

Georges Bernanos, Max Milner (Desclée de Brouwer).

Le Chrétien Bernanos, Hans Urs von Balthasar (Editions du Seuil).

Présence de Bernanos, Luc Estang (Plon).

Georges Bernanos, Collection des Cahiers du Rhône (Editions du Seuil).

Etudes Bernanosiennes: seven issues published by La Revue des Lettres Modernes.

Georges Bernanos, Peter Hebblethwaite (Bowes & Bowes).

Bernanos, Les Cahiers de l'Herne.

Bernanos no Brasil (Vozes, Rio de Janeiro).

Georges Bernanos, Louis Chaigne (Editions Universitaires).

Further material may be found in the *Bulletins de la Société des Amis de Georges Bernanos*, although it is difficult to lay hands on a complete series of these. For their current sequel, *Courrier Georges Bernanos*, enquiries should be addressed to M. Jean-Loup Bernanos, 211 boulevard Raspail, Paris 14e. Foreign subscriptions are 32F per annum.

*

The page references in this book relate in every case to the original editions of the works in question, except for the novels where the reference is to the Editions de la Pléiade.

ACKNOWLEDGEMENTS
TO PUBLISHERS

I am indebted to the following for permission to translate, and quote from, the works of which they hold the English copyright:

M. Jean-Loup Bernanos: *Bulletin de la Société des Amis de Georges Bernanos;*
Editions de la Baconnière: *Georges Bernanos: Cahiers du Rhône*;
Editions Gallimard: *Scandale de la Vérité, Le Chemin de la Croix des Ames, Français, si vous saviez, Les Enfants humiliés, Le Crépuscule des Vieux*;
Editions Bernard Grasset: *La Grande Peur des Bien-Pensants*;
Librarie Plon: *Dialogue d'ombres, L'Imposture, La Joie, Journal d'un Curé de campagne, Les Grands Cimetières sous la lune, Un Mauvais Rêve, Monsieur Ouine, Maurras et notre temps*;
Editions du Seuil: *Bernanos par lui-même*;
Editore Vozes: *Bernanos no Brasil*;
The Bodley Head: *Sous le Soleil de Satan, Nouvelle Histoire de Mouchette*;
Dennis Dobson: *Lettre aux Anglais*;
Sheed & Ward: *Jeanne – relapse et sainte*.

I must also thank the editor of *The Times Literary Supplement* for permission to reproduce in chapter 5 certain passages which originally appeared in that journal.

INDEX

INDEX